THEORIES OF SOCIAL REMEMBERING

THEORIZING SOCIETY
Series editor: Larry Ray

THEORIES OF SOCIAL REMEMBERING

Barbara A. Misztal

Open University Press
Maidenhead · Philadelphia

Open University Press
McGraw-Hill Education
McGraw-Hill House
Shoppenhangers Road
Maidenhead
Berkshire
England
SL6 2QL

email: enquiries@openup.co.uk
world wide web: www.openup.co.uk

and
325 Chestnut Street
Philadelphia, PA 19106, USA

First Published 2003

A catalogue record of this book is available from the British Library

ISBN 0 335 20831 2 (pb)   0 335 20832 0 (hb)

Library of Congress Cataloging-in-Publication Data
CIP data applied for

Typeset by RefineCatch Limited, Bungay, Suffolk
Printed in Great Britain by Bell and Bain Ltd, Glasgow

In memory of my mother

CONTENTS

SERIES EDITOR'S FOREWORD

Sociology is reflexively engaged with the object of its study, society. In the wake of the rapid and profound social changes of the later twentieth century, there is extensive debate as to whether our theoretical frames of reference are appropriate for novel configurations of culture, economy and society. Sociologists further need to ask whether recent theoretical pre-occupations – for example with the 'cultural turn', post-modernism, decon-struction, globalization and identity – adequately grasp social processes in the Millennium. One crucial issue here is the relationship between contempor-ary social problems and theories on the one hand and the classical heritage of Marx, Durkheim, Weber and Simmel on the other. Sociology is still reluctant to forget its founders and the relevance of the classical tradition is both powerful and problematic. It is powerful because the classics constitute a rich source of insights, concepts and analyses that can be deployed and reinterpreted to grasp current problems. But it is problematic because the social world of the classics is largely that of industrial, imperial and high bourgeois European societies prior to the First World War. How do we begin to relate the concepts formed in this milieu to the concerns of the globalized social world that is post-colonial, post-industrial and has seen the rise and collapse of Soviet socialism? Social theory in the twenty-first century further needs to grasp the fateful contemporary paradox that resurgent nationalism and religious attachments, exposing the fractured and dispersed basis of intolerance, accompany the growth of globalized culture, politics and econ-omies. How does sociology reconfigure the understandings of identity, cul-ture, history and society in appropriate ways? These are some of the major challenges for sociology that this series, *Theorizing Society*, aims to address.

This series intends to map out the ways in which social theory is being transformed and how contemporary issues have emerged. Each book in the series offers a concise and up-to-date overview of the principle ideas, innovations and theoretical concepts in relation to its topic. The series is designed to provide a review of recent developments in social theory, offering a comprehensive collection of introductions to major theoretical issues. The focus of individual books is organized around topics which reflect the major areas of teaching and research in contemporary social theory, including modernity, post-modernism, structuralism and post-structuralism; culture and economy; globalization; feminism and sexuality; memory, identity and social solidarity. While being accessible to undergraduates these books allow authors to develop personal and programmatic statements about the state and future development of theoretically defined fields.

Barbara Misztal's *Theories of Social Remembering* addresses the key issues identified in this series. The main aim of this book is to provide an overview of theories of social remembering and to show to what extent they have challenged sociological understandings of the formation of social identities and conflicts. Although memory is essential to the ability of individuals and groups to sustain identities over time it has received relatively little attention in sociology (since Halbwachs' seminal work in the 1920s) by contrast with other disciplines, such as psychology. Yet, as Misztal shows, since the 1980s there has been an explosion of interest in memory following the emergence of new communication media, sites of remembrance, heritage movements, and reassessments of national pasts in new democracies in eastern Europe, South America and South Africa. She argues that in the post-Cold War world, all societies, especially those that have recently gone through difficult, 'heroic' or simply confusing periods, are involved in the deep search for truth about their past. While sociological theories try to shed light on the workings of collective memory, this rapidly expanding field of research is assisted by the shift taking place in sociology from the study of social structures and normative systems to the study of 'practice', stimulated by the growing interest in culture as the constitutive symbolic dimension of all social processes.

In a wide-ranging analysis of theories of memory as a social and cultural process Misztal identifies questions to which there have not yet been coherent answers. These include questions about how societies remember and why the past is of any relevance? *Who* is a remembering subject and *what* is the nature of the past? Misztal argues that for the notion of memory to be a useful analytical concept it needs to retain a sense of both its individual and collective dimensions. She outlines major theoretical approaches with the intention of moving beyond these through close attention to the dynamics of the remembering process. Developing an inter-subjectivist approach Misztal avoids both social determinism and visions of an atomistic individualistic social order. Collective memories are seen as intersubjectively constituted results of shared experience, ideas, knowledges and cultural practices through which people construct a relationship to the past. The main 'memory groups' (nations, ethnic groups and families) are all, however, affected by processes of social differentiation and globalization. At the same time the decline of traditions and their selective re-appropriation in increasingly plural and fluid social settings creates highly complex relationships between memory and history, memory and time and memory and imagination. Thus Misztal weaves together a theory of social memory that draws on classical studies such as Halbwachs but also regards 'memories' as the embodied accomplishments of agents in a complex world. One consequence of this is that the sites and symbols of collective memories such as museums, monuments, and landscapes become increasingly contested such that memory needs to be viewed as the product of multiple competing discourses.

Understanding memory as a contested terrain is central to understanding the particular character of modernity. Although the recording of personal and collective memory is archaic, modernity encounters 'social amnesia' brought about by the dislocation between traditional and modern forms of cultural transmission. This has been compounded by the way the modern era has been uniquely structured by trauma, of wars, genocide and especially the Holocaust. Whereas memory and the politics of memory are ancient (and Misztal traces their appearance in Ancient Greece) the idea of memory as the recovery of trauma is modern and draws particularly on the unique impact of Freud. The linking of traumatic memory with the struggle for justice poses new challenges for societies to remember their collective wrongs while moving towards forms of reconciliation. *Theories of Social Remembering* brings fresh insight and systematic theorizing to this emerging area and will contribute to deeper understanding of the core theoretical challenges to sociology in the early twenty-first century.

Larry Ray
Professor of Sociology
University of Kent

INTRODUCTION

This book explores the workings of collective memory by presenting theories and research in this rapidly expanding field. As a result of many recent studies investigating how social memory is generated, maintained and reproduced through texts, images, sites and experiences, the concept of collective memory has become one of the more important topics addressed in today's social science. Although the conceptualization of the notion of memory varies, the increased number of approaches across all disciplines recognizes the importance of social frameworks and contexts in the process of remembering. This recent revival of interest in the concept of collective memory in inter- and cross-disciplinary studies of remembering presents sociology with a unique opportunity. In order to take full advantage of this, we must start with an overview of theories of social remembering. Moreover, if the role of sociology is to investigate the different ways in which humans give meaning to the world (Trigg 2001: 42), and if memory is crucial to our ability to make sense of our present circumstances, researching collective memory should be one of its most important tasks. The aim of this book, therefore, is to examine the contribution of sociological theories to our understanding of the workings of memory, and to evaluate to what extent such studies have challenged our understanding of various forms of collective memory and their role in different societies.

The process of remembering has always fascinated people because it is so fundamental to our ability to conceive the world. Memory, because it 'functions in every act of perception, in every act of intellection, in every act of language' (Terdiman 1993: 9), is the essential condition of our cognition and reflexive judgement. It is closely connected with emotions because emotions are in part about the past and because memory evokes emotions. Memory is also a highly important element in the account of what it is to be a person, as it is the central medium through which identities are constituted: 'A really successful dissociation of the self from memory would be a total loss of the self – and thus of all the activities to which a sense of one's identity is important' (Nussbaum 2001: 177). It can be seen as the guardian of difference, as it allows for the recollection and preservation of our different selves, which we acquire and accumulate through our unique lives (Wolin 1989: 40).

The re-emergence of interest in the concept of memory in social sciences was triggered by the 'commemorative fever' of the 1980s and 1990s. In those decades scarcely a month, let alone a year, passed without some celebrations. This astonishing burst of interest in social memory can be explained by such factors as the impressive number of civic anniversaries (from the American Bicentennial in the USA to the fiftieth anniversary of the end of World War II), the growing interest in ethnic groups' memories, the revival of fierce debates over the Holocaust and the Vichy regime, and the end of the Cold War, which brought about an explosion of previously suppressed memories (Kammen 1995a; Ashplant *et al.* 2000a, 2000b). Among other trends responsible for the present-day 'obsession with memory' (Huyssen 1995) are the increasingly 'authoritative' role of films which try to tell us how it 'really was', the growing importance of sites of remembrance for tourism and heritage movements, the popularity of the genre of autobiography and the reassessment of national pasts and cultures in the newly democratized countries of Eastern Europe, South America and South Africa, where reckoning with past wrongs has been publicly debated.

While we will return to a detailed account of the factors responsible for the recent visibility and importance of social memory in social and political practice in the following chapters, here it is worth noticing that the 'recent passion for memory' (Nora 1996a) has established it as one of the main discourses that is increasingly used in social sciences, not merely to explain the past but also to explore the present. This high status of memory discourse can be seen as a result of three general trends. First, it can be viewed as an effect of the nature of present-day intellectual culture in which a broad pattern of 'explanatory pluralism' is increasingly accepted (Kammen 1995a). Second, the recent interest in memory can be explained by the growing use of the past as a screen into which different groups can project their contradictions, controversies and conflicts in objective forms (Huyssen 1995). Finally, the rapid expansion of the study of memory has fuelled the rise of sociological interest in culturally acquired categories of understanding, which itself has been stimulated by the development taking place in cultural studies. These three trends, in the context of the development of electronic media and artificial memory storage, ensure the popularity of the notion of memory in sociological texts. The identification of memory and culture directs the search for the sources of stability and consistency of memories – first to 'schematic organization, which makes some ideas or images more accessible than others, and secondly, to cues embedded in the physical and social environment' (DiMaggio 1997: 267). Hence, recent scholarship views the construction of memory as a social and cultural process and analyses institutions' aims and operations responsible for that construction, while also examining objects, places and practices in which cultural memory is embodied.

Since remembering 'is nothing but tracking down what is concealed in the memory' (Albertus Mangus, quoted in Draaisma 2000: 35), studies of remembering are nothing less than research into the investigation of memory. Remembering is, writes Draaisma, a process of investigation of the hidden nature of memories. Over the centuries, everyday language has provided people with various comparisons which, through their combination of image and language, are capable of describing the complexity of remembering and forgetting. These analogies, such as caves, labyrinths, grottoes and mineshafts, have always been accompanied by a range of strategies used to assist memory. Various procedures employed as memory aids tend to reflect techniques of their time. In place of the mnemonic aids that supported the memories of the ancient Greeks or the knots tied at the corner of a handkerchief that helped our grandmothers to remind themselves of something, we now rely on external devices such as libraries, electronic diaries and the internet. We also use various emblems of remembrance: from rosemary, carried by Ophelia, who in Shakespeare's *Hamlet* says 'There's rosemary, that's for remembrance' (Act IV, Scene V) to poppies, which are symbols of our remembrance of the victims and veterans of the Great War. The complexity of the process of remembering has likewise been reflected in numerous metaphors developed by philosophers and scientists through the centuries, from Plato's wax tablet and Locke's 'storehouse of our ideas', through Freud's 'mystic writing pad', which erases yet keeps traces of what disappears, to today's comparison of memory to artificial computer memory (Sutton 1998: 13–19). Since the nineteenth century, memory has become the subject of scientific research, yet neither the large and interdisciplinary field of memory studies nor any system of thought provides us with a full picture of human memory. Apart from a common consensus that memory is a complex and hard to grasp phenomenon, scientists – who, by comparison with artists and philosophers, have only approached the topic of memory relatively recently – have not yet produced a full, integrated explanation of the working of memory. While scientists' ideas generally take longer to permeate down into the stratum of everyday society, artists, who have always been fascinated by memory, seem to be better equipped not only to grasp the depth of memory but also to popularize their penetrating insights into its workings.

We owe a deeper and more insightful understanding of the workings of memory to creative writing, particularly the novel, which is capable of providing the kind of inward, authentically objective account of the past that enables us to understand it (Bakhtin 1981). One of the best descriptions of the complexity of the process of remembering, understood as an act of representation in the memory of things past, can be found in novels of the late nineteenth and early twentieth century. It is enough here to mention the impact of Proust's famous masterpiece *Remembrance of Things Past* ([1922] 1989). The unique impact of Freud, who is commonly recognized as one of the forebears of the idea that the past continues to shape the present, can be attributed to his imaginative defiance of disciplinary boundaries which produced the creative combination of both literary and scientific insight. Although another important step in increasing our awareness of the complexity of the process of remembering belongs to sociology, until recently the topic of social memory has received relatively little attention from social scientists generally. Since memory has been seen as a characteristic of societies in which custom or tradition plays a decisive role, and since sociology has been from its beginning interested mainly in societies that place greater value upon change, the role of social remembering has not been an important subject of sociological debates. This was the situation at least until the development of the Durkheimian perspective which has expanded our understanding of the role of commemorative symbols and rituals in crystallizing the past and preserving order and solidarity. Although Durkheim ([1925] 1973) addresses memory directly only in his discussion of commemorative rituals and in relation to traditional societies, he stresses that every society displays and requires a sense of continuity with the past. Durkheim's idea of the importance of a sense of collective identity, seen as being reinforced through links to the past, is further elaborated by Maurice Halbwachs ([1926] 1950). He initiated the conceptualization of collective memory as shared social frameworks of individual recollections and, in the Durkheimian spirit, stressed that the coherence and complexity of collective memory tend to correspond to coherence and complexity at the social level and that this seemingly individual capacity is really a collective phenomenon.

Yet, despite this underlying understanding of the essential role of remembering in social life, and despite Halbwachs' discussion of the notion, it is difficult to find in sociological texts a direct definition of memory or an explicit account of how we remember the past. Collective memory does not seem to enjoy an independent standing, but rather has the status of an ephemeral or residual concept. Nonetheless, because of its crucial role in social life, the notion of social memory has played an important, although maybe not always explicitly formulated as such, role in the social sciences. For example, Weber (1978), who hardly mentioned memory, by rooting claims to legitimacy in tradition, drew our attention to the relations between collective memory and power. Mead (1932) argued that only the present is real, while the past is being continually constructed in and through the present. Following the Durkheimian link between memory and social order, Shils (1981) stressed the connection between collective memory and tradition-building and argued that culture depends upon chains of memory, or tradition, seen as the storage of inherited conceptions, meanings and values essential for the social order. While such an approach disconnects social remembering from the actual thought process of any particular individual, it establishes the importance of social remembering as closely connected with the unity of a society and the conceptualization of collective memory as guaranteeing social identity, and as dependent on ritualized collective symbols. More recently, Giddens (1984), who does not explicitly rely upon this notion, viewed structures as memory traces which are constantly instantiated in social practices, or, in other words, as existing in the memory of knowledgeable agents.

What is lacking in all these examples is a direct and coherent answer to questions about how societies remember and why the past is of any relevance. This is a surprising absence, especially if we notice that sociological theories' concern with continuity and change entails the passage of time. However, with current sociology becoming aware of the issues of time (see Chapter 5) and with the publication of Connerton's book *How Societies Remember* (1989), which directly addresses the issue of collective memory (see Chapter 4), there are some signs of changes. This temporal turn in sociology, by addressing the question of how to link synchrony and diachrony, facilitates investigations of mechanisms by which societies incorporate of the past into the present. The resulting research is still, nevertheless, open to criticism as many of these new works are tinted by a social determinism of Halbwachs' groundwork analysis of memory. On the other hand, the impressive research in cognitive psychology is under attack for ignoring the social context of remembering, and for overlooking social rules of remembrance that tell us what we should remember and what should be forgotten. In order to overcome the individualistic bias of psychological theories and the social determinism of many sociological studies, this book aims to review traditional and recent interpretations of the idea of collective memory.

The main issue requiring clarification is the question of *who* is a remembering subject and *what* is the nature of the past. Following the claim of many writers, we argue here that in order for the notion of memory to be a useful analytical concept we need to retain a sense of both its individual and collective dimensions (Funkenstein 1993; Schudson 1997; Zerubavel 1997; Prager 1998; Sherman 1999). While societies, to use Funkenstein's (1993) instructive comparison, do not remember in the same way as they do not dance, individual remembering takes place in the *social context* – it is prompted by social cues, employed for social purposes, ruled and ordered by socially structured norms and patterns, and therefore contains much that is social (Schudson 1995; Zerubavel 1997). Such a perspective, by pointing out that individual memory is socially organized or socially mediated, emphasizes the social dimension of human memory, without, however, necessarily being a straightforward projection of the shared remembering. In other words, the main assumption of the intersubjectivist sociology of memory is that, while it is the individual who remembers, remembering is more than just a personal act. The intersubjectivist approach, the significance of which becomes clear to its full extent in the course of the whole book, advocates the study of social contexts in which even the most personal memories are embedded, and the investigation of the social formation of memory by exploring the conditions and factors that make remembering in common possible, such as language, rituals, commemoration practices and sites of memories.

Turning now to the question about the nature of the past, we can, following Sartre, say that the past is not over and done with. It, like the present, is to some extent also part of a social reality and 'that, while far from being absolutely objective, nonetheless transcends our subjectivity and is shared by others around us' (Zerubavel 1997: 81). The past is not simply given in memory, 'but it must be articulated to become memory' (Huyssen 1995: 3). This unavoidable gap between experiencing an event and remembering it, filled up by our creative interpretation of the past, constitutes memory. Moreover, we recall and memorize the past which is passed to us in various cultural practices and forms, which further suggests the social construction of the past as its memory is located in a wide range of cultural routines, institutions and artefacts (Schudson 1995: 346–7).

The argument that memory is intersubjectively constituted – which assumes that while it is an individual who remembers, his or her memory exists, and is shaped by, their relation with, what has been shared with others and that it is, moreover, always memory of an intersubjective past, of a past time lived in relation to other people – seems to be a central characteristic of new sociological theories of memory. Following this development, the book is primarily concerned with the social aspects of remembering and the results of this social experience – that is, the representation of the past in a whole set of ideas, knowledges, cultural practices, rituals and monuments through which people express their attitudes to the past and which construct their relations to the past.

The outline of the book

The book consists of six chapters, with the first two devoted to elaborating the conceptualization of the process of remembering by analysing memory's function and history. Chapters 3 and 4 directly explore and discuss theories of social remembering, and Chapters 5 and 6 examine the location of memory in a broader field of social science and review the main fields of memory studies. After a short conclusion, the glossary offers a concise and up-to-date overview of the development of relevant theoretical concepts.

Chapter 1 directly addresses the issues concerning the functions and forms of memory. After a short presentation of the various forms and kinds of memory, sociological definitions of memory and collective memory's significance in modern societies are discussed. Collective memory is defined as the representation of the past, both that shared by a group and that which is collectively commemorated, that enacts and gives substance to the group's identity, its present conditions and its vision of the future. The next two sections examine the social formation of memory by looking at communities and institutions of memory. The chapter concludes with a discussion of the evolution of the status of memory, where it is argued that the shift in the prestige of memory can be linked to cultural change, seen as associated with the advancement of the means of communication and the transformation of techniques of power.

In order to throw light on changes in the status and meanings of memory, Chapter 2 briefly examines how cultures have been affected by the shift in the means of communication and social organization. It presents the history of memory by discussing the changes in aids to memory, from visual mnemonic techniques, through writing and print, to today's computer-enhanced methods of storing, transferring and constructing memory.

Chapter 3 is a summary presentation of the main theories of social remembering. It starts with Halbwachs' theory of social memory which draw on the Durkheimian perspective. This is followed by an overview of another influential approach, known as the invention of tradition, or the presentist approach. This approach describes how the social past has been constructed or reappropriated in order to serve current social interests and needs. In the next part of the chapter we critically evaluate the popular memory approach that explores how, when and why some social events are likely to form part of popular or unofficial memory. The final section examines recent works on social memory and directs our attention to the social and institutional relations of the production of memory, arguing that memory, far from being mechanical or stable, is actively restructured in a process of negotiation through time.

Chapter 4 addresses the issue of the nature of remembering by exploring how collective consensus is connected with the actual thought processes of any particular person. It discusses the embodiedness of memory as well as what makes an individual memory social. The role of generation and the significance of tradition, as a chain of memory, in shaping processes of remembering is also examined.

Chapter 5 examines the complex relationships between social memory studies and historiography, philosophy and psychology and argues that there is a need for an interdisciplinary integration of memory studies. After suggesting that further developments in our understanding of social memory should be built upon careful integration of various vocabularies and ideas with a continuation of the sociological tradition in the study of memory, the chapter concludes with several illustrations of battles over memory.

The final chapter, which is devoted to an examination of the main trends in studying memory in the social sciences, provides an overview of four of the most important fields of research. The first section looks at the high-profile commemorative activities of recent years which have been reflected in numerous studies of war memory, commemoration rituals and public and personal remembrance of conflicts. Following the widespread interest in the subject of identity in recent sociological writings, the next section looks at the growing number of studies trying to shed light on the links between memory and identity and on the conditions behind various groups' attitudes towards their past in different periods of their history. Turning to studies of memory and trauma, we discuss investigations of Holocaust memory and look at how they explain the shifts and changing phases in countries' responses to the Holocaust throughout the postwar decades. The recent search for explanations about why certain social events are either retained or forgotten and how, when and why some social events are more likely to form part of social memory, is also of great importance in studies of the role of memory in securing social justice. The final section looks at the issue of retrospective justice and shows how and why newly democratized regimes construct new memories by addressing, with a help of their legal systems, the wrongdoings committed in the past era.

Since memory practices are increasingly seen as the central characteristic of contemporary cultural formations, studies of social memory are becoming an important part of any examination of contemporary society's main problems and tensions. Thus, it is concluded that studies of collective memory can provide important insights for a general theory of modernity.

Further reading

Olick, J.K. and Robbins, J. (1998) Social memory studies, *Annual Review of Sociology*, 24(1): 105–41.

Zelizer, B. (1995) Reading the past against the grain, *Critical Studies in Mass Communication*, 12: 214–39.

Zerubavel, E. (1997) *Social Mindscape: An Invitation to Cognitive Sociology*. Cambridge, MA.: Harvard University Press.

CHAPTER I

MEMORY EXPERIENCE

The forms and functions of memory

'... whatever takes place has meaning because it changes into memory'

(Milosz 2001)

Human ability to retain and recollect a fact, event, or person from memory has been a topic of considerable interest to both scientists and artists for a long time. Yet, taking into account varieties of personal remembering (ranging from remembering an emotional feeling, through remembering where I left my car keys, or how to run the spelling check on my computer, or the date of the Battle of Hastings or how my daughter looks), it seems almost impossible to find a common underlying conceptualization of the process. Moreover, as its task involves summarizing, condensing or rewriting past events, memory is a complex but fallible system of storing information (Baddeley 1989: 51). Because of this difficulty in analysing memory we should view this faculty as some kind of active orientation towards the past, as an act of 'thinking of things in their absence' (Warnock 1987: 12). By referring to the process of remembering as 'memory experience' (Warnock 1987), we focus on the uniqueness of memory as a 'dialogue with the past' (Benjamin quoted in Lash 1999).

Memory has many forms and operates on many different levels, and the things that we remember are of many different kinds and are remembered for many different reasons. For example, there is the memory of how to ride a bicycle, which has been defined as a *procedural* memory; there is also the memory of such facts as that bicycles have two wheels and sometimes a bell, which has been defined as a *declarative* or *semantic* memory (Baddeley 1989: 35–46). Another type of memory is personal memory or *autobiographical* memory, which is the way we tell others and ourselves the story of our lives. Although autobiographical memories are not necessarily accurate, they are 'mostly congruent with one's self knowledge, life themes, or sense of self' (Barclay and DeCooke 1988: 92). When talking about *cognitive* memory, we refer to remembering the meaning of words and lines of verse: 'What this type of remembering requires is, not that the object of memory be something that is past, but that the person who remembers that thing must have met, experienced or learned of it in the past' (Connerton 1989: 23). Yet another kind of memory is *habit* memory, which refers to our capacity to reproduce a certain performance and which is an essential ingredient in the successful and convincing performance of codes and rules. Habit is the mode of inscribing the past in the present, *as* present. In this case, memory denotes a habitual knowing that allows us to recall the signs and skills we use in everyday life. This kind of memory, like all habits, is sedimented in bodily postures, activities, techniques and gestures. Such conceptualization of the process of remembering, where memory 'gets passed on in non-textual and non-cognitive ways' (Connerton 1989: 102), allows us to study social remembrance by focusing on the performance of commemorative rituals.

Habit-memory differs from other types of memory because it brings the past into the present by acting, while other kinds of memory retrieve the past to the present by summoning the past *as past* – that is, by remembering it. Remembering submits the past to a reflective awareness and it permits, by highlighting the past's difference to the present, the emergence of a form of critical reflection and the formation of meaningful narrative sequences. Although remembering, like habit, can be seen as a constant effort to maintain and reconstruct societal stability it, unlike habit, is also a 'highly active, effortful process' (Young 1988: 97). While remembering, we deliberately and consciously recover the past, so whatever memories 'route into consciousness, they need to be organized into patterns so that they make some kind of continuing sense in an ever-changing present' (Young 1988: 97–8). Hence, memory, as the knowing ordering or the narrative organization of the past, observes rules and conventions of narrative. For example, successful narratives about the past must have a beginning and an end, an interesting storyline and impressive heroes. The fact that memorizing is not free of social constraints and influences suggests the importance of another type of memory – namely, *collective* or *social* memory, which is our main concern here.

This book focuses on similarities between the ways in which people assign meanings to their common memories, while adopting the intersubjectivist approach which allows us to avoid both theories rooted in social determinism (which subordinate individuals totally to a collectivity) and visions of an individualistic, atomized social order (which deny the importance of communicative relations between people and their social embeddedness). Its main assumption is that remembering, while being constructed from cultural forms and constrained by our social context, is an individual mental act. Therefore, our intersubjectivist explanation of how we remember also acknowledges that – despite the fact memory is socially organized and mediated – individual memory is never totally conventionalized and standardized. The memories of people who have experienced a common event are never identical because in each of them a concrete memory evokes different associations and feelings. The relation between collective and individual memory can be compared to the relation between language (*langue*) and speech (*parole*), as formulated by Saussure (Funkenstein 1993: 5–9). Language, as a collective product, is separated from the variety of uses to which particular speech acts may be put; thus it is, like collective memory, an idealized system. Variations in individual memories, which can be compared to the scope of freedom with which we use language in particular speech, reflect the degree to which a given culture permits conscious changes and variations of the narrator in the contents, symbols and structures of collective memory.

Underscoring the intersubjectivity of memory, the sociology of memory asserts that the collective memory of a group is 'quite different from the sum total of the personal recollections of its various individual members, as it includes only those that are *commonly shared* by all of them' (Zerubavel 1997: 96). The collective memory, as the integration of various different personal pasts into a single common past that all members of a community come to remember collectively, can be illustrated by America's collective memory of the Vietnam War, that is more 'than just an aggregate of all the war-related recollections of individual Americans' (Zerubavel 1997: 96). Moreover, the prominent place of the Vietnam War (rather than, for example, the Korean War) in the memories of Americans also suggests that the division of the past into 'memorable' and 'forgettable' is a social convention, as it is society that ensures what we remember, and how and when we remember it.

Memory is social because every memory exists through its relation with what has been shared with others: language, symbols, events, and social and cultural contexts. Much research illustrates that memory is intersubjectively constituted because it is based on language and on an external or internal linguistic communication with significant others (Paez *et al.* 1997: 155). The way we remember is determined through the supra-individual cultural construction of language, which in itself is the condition of the sharing of memory, as a memory 'can be social only if it is capable of being transmitted and to be transmitted, a memory must first be articulated' (Fentress and Wickham 1992: 47). As the past is made into story, memories are simplified and 'prepared, planned and rehearsed socially and individually' (Schudson 1995: 359). Any retrospective narratives' chance of entering the public domain is socially structured: 'Within the public domain, not only the recording of the past but active re-working of the past is more likely to be transmitted if it happens in high-prestige, socially consensual institutions than if it happens at or beyond the edges of conventional organization' (Schudson 1995: 359). That remembering is social in origin and influenced by the dominant discourses is well illustrated by Zerubavel's (1997: 12) example of cognitive battles over memory, which are typically between social 'camps' rather than simply between individuals. The fact that major changes in the way we view the past usually correspond to major social transformations that affect entire mnemonic communities, as shown in many studies of changes in attitudes to the past in postcommunist countries after the collapse of communism (Szacka 1997), also provides the evidence that remembering is more than just a personal act and the nature of political power can influence the content of our memories.

Memory is also social because remembering does not take place in a social vacuum. We remember as members of social groups, and this means assuming and internalizing the common traditions and social representation shared by our collectivities. Memory cannot be removed from its social context, since whenever we remember something – for example, our first day at university – we also recall the social circumstances in which the event took place: the city, the university, friends and so on. Moreover, collective memory constitutes shared social frameworks of individual recollections as we share our memories with some people and not others, and – in turn – with whom, for what purpose and when we remember, all of which contributes to what we remember. Furthermore, memory is social because the act of remembering is itself interactive, promoted by cultural artefacts and cues employed for social purposes and even enacted by cooperative activity (Schudson 1997).

In today's societies, which 'are no longer societies of memory' (Hervieu-Leger 2000: 123), social memory refers not so much to living memory but to organized cultural practices supplying ways of understanding the world, and providing people with beliefs and opinions which guide their actions. As modern societies suffer from amnesia, we witness the transformation of living memory into institutionally shaped and sustained memory (Assmann 1995). *Cultural memory*, memory institutionalized through cultural means, is 'embodied in objectivations that store meaning in a concentrated manner' (Heller 2001: 1031). As 'memory that is shared outside the avenues of formal historical discourse yet . . . is entangled with cultural products and imbued with cultural meaning' (Sturken 1997: 3), cultural memory refers to people's memories constructed from the cultural forms and to cultural forms available for use by people to construct their relations to the past (Schudson 1995: 348). These cultural forms are distributed across social institutions and cultural artefacts such as films, monuments, statues, souvenirs and so on. Cultural memory is also embodied in regularly repeated practices, commemorations, ceremonies, festivals and rites. Since the individual 'piggybacks on the social and cultural practices of memory', cultural memory can exist independently of its carriers (Schudson 1995: 347). Cultural memory, as memory constituted through cultural means, comes close to Warburg's concept of the 'social memory' as communicated in visual imageries (Assmann 1995) – a notion which is popular mainly in the vast literature concerning museums, monuments, sculpture and festival culture in art and cultural history.

This approach, therefore, suggests that collective memory is not limited to the past that is shared together but also includes a representation of the past embodied in various cultural practices, especially in commemorative symbolism. Collective memory is not only what people really remember through their own experience, it also incorporates the constructed past which is constitutive of the collectivity. For instance, although citizens of Quebec, whose licence plates proudly state 'I remember', do not really remember the French colonial state, this past is a crucial element of the national memory of Quebec. Thus, the notion of collective memory refers both to a past that is *commonly shared* and a past that is *collectively commemorated*. As the word 'commemorate' derives from Latin *com* (together) and *momorare* (to remember), it can be said that the past that is jointly remembered and the past that is commonly shared are the crucial elements of collective memory (Schwartz 2000: 9). The fact that a commemorated event is one invested with extraordinary significance and assigned a qualitatively distinct place in a groups' conception of the past prompts some writers to assert that if 'there is such a thing as social memory . . . we are likely to find it in commemorative ceremonies' (Connerton 1989: 4).

Memory's essential role in social life is connected with the fact that 'collective memory is part of culture's meaning-making apparatus' (Schwartz 2000: 17). Our need for meaning, or, in other words, for being incorporated into something that transfigures individual existence, grants enormous importance to collective memory since it 'establishes an image of the world so compelling as to render meaningful its deepest perplexities' (Schwartz 2000: 17). In this way, collective memory not only reflects the past but also shapes present reality by providing people with understandings and symbolic frameworks that enable them to make sense of the world. Because the past is frequently used as the mirror in which we search for an explanation and remedy to our present-day problems, memory, is seen 'as [a] cure to the pathologies of modern life' (Huyssen 1995: 6). By mediating and paring the past and the present, as well as providing analogies to events of the present in past events, collective memory is strategic in character and capable of influencing the present. In other words, as we search for a means to impose a meaningful order upon reality, we rely on memory for the provision of symbolic representations and frames which can influence and organize both our actions and our conception of ourselves. Thus 'memory at once reflects, programs, and frames the present' (Schwartz 2000: 18).

Furthermore, the importance of memory lies in the identity that it shapes. The content of memory is subject to time as it changes with every new identity and every new present, so memory and temporality cannot be detached from each other. As self-identity presumes memory and because perception hinges upon remembered meanings, two processes are at work here. On the one hand, collective memory allows people to have a certain social identification, both on an individual and a societal level. On the other, following the old sociological assertion that the present influences the past, it can be said that the reconstruction of the past always depends on present-day identities and contexts. Memory can also play an important role as a source of truth. This happens where political power heavily censors national history and where oppressed nations have a profound deficit of truth. Therefore, they tend to look towards memory for authentic stories about their past. This inseparability of the content and form of memory and the issue of power is well illustrated by the situation in Soviet Latvia from 1940 to 1991, where people's memories conflicted with the official version of history and therefore they acquired 'a central importance of the preservation of authenticity and truth' (Skultans 1998: 28).

Social memory is also the crucial condition of people relations, since both conflict and cooperation hinge upon it. Groups' cooperative attitudes are the result of their ability to critically evaluate their respective pasts in a way that secures tolerance and removes barriers to mutual understanding. On the other hand, memory which is used to close boundaries of ethnic, national or other identities and which accepts some versions of the past as 'the truth' can aggravate conflicts. For example, the central memory of the Serbs, the lost Battle of Kosovo in 1389, symbolizes the permanent Muslim intention to colonize them and therefore is one of the obstacles to harmonious relations between Serbs and Muslims (Ray 1999). Another very important function of social remembering, which is best expressed in Karl Deutsch's remark that 'memory is essential for any extended functioning of autonomy' (quoted in Hosking 1989: 119), emphasizes the role of memory as helping us to ensure and improve the conditions of freedom by mastering our democratic institutions. Without memory – that is, without the checking of, and reflection upon, past records of institutions and public activities – we will have no warnings about potential dangers to democratic structures and no opportunity to gain a richer awareness of the repertoire of possible remedies. Memory, understood as a set of complex practices which contribute to our self-awareness, allows us to assess our potentialities and limits. 'Without memory', writes Deutsch, 'would-be self-steering organizations are apt to drift with their environment' because they are unable to reassess and reformulate their rules and aims in the light of experience. This statement is supported by many empirical studies which show that the lack of interest *in* the past and the lack of knowledge *of* the past tend to be accompanied by authoritarianism and utopian thinking, and that 'the root of oppression is loss of memory' (Gunn Allen 1999: 589). However, we need also to remember that since the nineteenth century, 'memory has seemed the mechanism by which ideology materializes itself' (Terdiman 1993: 33).

Memory, functioning as organized practices designed to ensure the reproduction of social and political order, is a source of 'factual' material for propaganda. Its task is to provide social groups or societies with identities and a set of unifying beliefs and values from which objectives are derived for political programmes and actions. Memory, when employed as a reservoir of officially sanctioned heroes and myths, can be seen as a broad and always (to some degree) invented tradition that explains and justifies the ends and means of organized social action and provides people with beliefs and opinions. This role of memory has been important since the end of the eighteenth century, when the new nation states started to construct their citizens' national identities with commemoration rituals, marches, ceremonies, festivals and the help of teachers, poets and painters (Hobsbawm and Ranger 1983). Thus, collective memory is not *just* historical knowledge, because it is experience, mediated by representation of the past, that enacts and gives substance to a group's identity. In order to understand the production of social memory we need to examine how a group maintains and cultivates a common memory. One way to start studying the social formation of memory is to analyse social contexts in which memories are embedded – groups that socialize us to what should be remembered and what should be forgotten; so-called *mnemonic communities.*

The communities of memory

In many languages 'memory stands, originally, not only for the mental act of remembering but also for the objective continuity of one's name – the name of a person, a family, a tribe or a nation' (Funkenstein 1993: 30). These groups – the family, the ethnic group and the nation – are examples of the main mnemonic communities which socialize us to what should be remembered and what should be forgotten. They affect the 'depth' of our memory; they regulate how far back we should remember, which part of the past should be remembered, which events mark the beginning and which should be forced out of our story. The process of our mnemonic socialization is an important part of all groups' general effort to incorporate new members. As such it is 'a subtle process that usually happens rather tacitly; listening to a family member recount a shared experience, for example, implicitly teaches one what is considered memorable and what one can actually forget' (Zerubavel 1997: 87). Mnemonic communities, through introducing and familiarizing new arrivals to their collective past, ensure that new members, by identifying with the groups' past, attain a required social identity. Since we tend to remember what is familiar – because familiar facts fit easily into our mental structures, and therefore make sense to us – groups' identities and collective memory are continuously reinforced. Due to a group's mnemonic tradition, a particular cognitive bias marks every group's remembering. Typically, such a bias expresses some essential truth about the group and its identity and equips the group with the emotional tone and style of its remembering. For instance, the partition of Poland in the eighteenth century gave that country an essential identity as 'the Christ among nations: cruci-fied and recrucified by foreign oppression', and through this established prism of victimhood many Poles still interpret their national fate.

Furthermore, a group's memory is linked to places, ruins, landscapes, monuments and urban architecture, which – as they are overlain with sym-bolic associations to past events – play an important role in helping to pre-serve group memory. Such sites, and also locations where a significant event is regularly celebrated and replayed, remain 'concrete and distinct regardless of whether they are mythological or historical' (Heller 2001: 1031). The fact that memories are often organized around places and objects suggests that remembering is something that occurs in the world of things and involves our senses. This was well understood by the ancient Greeks (see Chapter 2). Halbwachs, on the other hand, brings to our attention the fact that there are as many ways of representing space as there are groups and that each group leaves its imprint on its place. Arguing that our recollections are located with the help of landmarks that we always carry within ourselves, Halbwachs observes that space is 'a reality that endures', thus we can understand how we recapture the past only by understanding how it is preserved by our physical surroundings ([1926] 1950: 84–8). In *The Legendary Topography of the Gospels in the Holy Land*, Halbwachs (1941) demonstrates the work-ing of memory. He shows how Jews, Romans, Christians and Muslims rewrote the history of Jerusalem by remodelling the space according to their religious beliefs. Hence, 'When one looks at the physiognomy of the holy places in successive times, one finds the character of these groups inscribed' (Halbwachs [1941] 1992: 235). The discovery of several strata of memory superimposed on the Holy Land leads Halbwachs to argue that memory imprints its effect on the topography and that each group cuts up space in order to compose a fixed framework within which to enclose and retrieve its remembrance.

The link between landscape and memory is also present in Benjamin's (1968) viewing of the city as a repository of people's memories. Seeing the urban landscape as the battleground for the past, where the past remains open and contestable, he argues that the city can be read as the topography of a collective memory in which buildings are mnemonic symbols which can reveal hidden and forgotten pasts. Although the city offers us 'an illusionary and deceptive vision of the past' as many real histories are buried and covered (Gilloch 1996: 13), new events or new encounters can help us to uncover the city's true memories. So, memory and the metropolis are interwoven as memory shapes and is in turn shaped by the urban setting.

The nation is the main mnemonic community, for its continuity relies on the vision of a suitable past and a believable future. In order to create a required community's history and destiny, which in turn can be used to form the representation of the nation, the nation requires a usable past. Typically the creation of such a past is the task of nationalist movements, which propagate an ideology affirming identification with the nation state by invoking shared memories (Gellner 1993). Such movements owe their success, therefore, to memory, which they effectively employ to establish a sense of continuity between generations. The main way to shape societal aspiration for a shared destiny is by the rediscovery of memories of the 'golden age' and a heroic past (Smith 1997). In addition, appeals 'to the earliest individual memories of childhood – turns of phrase, catches of song, sights and smells – and [linking] them to the idea of the historical continuity of people, its culture and land' (Wrong 1994: 237), contributes significantly to the success of nationalist movements. However, as nations need to establish their representation in the past, their memories are created in tandem with forgetting; to remember everything could bring a threat to national cohesion and self-image. Forgetting is a necessary component in the construction of memory just as the writing of a historical narrative necessarily involves the elimination of certain elements. The role of forgetting in the construction of national identities has been noticed by Ernst Renan, who, in 1882, insisted that the creation of a nation requires the creative use of past events. He pointed out that, although nations could be characterized by 'the possession in common of a rich legacy of memories', the essence of a nation is not only that its members have many things in common, but also 'that they have forgotten some things' (Renan [1882] 1990: 11). In order to ensure national cohesion there is a need to forget events that represent a threat to unity and remember heroes and glory days. Renan's interpretation of collective memory continues to exert considerable influence on the way in which nations articulate themselves in the twentieth and twenty-first centuries. Anderson (1983) argues that being reminded of what one has already forgotten is a normal mechanism by which nations are constructed. He demonstrates how national memories, themselves underscored by selective forgetting, constitute one of the most important mechanisms by which a nation constructs a collective identity or become an 'imagined community'. Hobsbawm and Ranger (1983: 14) show that states engaged in historical construction of modern nations claim nations 'to be the opposite of novel, namely rooted in the remote antiquity'.

It has also been argued that our relation to the national past can be better described not so much as remembering but as forgetting. Billig (1995) suggests that established nations depend for their continued existence upon a collective amnesia. In such societies, not only is 'the past forgotten, but also there is a parallel forgetting of the present' (Billig 1995: 38). Forgetting, however, can also be highly organized and strategic, as examples from less open and democratic societies illustrate. Forced forgetting (Burke 1989) was of particular importance in communist countries, where people understood that 'the struggle against power is the struggle against forgetting' (Kundera 1980: 3). As the majority of communist regimes were also nation-building regimes, they 'went to great lengths to create new myths and to instill these in society through . . . political socialization mechanisms' (Cohen 1999: 27). They, like all new states, were busy constructing the national self-consciousness and used official ceremonies, education and socialization to create and foster a single, national, Marxist-Leninist class-based interpretation of the national history (Wingfield 2000). Politically and culturally oppressive states impose forgetting not only by rewriting and censorship of national history, but also by the destruction of places of memory. The Chinese communist government, for example, aimed to destory all places of memory, such as temples and monasteries, after the occupation of Tibet in 1951.

In today's societies, with their diversity of cultures, ethnicities, religions and traditions, we are witnessing the fragmentation of national memory. The processes of globalization, diversification and fragmentation of social interests further enhance the transformation of memory from the master narrative of nations to the episodic narrative of groups. The denationalization of memory, on the one hand, and an arrival of ailing and dispersed memories, on the other, in the context of the growing cultural and ethnic pluralization of societies, have provided a new importance to ethnic identities, whose formation is based on traditional memory narratives. Among all the groups in need of memory, 'ethnic groups have had the easiest task, for they have never entirely lost their cultural memory' (Heller 2001: 1032). Moreover, many forgotten elements can be brought to light, 'fused with new myths and stories of repression and suffering, or combined with heterogeneous cultural memorabilia such as music, crafts, and religious lore' (Heller 2001: 1032). As we witness the emergence of small, surrogate ethnic memories and a growing reliance on the specific content of a group memory to legitimize the group's political claims, battles 'for minorities' rights are increasingly organized around questions of cultural memory, its exclusions and taboo zones' (Huyssen 1995: 5). With ethnic memories surfacing in affiliation with the politics of identity, which itself is a result of the increasing importance of discourses of human rights in the global and postcolonial world, memories of past injustices are a critical source of empowerment. Today's fascination with ethnic memory, in the context of the declining of authoritative memories (traditional religious and national memories), poses new challenges for democratic systems (see Chapter 6).

The family is another group that plays a crucial role in the construction of our memories. As long as the family jointly produces and maintains its memory, its cohesion and continuity is ensured. The content of the shared family's narrative, symbolic of family unity across generations, reproduces family traditions, secrets and particular sentiments. These memories, objectified in old letters, photographs and family lore, are sustained through family conversations, as past events are jointly recalled or co-memorized (Billig 1990). Middleton and Edwards (1988) illustrated this process by researching how families collectively remembered past events by talking about photographs. As much research shows, children learn to remember in the family environment, guided by parental intervention and shared reminiscence. We do not remember ourselves as very young kids very clearly, so we rely on the memories of older members of our family, with the result that many of our earliest memories are actually recollections of stories we heard from adults about our childhood. Our memory is more accurately described as a collection of overlapping testimonies from our narrative environments, which influence our memory's emotional tone, style and content.

Presently we witness two processes: on the one hand, the growing impact of what might be described as the quest for family roots; and on the other the decline in the family's capability to maintain a living chain of memory. Family history was one of the most striking discoveries of the 1960s and has given rise to the most remarkable 'do-it-yourself archive-based scholarship of our time' (Samuel 1999: 169). This trend has been popularized by the mass media, with many books and films blending private and public memories. The growing interest in telling a family story has been recently assisted by new technologies such as the internet, where the numbers of family websites devoted to the construction of families' memory increases daily. At the same time there is a trend that suggests that families are less and less capable of maintaining their traditions due to changes in their structures and memberships, and this reflects the wider fate of memory in modern society. The decline of the extended, multi-generational family is leading to the destruction of a social framework that ensured the transmission of collective memories from one generation to the next. As family size and stability declines, the depth of family memory also suffers.

All three communities of memory (nation, ethnic group and family) are affected by the growing differentiation of society, the globalization of the world and by the development of new means of communication. These factors have also caused changes in the functioning of the institutions of memory.

The institutions of memory

In today's society, collective memory is increasingly shaped by specialized institutions: schools, courts, museums and the mass media. The growing number of 'ideas, assumptions, and knowledges that structure the relationship of individuals and groups to the immediate as well as the more distant past' (Sherman 1999: 2) is formed, interpreted and preserved by public institutions. The ideological themes that pervade the rhetoric of public authorities and the educational curricula, with history classes in school being the main example, 'tutor' public memory and promote a specific version of the past. Schools and textbooks are important vehicles through which societies transmit the idealized past and promote ideas of a national identity and unity. Textbooks have always been updated and rewritten to present the acceptable vision of the past, and although now, due to international pressures and national voices, textbooks are frequently the subject of external and domestic scrutiny, in many national narratives past events that could harm social cohesion and the authority of the state are still underplayed. Where the state controls the educational and media system, collective memory is fragmented, full of 'black holes', dominated by ideological values and used to produce legitimacy for the ruling élite. For example, in Tito's Yugoslavia, the official sanctioned memory of World War II, around which textbook narratives were structured, was a crucial element in the creation of legitimacy, myth and identity for the new communist state (Hoepken 1999). In such a situation, where the legitimization of social and political order depends upon official censorship, socially organized forgetting and the suppression of those elements that do not fit the regime's image of past events, unofficial and informal institutions as well an oral memory transmitted informally, frequently with the help of jokes, gossip, doublespeak and anecdotes, are essential to the preservation of collective memory.

Another institution which increasingly shapes our collective memory is the legal system. The relationship between public memory and the law is at the foundation of many countries' original conceptions of themselves. For example, such legal documents as the Magna Carta (UK) or the Declaration of Independence (USA) are essential for understanding these societies' origins and values. Not only is the legal system itself an enormously influential institution of collective memory, but in many countries changes in collective memory are legally induced. In all societies, to a considerable extent, courts, through their input in deciding historical questions, form collective memory. Postwar Europe saw many criminal prosecutions which aimed to influence national collective memories, the Nuremberg trials being the main example. Despite controversies and debates surrounding attempts to punish state-sponsored mass murder and readdress national memories, the trials' achievements for constructing the basis for new memories and a new order cannot be overlooked. Today, due to the proliferation of the language of human rights and the new strength of the politics of identity, we see an increase in demands for governments to address historical injustices committed in their name. Consequently, many nations, and not only those emerging from their authoritarian past, use the legal system to bring justice and to teach a particular interpretation of the country's history (see Chapter 6).

Legal attempts to construct collective memory are not without tensions and difficulties (Misztal 2001) but because they allow for confrontation of various memories, they can serve the periodic need to reawaken and strengthen the public's feelings of moral outrage.

A further important institution of memory is the museum. Museums originated in the late eighteenth century as monuments to wealth and civic patrimony, in the form of collections of material objects in courts and churches. From the nineteenth century it was an educational imperative of the emerging nation state to form national identity and 'to elevate the working class' that was responsible for the opening of exhibitions to a national public. Although museums have much in common with other institutions of memory, their authoritative and legitimizing status and their role as symbols of community constitute them as a distinctive cultural complex (Macdonald 1996). Museums are unusual not only because their development is connected to the formation and honouring of the nation state, but also because of their role in the social objectification of the past and organized memory around diverse artefacts.

Until recently, museums were mainly devoted to the preservation of a memory that constituted one of the high points of a national history, and therefore they were collecting 'objects to which the observer no longer has a vital relationship and which are in the process of dying' (Adorno 1967: 175). 'Museum and mausoleum', in Adorno's famous phrase, were associated by more than phonetics. Today, however, their authority as the curators of national treasures and the dictators of distinction and taste is challenged. This is a result of several factors, such as the availability of new technologies, the fragmentation and denationalization of memory and the development of a popular passion for heritage – that is, for 'the interpretation of the past through an artefactual history' (Urry 1996: 53) – resulting in an interest in old places, crafts, houses, countryside, old railways and so on.

With many museums fundamentally transforming their practice of collecting and exhibiting, their function now bears a strong relationship to memory production (Crane 2000a). Thus, 'the museum is no longer simply the guardian of treasures and artefacts from the past discreetly exhibited for the select group of experts', but has moved closer to 'the world of spectacle, of popular fair and mass entertainment' (Huyssen 1995: 19). In this process of transformation from the position of traditional cultural authority to a new role as cultural mediators in a more multicultural environment, museums redefine their strategies of representation of the past and find spaces for marginalized memories. This new opportunity for excluded memories, in the context of the decline of the management of public memory by the state, has resulted in the increased articulation of memory by various agencies from civil society and the enormous explosion of heritage and conservation organizations and movements.

Today, the most important role in the construction of collective memories is played by the mass media (McLuhan 1962). Before the development of the mass media, most people's sense of the past and the world beyond their immediate milieu was constituted by oral traditions that were produced and reproduced in the social context of everyday life. The shift from relying only on face-to face exchanges to depending on mediated interaction has profoundly affected the ways in which people organize material for recall as well as their modes of reconstructing the past (Thompson 1996: 95). Rapid technological advancements in the field of communication in the late nineteenth and twentieth centuries and the creation of the mass audience have ensured that the media is an extremely powerful instrument of ordering our knowledge of the past. In the nineteenth century it was the press that was the central means of communication and that provided people with images of groups that they could identify with. The press helped the transition from the local to the national by turning existing societies, through highlighting the common past and a constant repetition of images and words, into national communities (Anderson 1983). Now, the function of memory-keeping and presentation is 'increasingly assigned to the electronic media' (Samuel 1994: 25). The nature of this media and their interest in meeting public demands for instant entertainment are not without impact on the content and form of representations of the past. Thus, the input of media into how and what we remember is a crucial factor influencing the status of memory in contemporary societies.

The shift from oral culture, through writing and print, to electronic processing of the word has induced changes in the experience of time, brought about a new conception of the past and created growing possibilities for abstract thought. Thus, it can be said that the evolution of the role and form of social memory has been shaped by technological changes in the means of communication, and this is one of the most important factors structuring the status of memory in modern society.

The status of memory

Our discussion so far suggests that we rely on many social frameworks, institutions, places and objects to help us remember. The relationship between memory and objects is rather complicated because material objects, operating as vehicles of memory, can be of various types (e.g., dynamic or stable). Moreover, they provide us either with images and words, or both, while at the same time memory does not reside specifically in any image or word. Not only does our ability to remember depend on images and/or words, but how images work depends largely on their complex linkage with words, since images have in part always depended on words for direct interpretation, although images also function differently from words. If words and images offer two different kinds of representation, we can expect that as 'modes of representation change, both the relationship between words and images changes as well as how we understand images and words independently of each other' (Zelizer 1998: 5). Thus, the dependence on either words or images results in contrasting cultural values and also in contesting roles of memory. In order to throw light on changes in the status and meaning of memory, it is useful to have a quick look at discussions of the cultural consequences of the shift from oral culture to literacy.

When discussing the role of memory it is often assumed that in an 'oral' society – that is, in a society where communication occurs in forms other than written documents – culture depends upon memory and hence memory is highly valued. A further argument is that the 'rise of literacy' threatens memory. The assertion that technological change means the devalourization of memory has been a permanent element of the history of memory since ancient times. Starting with Plato's argument that the development of writing itself is a threat to individual memory, the idea that memory is in crisis has become the focus point of the centuries-long debate about memory. However, many writers protest against misconceptions about the value of memory in oral cultures and against the notion of memory crisis with the rise of literacy (Ong 1983; Carruthers 1990; Le Goff 1992; Goody 1998).

These scholars argue that the distinction between oral and literary societies is misleading because, as the continuation of the oral component in literary societies illustrates, the possession of writing does not mean that a society has ceased to be an oral culture as well. The majority of researchers agree that the rise of literacy does not necessarily bring the devalourization of memory and that learning by hearing material and reciting it does not necessarily imply an ignorance of reading. The reliance on living memories, associated with the oral transmission of a living past persisted long after the advent of print, and indeed continues to the present day (Ong 1983). In all cultures, not only in those without writing, memorizing is a part of everyday life (Goody 1977: 35). Moreover, basing the distinction between preliterate and literate cultures on a difference in levels of rationality embedded in those cultures needs to be rejected, as the extent to which a society is capable of transmitting its social memory in a logical and articulate form is not dependent upon the possession of writing but is rather connected with that society's representation of language and its perception of knowledge (Fentress and Wickham 1992: 45). Many studies illustrating a continuity between the mnemonic habits of preliterate and literary cultures argue that the privileged cultural role of memory depends 'on the role which rhetoric has in a culture rather than on whether its texts are presented in oral or written forms' – so in societies where literature is valued for its social function, rhetoric and interpretation works to provide the sources of a group's memory (Carruthers 1990: 10, 12). In similar vein, Assmann (1997), stresses the importance of oral transmission in cultures which, despite the possession of written means for preserving the past, keep their main texts alive through commentary.

Nevertheless, although preliterate cultures do not necessarily differ in terms of tasks and the value they assign to memory, the content of memory and the principal domain in which memory crystallizes have been affected by various processes such as the transformation of the technical means of preserving the past, changes in the experience of time, the increased interest in the past and the occurrence of dramatic events. For example, writing, because it generates cultural innovation by promoting economization and scepticism, encourages 'the production of unfamiliar statements and the thinking of novel thoughts' (Connerton 1989: 76). Furthermore, while speech can preserve memories over long intervals of time, it is too fleeting to permit any listener to pause for recollection; thus a sense of the past 'that is primarily based on hearing tales from others is different from one that is primarily based on reading oneself' (Eisenstein 1966: 49). As the 'pastness' of the past depends upon a historical sensibility, this can hardly begin to operate without permanent written records. Hence, literate societies, where records reveal the past is unlike the present, differ from oral cultures in their attitudes to the past. The repetitive regularity of most orally transmitted history means that most knowledge of the past is in fact shared, while in literate societies 'printed historical texts are widely disseminated but most knowledge of the past is fragmented into segments exclusive to small clusters of specialists and the consensually shared past shrinks to a thin media-dominated veneer' (Lowenthal 1998: 238). In literary cultures, past events, removed from living memories and fixed to printed pages, lose their vividness and immediacy. Moreover, as nobody could be expected to remember the content of continuously expanded libraries, the past is not entirely known. However, printed texts facilitate critical approaches and open inquiry into the past (Ong 1983). The new awareness of historicity came into being 'when it became possible to set one fixed account of the world beside another so that the contradictions within and between them could literally be seen' (Connerton 1989: 76). In contrast, oral societies live very much in the present and only with memories which have present relevance and which articulate inconsistent cultural inheritance.

The 'electronification' of memory provides a new dimension to the role memory plays in our image-fed society (Urry 1996: 63). Digital technology, interactive media and information systems have greatly changed the facets of memory practices in our time, and as a result today's memory is 'composed of bits and pieces' (Hervieu-Leger 2000: 129). The immediacy of communication, information overload, the speed of changing images, the growing hybridity of media, all further expand and problematize the status of memory. We have unlimited access to facts, sources and information, which we can store, freeze and replay. At the same time, visual images can interfere with and confuse our memories. For example, computer-generated graphics can fake the truth about the past, as they do in films like *Forrest Gump* and *Zoolander*). This decline of the credibility of photographic images and other visual evidence, together with the overabundance of flickering and changing narratives and images, is a threat to the status of memory as it raises the question of whose vision of the past and whose memories should be trusted. In the same vein, just as in print culture, readers' assessment of trust in the book underwrote the stability of knowledge and society (Johns 1998), trust in media (in other words, institutional trust) is crucial in making narratives of memory and identity into dominant cultural representations of reality.

The importance of institutional trust means that technological change is not the sole factor responsible for the status of memory. Both the shift in means of communication and the changes in modes of social organization, including changes in the practice of power, influence the nature of mnemonic practices. In other words, the structuring of memory in society is shaped by technological changes in the means of communication and the transformation of the dominant institutions of society. Memory, as the main source of collective identity, has always been employed by various social forces to boost their control and standing. When the main social authority was religious institutions, for example (as in ancient Israel), religious memory was called upon to sustain followers' allegiance; thus the biblical continuous appeal to '*Zakhor*' ('remember') that ensured that remembering was 'felt as a religious imperative to an entire people' (Yerushalmi 1982: 9). Similarly, the emergence of the nation state was accompanied by inventions of new memories to enhance national identities. Today, memory is more distant from traditional sources of power, while at the same time it becomes increasingly shaped by mass media.

To sum up, this chapter, after describing different forms of memory, defined collective memory as the representation of the past, both the past shared by a group and the past that is collectively commemorated, that enacts and gives substance to the group's identity, its present conditions and its vision of the future. The following presentation of the role of main mnemonic communities and institutions of memory aimed to expand our understanding of the social formation of memory. Discussing further the status of memory, we noted how changes in modes of communication and social organization influence the structure and status of memory. Since memory has travelled from oral expression through print literacy to today's electronic means of communication, we can conclude by saying that memory has its own history. This history, linked to a large degree to the history of changing modes of communication and techniques of power, will be discussed in the next chapter.

Further reading

Baddley, A. (1989) The psychology of remembering and forgetting, in T. Butler (ed.) *Memory: History, Culture and the Mind*, pp. 33–60. Oxford: Basil Blackwell.

Goody, J. (1998) Memory in oral tradition, in P. Fara and K. Patterson (eds) *Memory*, pp. 73–94. Cambridge: Cambridge University Press.

Renan, E. ([1882] 1990) What is a nation?, in H.K. Bhabha (ed.) *Nation and Narration*. London: Routledge.

Schudson, M. (1995) Distortion in collective memory, in D.L. Schacter (ed.) *Memory Distortion*, pp. 346–63. Cambridge, MA: Harvard University Press.

Sennett, R. (1998) Disturbing memories, in P. Fara and K. Patterson (eds) *Memory*, pp. 10–46. Cambridge: Cambridge University Press.

CHAPTER 2

METAMORPHOSIS OF
MEMORY

*'Memory has always had political or ideological overtones, but
each epoch has found its own meaning in memory'*
(Hacking 1995: 200)

As we concluded in the previous chapter, memory has its own history as its
status has been affected by the shift from preliterate culture through literacy
to today's capacity to freeze, replay and store visual memories. The history
of collective memory can be divided into five periods (Le Goff 1992). The
first phase refers to the collective memory of people without writing. The
second period, antiquity, is characterized by the predominance of oral
memory alongside written memory. The medieval period is seen as expressing itself in equilibrium between the oral and the written and in the transformation of the two memories' function. The period from the sixteenth
century until the present is characterized by the progress of written memory
connected with printing and literacy. The last, current phase is parallel to the
revolutionary changes of the present day and results in memory expansion
(Le Goff 1992: 54–5).

Memory in oral cultures

The notion of an oral culture refers to a society without writing or to a
society in which the capacity to produce and understand written symbols
(i.e. literacy) is confined to a small social, political or religious élite. Goody
and Watt (1968) offer a fascinating set of studies of the impact of literacy on
societies ranging from Greece in the seventh century BCE to pre-Columbus
America (i.e. before 1450), to pre-colonial Africa, India and Asia (i.e. before
the nineteenth century). Oral cultures, like all cultures, depended upon

stored knowledge. However, the accumulation and transmission of know-ledge in such societies largely relied on so-called 'ethnic memory' (Le Goff 1992: 55) which differs in its content, orientation and precision from memory in literary societies. In 'ethnic memories', the past was fused with the present, the collective identity based on myths, while handing down modes of life from the past, was expressed by genealogies and was more a matter of ingrained habit than deliberate effort. The past in oral cultures was not felt as an itemized terrain consisting of verifiable facts but was the domain of 'the ancestors, a resonant source for renewing awareness of present exist-ence' (Ong 1983: 98). In oral cultures people assumed that things were as they had always been, because oral transmission accumulates actual alter-ations unconsciously, continually readjusting the past to fit the present (Goody 1998: 74–93).

The main contrast between memory in a society in which communication occurs in forms other than written documents, and memory in societies collecting written documents and transforming them into testimony, is con-nected with their different conceptualization of the distinction between past and present (Le Goff 1992: 55–7). Oral cultures provide a milieu of living memory where the past expands beyond 10 to 12 generations in lineage structure or a 50–100 year span. The oral transmission of the past means that the past is bound to the present for its survival. The past exists only in so far as it continues to be held in living memory, and it is so remembered only as long as it serves present needs. Due to the limitations of memory in oral cultures, such societies' response to time is limited to an annual cycle and therefore cannot be used to differentiate longer periods than seasons. In oral societies, time is not a continuum as it is 'an order of events of outstanding significance to a group' (Evans-Pritchard 1968: 109). It is also relative to structural space because 'each group has its own points of reference'.

The second significant difference is connected with the orientation of col-lective memory in oral societies towards the time of origin and mythical heroes. In an oral culture, the past refers essentially to a mythical creation or Golden Age, with personal genealogies claiming to run to the beginning of time. Furthermore, due to the attraction of the ancestral past, the 'peculiar-ity of primitive thought is to be atemporal; it tries to grasp the world simul-taneously as a synchronic and as diachronic totality' (Levi-Strauss 1966: 55). Memory, moreover, is the only frame of reference by which to judge the past, and therefore it plays an important role in maintaining the order and cohesion of the group. Since in oral cultures all relationships must be explained in terms of the past, memory coordinates and cements social relations (Evans-Pritchard 1968: 105).

Oral traditions consist of records of mythology, lists of kings, genealogies, legends and clan names, so the memory of people without writing provides a parallel historical foundation for the existence of ethnic groups or families – that is, myths of origin. Since spirits of the departed remain intimately involved with everyday life, for many people in these societies 'the past was not a foreign country but their own' (Lownethal 1998: 13). In other words, oral tradition 'combines mythology, genealogy and narrative history, rather than holding them apart' (Fentress and Wickham 1992: 82). In many such cultures oral tradition is helped by a specialist (e.g. in many African societies, where the main practices of memorization rely on songs, a memory-man is a 'lore master' or 'praise singer') who preserves rituals, technologies and local knowledge. Ritualistic chants are repeated from performance to performance, while habit and custom ensure the memorization of practical, technical and professional knowledge without revealing the specific nature of the habit (Ong 1983: 63–5; Le Goff 1992: 56; Hutton 1993: 17). This type of memory is gained through apprenticeship and is based on a respect for custom and habit. Hence, memory in oral traditions can be 'identified primarily with habit; its authority is derived from the felt need to reiterate the wisdom bequest by the past' (Hutton 1993: 17).

However, memory transmitted through custom and habit does not stand still because it is not 'word-for-word memory' and because the past is continually updated as new realities present themselves (Levi-Strauss 1966, Le Goff 1992; Goody 1998). The unique flexibility of oral traditions is linked to the transformative nature of their knowledge, which is stored in a way that cannot be recalled precisely. As oral versions of events are recited in different times and places, oral memory becomes 're-worked experience' (Goody 1998: 88–94). Due to the role of forgetting, human diversity and the generative use of language and gesture, memory seems to function in these societies in accordance with 'generative reconstruction' rather than mechanical memorization. Hence 'every performance is also a creative act, there is no distinct separation between performer and creator' (Goody 1998: 91). The same argument is developed by Le Goff (1992: 57), who notes that societies without writing 'grant memory more freedom and creative possibilities'. In other words, mnemonic reproduction word is characteristic of literate societies rather than societies without writing where 'imagination and memory are virtually interchangeable because each is defined by its capacity to form images in which past, present and future are intimately joined' (Hutton 1993: 17). Therefore, since in oral cultures 'word-for-word memory' is impossible, the practice of memorization is not assigned an important role and it 'is rarely felt to be necessary' by members of this type of society (Goody 1977: 38).

Stressing that oral cultures are in a state of continuous creation, Goody warns against the danger of speaking about a collective memory in such societies: 'An oral culture is not held in everybody's memory store. Memories vary as does experience. Bits may be held by different people' (Goody 1998: 94). However, the same warning, although for different reasons, can be issued with regard to the nature of social memory in today's societies. Whereas the fluidity and creativity of memory in oral cultures is connected with the means of creation and transmission of memory available in those societies, memory's selectivity and plurality in literary cultures is a result of phonetic writing's ability to generate cultural innovation as well as of a more complex modern social structure. Although with the rise of literacy, improvisation becomes increasingly difficult and innovation is institutionalized, social memory, freed from dependence on rhythm and being the subject of systematic criticism, is in the process of continuous change (Goody and Watt 1968). Furthermore, since modern societies offer individuals the possibility of belonging to many groups and a choice of different sets of identities, social memories in those systems are not exclusive but multilayered and overlapping. Today an individual can be a member of an array of different groups, whereas in oral cultures membership was limited, and therefore, generally, a single group's memory informed the individual identity.

There is yet another similarity between social memory in oral cultures and memory in modern societies. In both cases we can observe the workings of a general principle of structural amnesia, which directs our attention to the role of social institutions in guiding and controlling memory (Evans-Pritchard 1968). In both type of society, remembering and forgetting is selective but not accidental – what is forgotten is not forgotten randomly. This phenomenon of structural amnesia suggests that 'the strength and weakness of recall depend[s] on a mnemonic system, that is the whole social order' (Douglas 1986: 72), and thus it points to the link between memory and social systems. In other words, collective memory in both oral and in literary cultures, is 'the storage for the social order' (Douglas 1986: 70) and therefore it is always a provisional, dynamic and selective interplay of opinions and narratives.

The art of memory

Despite the invention of script, antiquity was characterized by the predominance of oral memory, as oral modes of expression continued to convey a sense of the past that did not discriminate between the mythical and the historical (Eisenstein 1966: 51). In Greek mythology, memory, the goddess Mnemosyne, is a mother of nine Muses and her name symbolizes the power of imagination and stands for the totality of cultural activities – thus our contemporary term 'cultural memory'. By subsuming all cultural activities under 'the personification of memory, the Greeks were viewing culture not only as based on memory but as a form of memory itself' (Assmann 1997: 15). For ancient philosophers, who held memory in the highest esteem, remembrance was that of pure and timeless forms, not of temporal constructs. They viewed memory as a source of immortality and wisdom and did not distinguish between the past and imagination, nor between the past and myth. Socrates, for example, admired memory because without it no one could enjoy what her daughters, custodians of the arts and sciences, produced as each 'sound would fade away without ever being included in a melody, every word in a poem would disappear before the rhyming word was heard' (Draaisma 2000: 5). In Plato's and Aristotle's presentations, 'the gift of memory', placed in the soul and thus a function of the soul, is seen as essential for a virtuous and just life. Such 'mystical divinization of memory' meant that even 'the greatest Greek philosophers never fully succeeded in reconciling memory and history' (Le Goff 1992: 65). However, the trend towards the secularization of memory and the discovery of the technique of improving memory induced a slow process of transformation in this relationship.

This new technique, *ars memoria*, or the art of memory, is attributed to the poet Simonides of Ceos (c.556–468 BCE), who discovered the importance of order and the sense of sight for memory. Proceeding from Aristotle's assertion that there is no thought without an image and that recollection means perceiving something as an image, *ars memoria* assigned a central role to mental images (Yates 1966: 3–5). The mnemotechnics involved locating each element to be remembered in imaginary palaces of memory so that it could be easily recovered in its proper place by conceptually 'touring' those palaces. Orators, in order to associate the texts and ideas to be remembered with the image of a place, relied on paintings, sculptures and buildings as aids in the process of the placement of allegorical images within a fictive architecture. Thus, when they were mentally walking around imaginary objects as if they were statues in a palace, gallery or theatre, their remembering was enhanced. As philosophers, such as Cicero, focused on the difference between artificial or trained, and conventional or natural memory, and insisted that a memory strengthened by training was an essential part of the orator's equipment, memory lost its mythical aspect and became 'desacralized and secularized' (Le Goff 1992: 65). This suited a rising literary culture which still relied on memory for the organization of knowledge, and hence on the art of memory, as a part of an education based on rhetoric.

To sum up, in the largely oral culture of Greek and Roman antiquity, where wax tablets were little more than a memory aid, most of what people wanted to say in a speech still had to be committed to memory and therefore they relied on a procedure to facilitate remembering that turned memory into an imaginary space; this was the art of memory. The power of memory was admired by many as it was assumed, following Plato, that all 'knowledge is but remembrance', and that therefore memory is, as Cicero said, 'the treasury and guardian of all things' (quoted in Shotter 1990: 136). The high status of the art of memory in the ancient world was also a result of the fact that it was an élite practice, associated with orators and later with scholars who greatly appreciated this technique's capacities for image-making and the preservation of knowledge. In ancient Greece, memory was seen as the source of all the arts and sciences, while in Roman culture memory was placed at the heart of all teaching, learning and thought (Samuel 1994: vii): 'No art was more carefully studied, or esteemed, from Plato until Enlightenment, than the art of memory' (Hacking 1995: 203).

Following antiquity's later metaphors of memory as a storage space, the neoplatonist St Augustine (354–430) saw memory as a 'vast, immeasurable sanctuary', and stressed the spiritual dimensions of memory. Augustine, seeing memory as 'a great field or a spacious place, a storehouse for countless images of all kinds', asks: 'Who can plumb its depths? And yet it is faculty of my soul' (McConkey 1996: 7). Memory was seen as a source of truth because it allowed the recall of 'a state of blessed happiness', and this memory of a lost happiness thus must contain 'an awareness of Truth' Cicero's insistence on the ethical status of memory, which he saw as 'the soul's highest ability' was further enhanced by Albertus Magnus and Thomas Aquinas' discussion of memory as a part of Prudence (Draaisma 2000: 31). Thus, with memory seen as an essential element of virtue, the technology of memory was continuously recommended as a vital factor in the formation of moral character.

Memory in pre-modern Europe

In the medieval period oral transmission still played an important role and a trained memory continued to be highly valued as the essential means of the preservation of knowledge and the main safeguard against the loss of manuscript scrolls (Yeo 2001: 83). Until the late Middle Ages, writing was still regarded as a mere adjunct to memory and the collected knowledge was seen as worth committing to memory. Thus the art of memory played a central role in the scribal culture of Western Europe. Even though medieval scholars' memories were supplemented by the spread of texts, memory was still envisaged as a kind of book in which images were engraved or impressed (Yeo 2001: 79). Despite the fact that the use of writing as a support for memory intensified, it was only after the invention of printing in the 1450s that books came to be seen as supplementing memory (Le Goff 1992: 74).

The importance of oral transmission was also due to the fact that the world of manuscript literacy in the Middle Ages was for the most part a sphere of élite culture, while folk memories, rooted in oral means of transmission, were dominant. It was also due to the nature of scribal culture 'which was more closely tied to oral and auditory memory-training than is often recognized' (Eisenstein 1966: 44). Although the invention of script in antiquity permitted more abstract ways of thinking, nonetheless the world of manuscript literacy in the Middle Ages represented less an opening into history 'than an attempt to hold onto the wisdom of time immemorial derived from oral tradition' (Hutton 1993: 18). Generally, it can be said that throughout most of the Middle Ages, literate élites shared with pre-literary folk a common reliance upon oral transmission to teach most of what they knew about the past (Eisenstein 1966: 53). As a result of both the dissemination of written material and memorization, medieval culture should be seen as characterized by 'the tension maintained between these two forms' (Innes 1998: 3).

In the Middle Ages history was not understood as an appreciation of the reality of change but was 'a unified Christian drama with no scope for or interest in differences between past and present' (Lowenthal 1985: 232). This lack of awareness about, or denial of, the difference between the past and the present, along with ignorance of the reality of the past meant that medieval interest in antiquity was predicated on its relevance to present concerns and experiences. However, the gradually increasing fascination with classical sources and the growing authority of old manuscripts brought about new attitudes towards the past, which was presented as being exemplary of human practices, and towards memory, which was reconsidered as a capacity to make the experiences of the past live again (Lowenthal 1985: 232–4). Consequently, the understanding of memory 'as a repetition, carried over from oral culture, was gradually replaced by one of memory as a resurrection' (Hutton 1993: 18). The rise of Christianity brought with it an attendant understanding of history as the unfolding of a divine plan. Medieval thinkers believed in God as being the cause of all historical processes, and saw humans as carrying out the will of God. The Christian experience of history, which was associated with expectations of salvation (Carruthers 1990: 123), meant that the past and memory were not seen as models for understanding the present or the future but as sources of evidence of divine intervention in history (Tosh 1991: 11–12).

The new relation between memory and religion, reinforced by the nature of Christianity and Judaism (both being 'religions of remembrance'), by the Bible's frequent insistence on the duty to remember and by Christian rituals of commemoration of saints, resulted in 'a circular liturgical memory' (Le Goff 1992: 68). Apart from 'a circular liturgical memory', the second element of collective memory in the medieval period was lay memory, which was also shaped by the Church calendar (Le Goff 1992: 68). Being rooted in oral transmission and commemoration practices, lay memory contained a popular recounting of the family-centred past and memories of the dead. There was no clear distinction between the past and the present as ordinary people felt the past to be so much a part of their present that they perceived no urgent need to preserve it (Duby 1988: 619–20). The pattern of remembering characteristic of peasant societies, with their structuring of the past through family and locality, meant that memories were local rather than 'national' (Fentress and Wickham 1992: 153).

The sense of the past, shaped by the interaction between written and oral traditions, also went through profound transformations because of the importance of mnemotechnolgy in education systems and the impact of Christianity (Le Goff 1992: 68–72). In the Middle Ages, the art of memory was placed in the context of logic and moral philosophy rather than rhetoric, with the scholastic philosophers – who were central to medieval scholarly life, literature and the arts – being its main practitioners (Yates 1966: 368). From the earliest medieval times, educators relied on visual and spatial images and locations to improve students' memories, while from the thirteenth century, the architectural mnemonic, the method of projecting images into architectural places, enjoyed a revival. The art of memory, inherited consciously from antiquity, 'governed much in medieval education, designed to aid the mind in forming and maintaining heuristic formats that are both spatial and visualizable' (Carruthers 1990: 32). With the value of the art of memory enhanced further by St Thomas Aquinas in the thirteenth century (Samuel 1999: vii), religious scholars' trained memories were regarded as more reliable than the imperfect copies of manuscripts scattered across Europe. The reliance of the Church on the art of memory provided the central support for texts, while the layout of libraries imitated the design of religious scholars' memories (Yeo 2001: 80). Memory, because of its identification with prudence, rigorous discipline and the highest pursuits, was highly valued, although practiced mainly by the preaching orders. All mnemonic systems underwent a process of Christianization, as a result of which 'the palaces of memory were replaced by abbeys and cathedrals', classical images were replaced by 'such virtues as Chastity and Moderation', while memory became 'the instrument for keeping in mind liturgies and saints, heaven, hell and purgatory' (Draaisma 2000: 41). A new mnemonic landscape, associated with the sacred landmarks of pilgrim routes, burial grounds, churches and shrines, became the essence of the early Middle Ages. Medieval Christianity's images of memory, pictured as 'a vast, immeasurable sanctuary', or as a series of buildings harmonized with the great Gothic churches (Yates 1966: 46). This connection between the medieval period's architectural style and the art of memory's imaginary canons resulted in 'the Great Gothic artificial memories of the Middle Ages' (Yates 1966: xii) and illustrates the observation, which opens this chapter, that each epoch finds its own expression and meaning in memory (Hacking 1995: 200).

In the Renaissance, the art of memory expressed the period's expanded power of imagination and harmonized intellectually with its geometric architecture (Yates 1966: 152–69). Although the humanist philosophers rejected the art of memory, for the hermetic philosophers it still had a special appeal as it allowed for the revival of the belief in the magical power of memory, alchemy, astrology, cabalism, and magic. In this mystical tradition of occult science, the magical practice of memory was conceptualized as a kind of 'ascent to the stars' (Samuel 1994: ix) and became connected with the issue of human immortality, with the result that spiritual theories of memory gained in significance (Draaisma 2000: 60–4). The Renaissance applications of the art of memory aimed to contain the 'soul' of things to remember (Yates 1966: 140), and thus to provide 'a way toward initiation into a state of spiritual enlightenment' (Hutton 1993: 19).

Soon, however, the relationship between memory and knowledge changed and this led to a gradual but systematic erosion of the value put on memory. Although in Bacon's influential classification of knowledge, published in *The Advancement of Learning* (1605), Memory, together with Imagination and Reason, were presented as the main faculties, in the early modern period the reliance on memory in the scientific field was already declining (Yeo 2001: 23). The role of memory was further diminished by the evolution of the classical mnemonic system, which transmuted from a 'method of memorizing the encyclopaedia of knowledge, of reflecting the world in memory' to an instrument to help in the discovery of the world (Yates 1966: 185). Even more importantly, the art of memory was seen as 'a method of investigation and a method of logical investigation' (Yates 1966: 185) and by developing scholars' need for the systematic organization of knowledge 'may have trained them in the kind of systematic thinking, that made possible the scientific revolution' (Hutton 1993: 12). With the spread of printing and the expansion of knowledge, now understood not as accepted truth but as an open search, the elaborate mnemonic techniques began to disappear, while scientists rejected memory because 'one does not require memory in all science' (Descartes, quoted in Le Goff 1992: 84). By the seventeenth century, with the decline of the art of memory, the function of transmitting messages from the past detached from the human voice and entrusted to books, and with the increasing dissemination of printed historical texts, the 'pastness' of the past slowly came to be appreciated.

The development of print culture, which ensured the standardization, dissemination and fixity of the text, underwrote the gradually established stability of the vision of the past (Eisenstein 1966). Additionally, the emergence of this new awareness and appreciation of the past was assisted by the Renaissance rediscovery of the classical world and the growing understanding of antiquity as a different realm. This new method of understanding antiquity was developed by the Renaissance humanists, who discovered that 'the clearer the image of antiquity became, the less it seemed to resemble the present' (Lowenthal 1985: 232) and insisted on the critical reading of 'the pure text' and the investigation of the authenticity of documents. While for ancient or medieval authors, historical facts were atomic entities, immediately perceivable and understandable and hardly in need of interpretation, from the sixteenth and seventeenth centuries onward a new perception of historical facts emerged. Now, the historical fact was 'not in and of itself meaningful: only its context endows a historical fact with meaning and significance. The context of historical facts is not at all given: it must be reconstructed by the historian from other facts' (Funkenstein 1993: 25). The strengthening of this new perception of the past, which led finally to seeing the past as a different realm, was further helped by the use of letters to preserve memory, the establishment of archives (from the thirteenth century), libraries, the dissemination of printed books, secularism and the increasing scrutiny of evidence (Lowenthal 1985: 233). All these trends gradually reinforced the importance of written documents beyond the monopoly of a small élite, therefore textualizing the past and historicizing memory in more concrete ways. By removing ideas, personalities and events from the milieu of oral tradition and giving them a specific time and place in collective memory, texts enabled readers to comprehend the historicity of the past in a more profound way: 'The textualization of collective memory depended on the readers' awareness of temporality, and this in turn led to the recasting of mnemonic schemes, previously conceived spatially, onto timelines on which historical events served as places of memory' (Hutton 1993: 19). Nevertheless, the trend towards seeing the past as a different realm was a slow process, as discrimination between 'the mythical and historical remained blurred for a full two centuries after printing' (Eisenstein 1966: 51).

In the Middle Ages, memory enjoyed a high status not only because it was valued enormously as a container of virtues and an instrument of thought, but also because of concern about loss of knowledge. Since until the eighteenth century even printed books were not perceived as a safe container of knowledge (Yeo 2001: 80), medieval works sought to summarize and record a stable body of knowledge, often by referring back to the vocal context (Ong 1983: 311–13). In the monastic tradition of the Middle Ages, the written word was treated differently as it was assumed that what was written in books must eventually find its way into the personal memory, and therefore the book was not regarded as an alternative to human memory, but as an aid to memory (Carruthers 1990). However, the spread of dictionaries and encyclopedias gave the public access to an enormous amount of knowledge about the past, as well as the progress of science and philosophy, and as a result transformed the role and content of memory (Le Goff 1992: 81–5). From the end of the Middle Ages, mnemonics were not invested 'with any moral authority or stature' (Hacking 1995: 203) and with the early modern period came the realization 'that knowledge, even the most important parts of it, could no longer be held in memory' (Yeo 2001: 78). During the Enlightenment, the art of memory was rejected in favour of observation, experience, intelligence and reason, which meant the end of the art of memory and the emergence of a clear difference between the mythical and the historical.

Although during the Enlightenment the mnemonic technique lost its standing, a concern with memory continued in many philosophical works. For example, John Locke famously discussed connections between personal identity and memory as well as the role of emotion in recovering memory. Nonetheless, as Hacking (1995: 203) notes, in the seventeenth century 'there was no systematic attempt to uncover facts about memory'. Yet, as the arenas for religious and political activity were broadening and as many fundamental issues became subjects of dispute, the rivalry over who owned memory and whose vision of the past was to be honoured in official memorials and monuments became one of the most important political issues, first in England and later in all modern societies.

Memory in modern society

The history of memory since the eighteenth century has been influenced by many factors, including new technological developments, the advent of a middle-class readership, a growing detachment from religious worldviews, an increasing process of industrialization and urbanization, as well as nationalism. All these trends led to expansion of the possibility of abstract thought and produced a new awareness of the distinctiveness of history (Olick and Robbins 1998: 110–12). Since it is beyond our capacity to discuss all these changes here, in this section we only briefly summarize the main trends related to the history of memory in this period.

The eighteenth century was a unique period in the history of memory because at that time the meaning of memory at once broadened and diminished. First, within this period the vast advancement of literacy and the expansion of sciences gradually expanded memory. As there was a lot more of the past, many historians, influenced by the Ciceronian model of rhetorical history, assembled 'beautifully written tales for the reading public' (Arnold 2000: 47, 52). The progressive mass of information produced by increasingly specialized disciplines and the multiplication of books meant that memory, however finely trained, was no longer an adequate container of knowledge (Yeo 2001: 80–7). This realization, that individual memory could not cope with the expansion of knowledge, provided a new rationale for the publication of dictionaries and encyclopedias, and the creation of museums, archives and libraries, which were supposed to condense and preserve knowledge and memories. Although encyclopedias of the Enlightenment sought to provide a solution to the situation in which there were too many books and nobody could be expected to remember the content of whole libraries, this does not mean that they were envisaged in strictly instrumental terms, or merely as 'machines that remember for us' (Van Doren, quoted in Yeo 2001: 116). However, with the still prevailing conviction that educated persons should attempt to embrace a range of science, Enlightenment encyclopedias were nevertheless designed to bring 'an increasingly rich technical, scientific and intellectual memory' to the reader (Le Goff 1992: 85).

Second, the Enlightenment undermined the authority of memory by making it clear in an 'encyclopedic tree', which replaced Bacon's classification of knowledge, that reason, not memory, 'controlled the largest number of arts and sciences' (Yeo 2001: 28). Third, the Enlightenment weakened the importance and status of memory as it set out to destroy the authority of tradition, seen as associated with backwardness and reactionary beliefs. Historians, who believed that their age surpassed any previous period in knowledge, not only studied the past but also made judgements upon it. Unfortunately, in the majority of cases, 'the past did not live up to their high expectations' (Arnold 2000: 52). The appeal of the notion of rationality and progress meant that the past was viewed as the bastion of ignorance and irrational tradition: 'The first entry of the agenda of the Enlightenment was therefore to do away with traditionality as such' (Shils 1981: 6). Seeing history as a kind of continuous progress of reason and knowledge gave tradition a bad name and resulted in a lack of interest in memories of the past. The belief that progress could be achieved through the development and application of scientific knowledge enhanced a fascination with the future and promoted a rejection of the traditional past. With the Enlightenment theorists' dislike of tradition, western societies of the eighteenth century displayed interest neither in how the past works nor in commemoration rituals (Aries 1981).

However, since the late eighteenth century, with the invention of the 'nation state', the political demands on memory have been strong in all Western European countries. With the emergence of many European nationalist movements it became clear that a 'free nation needs national celebrations' (Gambetta 1872 quoted in Le Goff 1992: 87). Consequently, each nation created its own commemorations, and supplied the collective memories with monuments of remembrance and new traditions, which were deliberately designed to symbolize national unity, to ensure state legitimacy and build political consensus. The expansion of the state's role in shaping and maintaining a nation's narrative of collective historical experience was most pronounced in France, where the 1789 Revolution, by providing the nation with an origin myth, became a founding moment for the historical imagery of the country (Fentress and Wickham 1992: 128–33). After the Revolution, the French constitution declared that: 'National celebrations will be established to preserve the memory of the French Revolution' (Le Goff 1992: 86). The revolutionary fascination with antiquity and French history resulted in an increased focus on the past, with the art in this period consequently becoming a 'factory of the past' (Le Goff 1992: 15). The French state organized and articulated narratives enhancing its legitimization through the introduction of a new calendar (which aimed to create a distinctive rhythm of social life that unified a group through shared recollection), celebrations and commemorations, all seen as powerful means to mark the discontinuity between the past and the present, between a former regime and a new one: 'All the calendar-makers and celebration-makers agree on the necessity of using the festival to maintain the memory of the Revolution' (Ozouf 1988: 199). The national celebration, anthem and flag became means to symbolize the uniqueness of the nation and were used in the service of national memory. From that moment on, state-designed and state-sponsored commemoration practices multiplied, while the style of celebrations broadened, particularly with the use of coins, medals, postage stamps, monuments and memorial days as new means of commemoration (Ozouf 1988). During the Revolutionary and Napoleonic periods, state patronage resulted in raising monuments which focused public attention on the aspirations of the state. At the same time, these eras initiated the democratization of memory by erecting memorials not to kings or generals but to ordinary warriors, with the first monuments to dead soldiers constructed in Lucerne and dedicated to the memory of members of the Swiss Guard killed on 10 August 1792 (Laqueur 1994: 159). The Third Republic also continued the construction of an official memory by developing, for example, secular education designed to replace religion as a source of collective identity, with Republican values and memory. The Republic likewise manipulated the practice of national unity by inventing public commemorative celebrations to enhance officially approved memories and to propagate the state glory. For instance, Bastille Day was 'invented' only in 1880, more than 90 years after the actual event took place (Hobsbawm 1983: 271).

In contrast, the continuity of the British state and a lack of comparable state patronage did not produce new commemorative practices, official holidays or patriotic celebrations. However, by the seventeenth century there was a insistent focus on public memory in England which was used for political and religious purposes. At this time, England's past became 'an issue of many political discourses, which revolved around interpretation, celebration and control of the past' (Cressy 1994: 61). A resulting accomplished vision of the past was incorporated into the calendar, reiterated in sermons, and exhibited in memorials and monuments. By the end of seventeenth century, following the English governments' construction and manipulation of national memory, 'a canon of memories that once bound the nation to its crown and its church had become the contested ground for rival ideologies and faith' (Cressy 1994: 71). In the next century, the break with the past brought about by the industrial revolution was remembered by all classes: 'Memory was central to the making of English working-class identities as it was to the class consciousness of the British bourgeoisie, both of which were constructed in the nineteenth century' (Gillis 1994b: 8).

The nineteenth-century trade union movement in England established its own labour rituals, celebrations and parades, while the bourgeoisie expressed its civic pride by collecting national treasures and contributing to the creation of museums. The British Museum, founded in 1753 when parliament voted to buy, with public money and gifts, a vast private collection, was quite different from the collections of the previous century, not only because it was 'the strongest, and not only in art and antiquity, but also in natural history', but also because its intellectual rationale was rooted in the wealthy middle-class belief in progress, knowledge and 'the idea of the present as the product of the past' (Pearce 1992: 100–1). The creation of museums in most cities and large towns in Britain can be seen as the manifestation of the civic pride of the emerging middle classes, whose nationalism expressed itself in the celebration of the lives of great men and artists. Also the National Trust, created at the end of the nineteenth century as a bulwark of the aristocracy, soon became a middle-class heritage mass movement (Wright 1985; Hewison 1987).

The further expansion of social movements concerned with conservation and heritage, together with the rise of an enthusiasm for voluntary subscription for the construction of monuments commemorating national heroes, suggests that national memory was created not just from the sense of a break with the past. Public monuments at the beginning of the nineteenth century 'were a means of expressing the emerging national and civic pride of the British people, particularly in expanding provincial towns and cities' (Yarrington 1988: 326). In the second part of the nineteenth century, as the public directed its attention towards monuments of men of peace, local demands for neoclassical monuments of war heroes decreased. It can be said that modern British memory was born 'from an intense awareness of the conflicting representations of the past and the effort of each group to make its version the basis of national identity' (Gillis 1994b: 8), while the wealth of the nation created conducive conditions for a public interest in the past.

The nineteenth-century citizen's civic pride was closely linked with the growing significance of history, which, fuelled by the ascendancy of positivism, established itself as a 'scientific' discipline. History, being hostile to abstraction and generalization, aimed to describe the past as it 'actually had been', as famously expressed by Leopold von Ranke (Tosh 1991: 13–16). National historians enjoyed the status of 'cultural priests' and their work was 'read by a wide stratum of the educated public' (Funkenstein 1993: 20). As the nation state replaced 'the sacred liturgical memory with the secular liturgical memory – days of remembrance, flags, and monuments', the task of the national historian was to make 'the symbols concrete' (Funkenstein 1993: 20). In their efforts to separate history as a secular academic practice from a background of cultural religiosity, nineteenth-century historians 'identified memories as a dubious source for the verification of historical facts' (Klein 2000: 130). This suspicion of memories led historians to reject myth-making about the past and to rely on written documents. Yet, at the same time, ballads, proverbs, legends and songs (e.g. the Arthurian tradition in England) were making their way into the national history (Samuel 1994: 442–3). This appeal of popular memory can be seen as a result of the state's interest in history's ability to promote a national identity as well as the product of the new Romantic movement, which deliberately turned toward the past.

Following the earlier interest in antiquity, and rejecting the notion of uniformity among all cultures, the Romantic movement declared that each historical period had a unique character. Arguing that differences between the present and the past were incommensurable (Lowenthal 1985: 233), Romanticism rediscovered the attraction of memory as well as the links between memory and imagination, and memory and poetry. At the heart of the Romantic movement in nineteenth-century Europe was the concept of memory as a power of the soul, a nostalgia for the past and a focus on the imaginative power of memory. The idea of cultural diversity as intrinsic to human history, as expressed by Herder, meant that history does not move in straight lines, and that 'there is not a single key to the future or the past' (Berlin 1999: 36).

The Romantics claimed that each human group must strive after 'what lies in its bones', and concluded that other cultures could be understood with the help of empathic imagination (Berlin 1999: 66). For Herder, for example, a nation was not a state but a cultural entity whose members spoke the same language, possessed the same habits, had a communal past and common memories (Berlin 1999: 62–7). In this way, Romanticism destroyed the Enlightenment's axiom that if we apply proper scientific methods, valid and objective answers will be discovered to all questions and therefore a correct, perfect pattern of life taught to people: 'Romanticism built on time's ruin. Its idea of memory was premised on a sense of loss. It divorced memory-work from any claim to science, assigning it instead to the realm of the intuitive and instinctual' (Samuel 1994: ix). The passion of Romantic literature for memory, seen as a synonym for the notion of the spirit or the 'inner' character of the nation, was accompanied by an unprecedented interest in commemoration in Western European culture (Aries 1981), which contributed to the emergence of many European nationalist movements.

In contrast to the heyday of Romanticism, when memory could be described 'as a landscape full of woods and streams, ravines and plateaux, skies and gleaming lakes', at the end of the nineteenth century memory became the subject of experimental research (Draaisma 2000: 97). The memory discourse in this period was dominated by the metaphor of evolutionary progress in nature. The power of this naturalizing metaphor was so widespread that it can be said that memory at the time was 'first of all the story of an *organism*' (Matsuda 1996: 7). Darwin's concept of biological time, with its emphasis on conflict, competition and inheritance in evolutionary progress, shaped ways of thinking about memory. With the introduction of this 'hereditary and species memory into the traditional memories of rhetoric and language', memory was represented as a physical organism. Numerous evolutionary theorists, attempted to operationalize memory in biological terms as an inheritable or 'racial' characteristic (Assmann 1995), or conceived it as 'an objective indicator of inferiority' (Hacking 1995: 201). The biological-evolutionary reading of life histories also influenced Karl Marx's conceptualization of memory. Ideological dimensions of the evolutionary vision of progress, which implied a vision of the past as an 'unending record of pains and struggles which formed us into the creatures we are now', strengthened Marx's aversion to nostalgia and prompted him to denounce memory as false consciousness (Sennett 1998: 11). In his *The Eighteenth Brumaire*, Marx, claiming that 'the tradition of the dead generations weighs like a nightmare on the minds of the living', rejects the reactionary 'cult of the past' as well as the French people's nostalgia for the past and their inability to 'get rid of the memory of Napoleon', and declares that the 'drama of the French, therefore also the workers, is in great memories' ([1852] 1973: 248).

In the late nineteenth century, with the process of the secularization of thinking about the human mind underway, neurobiological studies of the functioning of memory, combined with experimental studies of recall and the psychodynamics of memory contributed to the development of empirical investigations of memory. These studies were underpinned by the assumption that there is objective scientific knowledge about memory. This has led, according to Hacking (1995), to the replacement of moral and spiritual reflection on the soul with empirical facts about memory. Memory, as the instrument through which positivist science sought to secularize the soul, has become the subject of the new sciences of memory which have profoundly influenced western culture. Laboratory work on recall, anatomical and statistical studies of memory, investigations in experimental psychology and pathological psychiatry all provided new knowledge about memory, as opposed to the art of memory, which taught us *how* to remember (Hacking 1995: 201). Being creatures of the nineteenth century, and being rooted in the French culture of the period, these sciences tried in a systematic way to uncover facts about memory and to establish scientific laws about its subject by studying pathological memory and forgotten traumas. Since then, forgetting rather than remembering has continued to be seen as the factor that 'forms our character, our personality, our soul' (Hacking 1995: 209).

The nineteenth century was a time of the great technological development. New inventions and new machines were 'defining characteristics of late nineteenth century European memory' (Matsuda 1996: 13). The spread of new technologies, such as photography, radiography and cinema cameras revolutionized ways of preserving and recalling memory. After 1839, human memory became compared to a photographic plate containing a record of our visual experience. By the 1880s the idea of a 'photographed reality' was a familiar means of recording the past (Caldwell 2000: 40). Photography became accepted as 'a vessel of accuracy, authenticity, verisimilitude, and truth' (Zelizer 1998: 9). In contrast to a painting or a piece of prose, a photograph was seen as realistic and objective, while also guaranteeing longevity: 'Memorialising the achievements of individuals considered as members of families is the earliest popular use of photography' (Sontag 2001: 43). The conceptualization of memory as 'images photographed upon the object itself' (Bergson quoted in Sherman 1999: 13) was further secured by the development of cinematography in 1895. As the eyes of the camera recorded experience, the collection of images captured on film resulted in a new opportunity to preserve images (Sontag 2001) and see them move. With the preservation of sound, following the invention of the phonograph by Edison in 1877, we had 'armed ourselves against the transience implicit in the mortality of memory by developing artificial memories' (Draaisma 2000: 2).

All these new means of storing and preserving historical events resulted in the proliferation of documents and archives. Those were used by various institutions, such as the medical profession and the police to record names, dates and cases. The institutionalization of memory in archives and museums, the increased opportunity, due to technological innovation, to keep a record of the past, combined with the fascination of nationalist movements with the past, the proliferation of national histories, a growing interest in the medieval past and the growing sophistication of historical methods made the nineteenth century 'the century of history' (Le Goff 1992: 15).

However, not all thinkers of that period accorded history such a prominent status. For instance, Nietzsche (1983), who rejected the view that meaning is revealed in history, saw memory as the imposition of values that become fixed and obligatory. He spoke about the 'heaviness' of history and stressed how the sheer volume of the past could weigh on the present, warning that an excess of history could destroy humanity. This new uncertainty about the relation of the present to the past, signalled the emergence of a crisis of memory, defined as people's experience of 'the insecurity of their culture's involvement with its past, the perturbation of the link to their own inheritance' (Terdiman 1993: 3).

In the late nineteenth century and early twentieth century, as a result of a massive disruption of traditional forms of memory, a feeling of anxiety about memory emerged as the dominant trend. In traditional societies, people's past and their conduct were open to easy interpretation as they carried 'their pasts and their meanings openly' (Terdiman 1993: 6). In contrast, in modern societies, due to a lack of transparency of the past resulting from the fact that people were disconnected from their past, the interpretation of people's behaviour became notoriously problematic. This increasing crisis of memory was further enhanced by upheavals in European societies which at that time were undergoing rapid industrialization, urbanization and modernization, as well as by a new questioning of the idea of 'progress'. Consequently, these processes led to the destruction of tradition and the insecurity of a culture's involvement with its past. The decline of oral traditions in villages, the rise of the popular press and the extension of compulsory education transformed the status of memory and the ways in which memory was preserved.

This crisis of memory manifested itself in an overwhelming sense of loss, anxiety and uncertainty, with the past being rejected on the one hand and appreciated as a lost mentality on the other (Terdiman 1993). The increasing tendency in this period to construct memory in physical monuments seems to be 'symptomatic of an increasing anxiety about memory left to its own unseen devices' (Savage 1994: 130). Matsuda (1996) speaks likewise of a memory discourse, which emerged in late nineteenth-century Europe as a response to the acceleration of history. Moreover, people's alienation from their past grew as modernism distanced itself from the past. As the connection between the past and the present grew uncertain, people tried to find a remedy in the 'vigorous and sensitive cultivation of historical understanding', replacing 'intellectual certainty by an emotional cohesion with which all experiences of the past could coexist' (Lowenthal 1985: 376).

Modernism's desire to 'wipe out whatever came earlier' paradoxically generated a greater dependence on the past – hence modernity's indecisive affiliations with memory (de Man 1970: 387–96). On the one hand, these relations manifested themselves in modernity's preoccupation with memory, and on the other in its orientation towards the future and its dislike of tradition. While modern science in general liberated itself from the guardianship of memory, some disciplines' interest in memory grew. In psychoanalysis (Freud) and in philosophy (Bergson) the most influential works on the topic of memory were created (see Chapters 5 and 6 for further discussion). For psychoanalysis, which can be seen as 'our culture's last Art Memory', memory has been both the problem and the core of its solution (Terdiman 1993: 240–1). Yet memory was absent from the social sciences, with the majority of scientists following the prejudices of the Enlightenment and rejecting tradition. Despite the widespread discussion of memory in late nineteenth-century culture, the 'classical' sociological theorists hardly mentioned it, as they believed that memory was a feature of pre-modern societies, and that in modern society, seen as on the road to 'traditionlessness', memory had no significance. Weber (1978), for example, argued that traditional modes of belief and conduct could not help us to stand up against the power of rationality and to stop the inevitable process of rationalization, and therefore were irrelevant for the modern world.

There were also opposing orientations to the role of memory in the artistic world. On the one hand, the nineteenth century avant-garde was interested solely in the future, invention, innovation and originality: 'The attack of the avant-garde was directed mainly against the store-room of collective memory: museums, libraries and academies' (Connerton 1989: 62). The avant-garde artists' demands, most stridently expressed in the manifestos of the *futurists,* called for the primacy of forgetting, and denounced museums as cemeteries and libraries as burial chambers. On the other hand, the role of memory was emphasized in many literary works proposing to look at memory not in historical terms but rather as an act of imagination. The best example here is Proust's seven-volume novel *Remembrance of Things Past*, the first volume of which was published just before World War I.

The most important changes in attitudes towards the past were brought about by World War, I, which created the 1914 generation's new ideas and perception of temporality as well as a new memory of war (Fussell 1975; Wohl 1979). For Walter Benjamin (1968), the war experience was a decisive moment in a longer-term trend, typified by a decline of storytelling that left people without the possibility to tell their tales and without communicable experiences to tell. However, the war, or 'shock' generally as the hallmark of modern experience, is also, according to Benjamin, a category of awakening, as it disrupts life's complacent conviction of its own immortality. Thus, the experience of the Great War engendered not only forgetfulness but also a distinctive form of memory. The war's myth, supplied with coherence by literary narratives, upgraded the status of national memory. The memory of the war, by becoming 'the total cultural form of our present life', established a new form of memory, where the culture of the past was 'our own buried life' (Fussell 1975: 335). The war influenced the nature of commemoration practices, forms of war memorial and types of mourning (Winter 1995). Widespread state-sponsored commemorative practices after the war (which, for example in France, practically left no town without a war memorial) (Sherman 1994), were exploited by nationalist leaders to create an identification of states with mass memory. In all countries, the 'We' who should remember 'Them' were mourning the loss by erecting so-called tombs of unknown soldiers, thereby 'remembering everyone by remembering no one in particular' (Gillis 1994b: 11). As the memory of the Great War became materialized in a single place, individual and family memories of the dead were 'to be blended and given purpose by identification with collective expressions presided over by the state' (Gray and Oliver 2001: 14). The interplay between private and collective memories, so characteristic of these type of practice, contributed to the democratization of the cult of the dead, and this further enhanced the impersonalization of national memory (Gillis 1994a).

In the interwar period, the debate about memory entered the field of sociology. The publication of Maurice Halbwachs' *Les Cadres Socioaux de la Memoire* in 1924 established memory as an object of sociological study and shifted the conceptualization of memory out of a biological framework and into a cultural one (Assmann 1995). Halbwachs' observation that the advent of capitalism and technology brought about the gradual alignment of all spheres of social life on the sphere of production, led him to suspect that the more advanced societies become, the more collective memory disintegrates ([1941] 1992). In other words, the development of industrial capitalism is seen as causing the disintegration and functionalization of collective memory in modern societies. This relationship, argues Halbwachs, can be attributed to two processes. First, it is an effect of the expansion and homogenization of collective memory that can be explained by the growing specialization and differentiation of modern societies. The emergence of the bourgeoisie and the modern capitalist economy, in particular, are seen as responsible for the destruction of a social framework and depth of collective memory (Halbwachs [1941] 1992: 115–25). Thus, at the end of 'this homogenizing, functionalizing process, the memory of modern societies took on the aspect of surface memory, dull memory, whose normative creative capacity seems to have dissolved' (Hervieu-Leger 2000: 128).

Second, the disintegration of collective memory in modern societies can be seen as a result of the process of the destruction of a social framework that ensured the transmission of collective memories from one generation to the next; a process brought about by the contemporary fragmentation of space, time and institutions, as well as by the growing number and plurality of groups to which individuals belong. Halbwachs' argument that modern societies are less capable of maintaining the common stock of memory provides us with a good opportunity to finish this chapter with a short discussion of collective memory in modern societies, which will be further developed in Chapter 6.

Memory today

Today's societies are often seen as those in which one no longer finds a minimal continuum of memory, or those in which life is not tradition-informed, past-oriented and memory-rich. This collapse of the comprehensive collective memory is, however, accompanied by a the fascination with memory. Thus, the end of the twentieth century, in a remarkably similar way to the end of the nineteenth, was characterized by a memory crisis. On the one hand, the cultural demise of authoritative memory has meant that contemporary societies have been described as 'terminally ill with amnesia' (Huyssen 1995: 1), 'amnesic' (Hervieu-Leger 2000) and 'without a living memory' (Nora 1996a), where the anniversaries and celebrations of the past are only media events (Collini 1999) and where there is no historical awareness or knowledge (Lowenthal 1998). On the other hand, they are described as suffering from an 'obsession with memory' and going through 'museumania and exhibition craze' (Huyssen 1995: 7, 21) the epidemic of commemoration and a passion for heritage. Even more importantly, the decline of comprehensive memory is accompanied by the spread of community-based small memories, which absorb the need for identity, and by the emergence of extra-territorial global memories, which are facilitated by 'the speed and imagery of the new global communications (Levy and

Sznaider 2002: 91). Consequently, we witness a process of denationalization of memory as well as trends towards the fragmentation and democratization of memory. As previously marginalized groups have access to
resources and to the public space to cultivate and express their memories,
they undermine, in turn, the authoritative memory of the dominant culture.
This process of the expansion of various group memories, in the context of
the growing importance of the politics of identity, has resulted in the politi-
cization of memory. Hence, as memory becomes a significant element in the
development of social and cultural identities, it establishes itself as not only
a source of a sense of lineage and inheritance, but also as identities' sole
justification and legitimization. This process, furthermore, often leads to
the sacralization of memory, or memory becoming a 'surrogate' religion.
The enhancement of the sacrality of memory manifests itself not only in the
growing significance of group memories but also in the proliferation of
conservation movements, museums and heritage sites (see Chapter 1).

   In the past 50 years historic sites around the globe have multiplied from
thousands to millions and 95 per cent of existing museums postdate
World War II (Lowenthal 1998: 3–8). The growth of the number of private
and public collections and museums has been followed by the expansion of
the 'heritage industry' – that is, 'the instrumental (commercially and/or
state-founded) use of representations and activities centred upon memorialising, preserving or re-enacting the past in order to protect and project a
nation's inheritance' (Evans 1999: 5). Britain, where popular enthusiasm for
the past has been visible since the 1960s, is seen increasingly as manufacturing heritage instead of manufacturing goods (Hewison 1999). The growing
significance of heritage, with the National Trust having over 2 million members, making it the largest mass organization in Britain (Urry 1996: 60), can
be explained by a loss of trust in the future and an ageing society's nostalgia
for a golden past. It can also be seen as motivated by economic interest as a
commodified heritage benefits local economies (Hewison 1987). This devotion to the past has, however, undergone a social transformation from a
conservative nostalgia and desire to preserve the past to a more democratic
representation of the past (Samuel 1999). Moreover, the past can also be
recreated for popular entertainment, as it is argued that 'the exploration of
the past need not be a serious endeavour, requiring time and commitment,
but should be in essence undemanding and diverting' (MacGregor, quoted in
Rojek 1999: 201). This trend expresses itself particularly in the development
of various theme parks, which aim to bring the past to life by immersing
people in direct sensory experiences. As the heritage industry enjoys new
developments, takes on new functions and moves to storing and presenting
cultural heritage in a digital form, it also faces new threats connected with its
further commercialization.

   New demands for the recreation of the past and for entertainment, as well
as the availability of new technologies, have also changed the role of the

museum and its modes of exhibiting. As the information age offers us access to images and more interactive ways of displaying exhibits, museums have become less like traditional archives and more like interactive libraries, while at the same time new archives' capacities for collection and filing are unlimited. Integrated digital systems have enriched our access to archives, museums and libraries, and the potential for greater visual literacy has also been expanded by the provision online exhibitions and new ways of collecting, storing and producing memories. The personal testimony constitutes the favoured form of memory production in many museums, as its 'intensely individuated meanings differentiate it from the monument, remembrance day or other "official" and collective markers of memory' (Ashplant *et al.* 2000b: 48). Projects of generating memory are now technologically complex and often include clips of oral testimonies and video interviews. One of the most fully developed memory projects is the Holocaust archive – a collection of 3400 witness accounts organized by the Fortunoff Video Archive and 50,000 testimonies collected by Steven Spielberg's Visual History of the Shoah Foundation.

The role of the media has also undergone change as a result of new technologies, which have increased our ability to store and transmit memory, allowing more freedom and creative possibilities. These new developments have been preparing us for the arrival of cosmopolitan memory (Levy and Sznaider 2002). However, although we witness the decline of the role of the media in legitimizing the nation, it remains – through its ability to create 'master narratives' and to make journalists into 'authoritative spokespersons for the story'(Zelizer 1993) – the main source of images of the past. Our growing reliance on new electronic means of communication (from TV to the internet) for memory-keeping and memory-construction makes us dependent on media representations of the past. Our contact with the past increasingly takes place through the electronic media, which are based upon a presupposition that they, unlike the press which reports and comments, represent the world (Tester 1999: 470). Generally, the importance and the nature of mass media have established the new role of mediated and delocalized traditions as a means of making sense of the world and creating a sense of belonging.

By presenting the changes in aids to memory, from visual mnemonic techniques, through writing and print, to today's means of storage, transition and construction of memory, this chapter has illustrated how cultures have been affected by the shift in the means of communication and social organization. It has shown changes in the status and meanings of memory, from its mythical and sacred status in antiquity, through its high position in the pre-modern period where memory was seen as source of knowledge and truth, to the erosion of its value in modernity. The history of memory reveals changes in the custodianship of remembering, from the religious authorities, through the state to the media. In order to further clarify social rules of remembering the next chapter will examine sociological theories of collective memory.

Further reading

Hacking, I. (1995) *Rewriting the Soul*. Princeton, NJ: Princeton University Press.

Hobsbawm, E. (1983) Mass-producing traditions: Europe, 1870–1914, in E. Hobsbawm and T. Ranger (eds) *The Invention of Tradition*, pp. 263–308. Cambridge: Cambridge University Press.

Le Goff, J. (1992) *History and Memory*, trans. S. Rendall and E. Claman. New York: Columbia University Press.

Lowenthal, D. (1985) *The Past is a Foreign Country*, Ch. 5. Cambridge: Cambridge University Press.

Matsuda, M.K. (1996) *The Memory of the Modern*. New York: Oxford University Press.

CHAPTER 3

THEORIZING REMEMBERING

This chapter discusses four main theories of remembering. It starts with a short presentation of the Durkheimian perspective, paying particular attention to Halbwachs' theory of collective memory. This is followed by a discussion of the presentist tradition which assumes that images of the past are strategically invented to suit present needs. The third part describes work on social memory which argues for a more complex view of the relation between the past and the present and between the dominant, or official, memory and popular memory. The final section presents some recent studies that conceptualize memory as actively restructured in a process of negotiations through time.

Halbwachs: the social context of memory

Maurice Halbwachs (1877–1945), as we have already mentioned, is responsible for the introduction of the concept of collective memory into the sociological vocabulary. Despite Halbwachs' highly original argument about the social context of collective memory, his books, *Les Cadres Socioaux de la Memorie* ([1941] 1992) *La Topographie Legendaire des Evangiles en Terre Sainte* (1941) and the posthumously published *The Collective Memory* ([1926] 1950), were neglected for a long time. Halbwachs, who was also the first to systematically explore the ways in which present concerns determine what of the past we remember, continued the legacy of Durkheim's belief that every society displays and requires a sense of continuity with the past. His affinity with Durkheim's ideas is also clearly visible in his emphasis on the collective nature of social consciousness and his assertion that a collectively imagined past is crucial for the unity of a society, while a shared past is the essential element for the reconstruction of social solidarity. Halbwachs, like Durkheim, assumes the persistence of what is remembered, as the function of remembering is not to transform the past but to promote a commitment to the group by symbolizing its values and aspirations.

Yet Halbwachs' concept of collective memory is more than a mere application of Durkheim's theorizing of collective memory as a *social fact* that confers identity on individuals and groups. Whereas Durkheim mentions memory solely in relation to traditional societies, which want to preserve a sacred memory of their origin, Halbwachs insists on the importance of memory in all types of society and argues that modern societies might prefer to refashion their past in order to further some present political objective. Halbwachs, moreover, expands Durkheim's idea of collective memory beyond its original connection with rituals. While Durkheim addresses memory directly only in his discussion of commemorative rituals, the notion of memory stands at the heart of Halbwachs' approach. Halbwachs enriches Durkheim's theory even further by uncovering and classifying the elements of social life that contribute to collective memory.

Halbwachs' ([1941] 1992) fundamental contribution to the study of social memory is the establishment of the connection between a social group and collective memory. His assertion that every group develops a memory of its own past that highlights its unique identity is still the starting point for all research in the field. Collective memory is, according to Halbwachs, always 'socially framed' since social groups determine what is 'memorable' and how it will be remembered: 'The individual calls recollections to mind by relying on the frameworks of social memory' (Halbwachs [1941] 1992: 182). For instance, individual memories of one's family cannot be dissociated from the whole images that comprise the 'family memory'. Halbwachs ([1926] 1950) also notices the relationship between the duration of a group and its memory. He argues that a group memory lasts only as long the group and that the prominence, and therefore also the duration, of a collective memory depends on the social power of the group that holds it. The social standing of the group provides an important indicator of its memory's durability, visibility and power, while the diversity and variable intensity of individual remembrance is explained by the existence of a multiplicity of collective influences.

Moreover, collective memory is by definition multiple because there are as many memories as groups. In other words, when there is a plurality of social frameworks or a multiplicity of memberships, there are many memories. The succession of remembrances and the plurality of memories are the result of changes occurring in our relationship to various collective milieus: my memory changes 'as my position changes' and 'this position itself changes as my relationships to other milieus change' (Halbwachs [1926] 1950: 48). Through all these changes groups need stable supports and frames of reference that enable them to rediscover the past in the present and feel their own continuity. Consequently, 'every collective memory requires the support of a group delimited in space and time' (Halbwachs [1926] 1950: 84). Both time (see Chapter 5) and space (see Chapter 1) play a crucial role in anchoring group recollections and hence in ensuring their preservation. Halbwachs ([1941] 1992: 172) notes that time and space are imposed upon us, and that from this comes a 'feeling of a reality' – that is, the point of departure for all our acts of memory. A group colonizes time by ordering important dates within a commemorative sequence. By conforming the past to its conceptions, the group's memory conveys an illusion of timelessness and continuity. The preservation of recollections also rests on their anchorage in space, which – because of its relative stability – gives us the illusion of permanence: 'The group's image of its external milieu and its stable relationships with this environment become paramount in the idea it forms of itself' (Halbwachs [1926] 1950: 13). Furthermore, the reason members of a group remain united, even after the group is dispersed, 'is that they think of the old home and its lay-out'. In other words, the spatial image alone, by reason of its stability, gives us 'an illusion of not having changed through time and of retrieving the past in the present' (Halbwachs [1926] 1950: 157).

According to Halbwachs ([1926] 1950), the persistence of memory, as the shared image of the past, which is a part of group common consciousness, explains the group's continuity. Halbwachs' theory views collective memory as 'a record of resemblance' which ensures that 'the group remains the same' ([1926] 1950: 86), while asserting that a group's identity has the central input into the process of the reconstruction of 'an image of the past which is in accord . . . with the predominant thoughts of that group' ([1926] 1950: 84). Collective identity precedes memory, therefore social identity determines the content of collective memory. Collective memory, being both a shared image of a past and the reflection of the social identity of the group that framed it, views events from a single committed perspective and thus ensures solidarity and continuity. It seems that Halbwachs' concern with the Durkheimian conception of solidarity and moral consensus leads him to argue that a group's memory is a manifestation of their identity.

Thus, memory is not only plural and changeable but is also a crucial condition of social order and solidarity. Halbwachs illustrates a link between collective memory and social solidarity on a national scale by showing that shared stories define the nature and boundaries of entire societies to whom the stories belong. Although he is aware that 'Ordinarily, the nation is too remote from the individual for him to consider the history of his country as anything else than a very large framework with which his own history makes contact at only few points' (Halbwachs [1926] 1950: 77), he argues that there are certain events that 'alter group life' and therefore that collective memory can play a solidifying role in societies ([1926] 1950: 62). So, despite the fact that 'between individual and nation lie many other, more restricted groups' ([1926] 1950: 77), each with its own history, there is the possibility of a link between collective memory and social solidarity on a national scale. The underlining argument is that a stable identity, personal or national, rests on an awareness of continuity with a beloved past.

For Halbwachs, collective memory is carried and supported by a group, while an individual memory can be understood only by connecting 'the individual to the various groups of which he is simultaneously a member' ([1941] 1992: 53). Individual remembrance is seen as 'the intersection of collective influences' ([1926] 1950: 44) or as the meeting point of networks of solidarity of which the person is a part. Such a conceptualization of individual memory means that individual remembrance changes as the individual's affiliation changes. In other words, memories adapt to our present connections, belongings and positions and therefore only we can be sure of the accuracy of our memory when it is supported by others' remembrances. Only in the group context are we able to 'reconstruct a body of remembrances' (Halbwachs [1926] 1950: 22) and more accurately describe past events. Only when people come together to remember do they enter a domain beyond that of individual memory (Halbwachs [1941] 1992: 45–56). Although collective memory encompasses individual memories, it always remains distinct from them and evolves according to its own laws. Furthermore, in recollection, we do not retrieve images of the past as they were originally perceived but rather as they fit into our present conceptions, which in turn are shaped by the social forces that act on us. Thus, only by recognizing the role of an affective community, within which our feelings and thoughts originate, can we comprehend how a memory is at once reorganized and reconstructed, and that the past is revealed more fully when we remember together.

By showing how a remembrance is at once reorganized and reconstructed, Halbwachs aimed to prove that it is an illusion that our memories are independent. This illusion, he maintains, is the outcome of the interweaving of several series of collective thoughts, which make most social influences unperceivable. People usually believe that they are free in their thoughts and feelings, when in fact they draw on the same part of common thinking and understanding (Halbwachs [1926] 1950: 45). Only in social contexts are individuals capable of transforming their private images into appropriate patterns which are kept by the entire group. These conceptual structures are determined by communities in the process of remembering, which starts from shared data or conceptions. By showing that different social groups, such as the family, the religious community or the social class, have different memories attached to their respective mental landmarks, Halbwachs asserts that an individual memory separated from collective memory is provisional and without meaning. Although we are 'participants in the events' as individuals, our memories remain collective because we always think as members of the group to which we belong, because our ideas originated within it and because our thinking keeps us in contact with that group (Halbwachs

[1926] 1950: 23). However, we do not need the actual presence of others to preserve our memories:

> In fact I continue to be subject to the influence of a society even when I have walked away from it: it is enough that I carry within me, in my spirit, all that allows me to classify myself with reference to its members, to reimmerse myself in their milieu and their own particular time, and feel myself very much a part of the group.
>
> (Halbwachs [1926] 1950: 128)

Halbwachs' rejection of the individualist perspective and his idea of collective memory as the conceptual schemes or 'social frameworks' in which individual memories come to be located and which provide the model which constrains individual memory show him as a faithful follower of Durkheim. Halbwachs is, however, a more conciliatory figure than Durkheim (Coser 1992: 4) and tries to introduce psychology into sociological enterprise. While Durkheim neglects the issue of individual consciousness, Halbwachs asserts that it is an individual who remembers, although this individual, being located in a specific group context, draws on this social context to remember or recreate the past. Yet, his interest in psychological explanations is rather limited as he quickly moves on to say that people remember only as members of social groups and thus collective memory is different from both the historical and the autobiographical forms. Furthermore, even though Halbwachs admits that only individual recollection exists, he nevertheless argues that our individual memories, if not located within conceptual structures that are defined by communities at large, tend to fade away, are less accessible and more difficult to recall because they do not enjoy group support. In contrast, the collective memory lasts longer since it draws strength 'from its base in a coherent body of people' ([1926] 1950: 48).

Halbwachs left us with a rather unclear legacy. He never really elaborated the theoretical foundation of the concept of collective memory and did not provide a clear definition of the notion. His idea of collective memory is often criticized for its inconcreteness and lack of clarity (Gedi and Elam 1996). It is even described as a confusing or 'woolly' concept which lacks any explanatory power (Osiel 1997: 18) or as coming close to 'the bad old Romantic notion of the spirit' or the 'inner' character of race or nation (Klein 2000: 9). While Halbwachs was right to say that social groups construct their own images of the world by establishing an agreed version of the past, he failed to explain how the dynamics of collective memory work. His effort to combine personal images and social manifestations of ideas has not resulted in a clear theory capable of explaining the way collective memory is formed. Halbwachs' belief in the power of society to shape individual memory neglects the dialectical tensions between personal memory and the social construction of the past. His social determinism is responsible for his failure to address the question of how individual consciousnesses might relate to those of the collectivities these individuals actually make up. By moving from the psychological unconscious to social thought without giving an adequate account of the place the individual memory occupies within the collective memory, Halbwachs was unable to explain the fact of the social persistence of images of the past (Connerton 1989: 38). Generally, Halbwachs puts too much emphasis on the collective nature of social consciousness and disconnects it from the actual thought process of any particular individual. Indeed, Fentress and Wickham argue that Halbwachs' vision of individuals comes too close to seeing them as 'a sort of automaton, passively obeying the interiorised collective will' (1992: x).

The explanatory power of Halbwachs' approach is further reduced by another essential element – namely his assumption that collective identity precedes memory (Megill 1999: 44). The assertion that identity is already well established, combined with the assumption that social identity is stable, makes Halbwachs' main argument (that social identity determines the content of collective memories), much less interesting. Due to the assumption that memory is determined by an already well established identity, his theory also undervalues other functions of collective memory. It seems that Halbwachs underestimates the importance of groups' living memories, because instead of seeing these memories in dialogue, interdependence and conflict with the tradition of the main collectivity, he views them as integrated into the tradition of the most powerful group. Thus, his conceptualization of the relations between past and present is rather one-dimensional and assumes the stability of the vision of the past in a group memory. Such an assertion not only prevents us from accounting for changes in a group's perception of the past, which could arise due to new conditions, but also presumes a vision of frozen social identity.

Halbwachs argues that memories are bound together and sustained due to the fact that they form part of a whole aggregate of thoughts and interests common to a group. Thus, complexity and coherence in public memory tend to correspond to complexity and coherence at the social level (Douglas 1986: 80). Because of his insistence on the way in which collective memory is continually revised to sustain solidarity, Halbwachs' approach is adopted by many studies of the invention of traditions. However, despite the fact that his work has inspired many such investigations, Halbwachs' position cannot be reduced to the narrow presentist approach. Because Halbwachs' preoccupation with the role of collective memory in securing stability, solidarity and continuity goes together with his insistence on the centrality of change and variation in societies, it can be said that his perspective does not exclude the possibility of collective memory having both cumulative and presentist aspects. Thus, Halbwachs' viewing of collective memory as simultaneously plural and changeable as well as a storage system for the social order and stability (Douglas 1986: 70) makes his ideas popular among both researchers interested in stability and order, and among writers who define collective memories as effective markers of social differentiation.

The presentist memory approach: the invention of traditions

This part of the chapter examines the presentist approach to social remembering as exemplified in works on the invention of public rituals as modes of social control. This perspective scrutinizes how public notions of history are manipulated by the dominant sectors of society through public commemorations, education systems, mass media, and official records and chronologies. The 'invention of tradition perspective' or 'theory of the politics of memory', as the presentist memory approach is also called, argues that the past is moulded to suit present dominant interests. Researchers working within this paradigm have illustrated how new traditions and rituals are 'invented' in the sense of being deliberately designed and produced with a view to creating new political realities, defining nations and sustaining national communities. Defining social memories as inventions of the past, they study the institutionalization of 'remembrance' within national ritual and educational systems. Such investigations show how nationalist movements create a master commemorative narrative that highlights their members' common past and legitimizes their aspiration for a shared destiny. While Hobsbawm and Ranger's *Invention of Tradition* (1983) still remains the main work written in this perspective, there are now many studies concerned with the role played in modern societies by constructed versions of the past in establishing social cohesion, legitimizing authority and socializing populations in a common culture.

While the Durkheimian tradition argues that we remember collectively and selectively, the invention of tradition approach suggests more directly who is responsible for memory's selectiveness and points to causes of this selectiveness. In other words, investigators working from this perspective show *who* controls or imposes the content of social memories, and that those 'invented' memories serve the current purposes of those in power. The official management of collective memory, while always designed to legitimize power, is seen as revolving essentially around the two poles of censorship and celebration, or socially organized forgetting and socially organized remembering. Both methods are frequently employed in the deliberate production of traditions serving states to legitimize and stabilize their political orders. However, it is the nature of the political regime that determines which methods are emphasized and relied upon to construct a 'useable past'. In this state-centred approach, the emphasis is on the mechanism of state rituals as the means of the production of official memory.

Analysing the role of these dominant narratives or official ideologies in establishing national cohesion, Hobsbawm and Ranger in *The Invention of Tradition* stress the primary role of the state in shaping collective memory. While examining the late nineteenth-century European states and the widespread progress of electoral democracy, they argue that the decline of traditional political structures led to invented traditions. The emergence of mass politics demanded the construction of traditions that could symbolize societal cohesion, legitimize new institutions, statuses and relations of authority, and inculcate new beliefs and values. Hobsbawm and Ranger define the notion of 'invented tradition' in a broad sense as contrived rather than growing up spontaneously. The term 'tradition' here means 'a set of practices, normally governed by overtly or tacitly accepted rules and of a ritual or symbolic nature, which seek to inculcate certain values and norms of behaviour by repetition, which automatically implies continuity with the past' (Hobsbawm 1983: 1).

Hobsbawn points out that many traditions which appear to be old are actually products, at most, of the past couple of centuries, and often only of several decades. Invented traditions tend to establish themselves relatively quickly and aim to imply a long-term continuity, as in the case of the kilt, the common symbol of Scottishness, which was invented by an English industrialist in the early eighteenth century. Invented traditions are not, therefore, genuine. In this respect they differ from customs, which dominated so-called traditional societies, and whose function was technical rather than ideological. Where 'the old ways are alive', traditions need be neither revived nor invented; however, where there is a need to provide a framework for action that can go largely unquestioned, and a justification of power, traditions are constructed (Hobsbawm 1983: 8). According to Hobsbawm and Ranger (1983), invented traditions are used as a means of exercising power, to establish or legitimize institutions, to symbolize social cohesion and to socialize individuals to the existing order.

The period 1870–1914 in Europe was unique in terms of a mass-production of traditions because there was an enormous need to understand and reflect on the rapid social transformations of the period: 'Quite new, or old but dramatically transformed, social groups, environments and social contexts called for new devices to ensure or express social cohesion and identity and to structure social relations' (Hobsbawm 1983: 262). Dramatic social changes such as industrialization, and the process of democratization, along with the expansion of the mass electorate, made the old rulings by the state inpractical and dramatized the problem of maintaining public loyalty. As the masses could not be relied upon to follow their masters, there was a need for new methods of establishing bonds of loyalty. With the emergence of electoral politics, the late nineteenth-century nation states tried to secure mass obedience with the help of new symbols, such as flags, national anthems, military uniforms and new celebrations and rituals. For example, in Britain, this period witnessed the revival of royal ritualism, which was seen as a necessary counterweight to the dangers of popular democracy. In new countries, where rulers were unable to reconstruct or reach back, nationalism invented the national self-consciousness. Among the main Western European states, only Italy had to start the process of national justification through the construction of traditions totally from scratch. Here Hobsbawm (1983: 267) quotes the writer and politician d'Azeglio's famous phrase, 'We have made Italy: now we must make Italians'. The implementation of new traditions was ensured through three different methods and institutions: the development of education, the invention of public ceremonies and the mass production of public monuments.

From the 1870s, with the notion that 'authority once achieved must have a secure and usable past' (Plumb 1969: 41), the British undertook a series of attempts to re-establish political order in their colonies through the construction of new traditions. In India (Cohen 1983) and in Africa (Ranger 1983), the British experimented with varying forms of ritual to mark public occasions and justify their role. In both cases, the most far reaching inventions of tradition took place when the British believed themselves to be respecting age-old local customs. So, for example, before 1860 both Indian and British soldiers wore western-style uniforms, but the Indian uniform was then modified to include turbans, sashes and tunics, because they were seen by the British as more 'authentic' (Cohen 1983: 167–90). After India's independence, many traditions invented by the British were rejected. With a new balance of power, India adopted new codes of conduct, as illustrated by Gandhi's new standards of dress: 'No longer were Indians to wear either western clothes or the "native" costumes decreed by their imperial rulers, but home-spun simple peasant dress' (Cohen 1983: 209).

In colonial Africa, 'what were called customary law, customary land-rights, customary political structure and so on, were in fact *all* invented by colonial codification' (Ranger 1983: 250). Here, white settlers constructed traditions both to define and justify their role as undisputed masters, and these invented practices were not counterbalanced by local cultures or social forces. In contrast with Europe, the majority of invented traditions 'became much more starkly a matter of command and control' (Ranger 1983: 211). Even more importantly, in Europe 'these invented traditions of the new ruling classes were to some extent balanced by the invented traditions of industrial workers or by the invented "folk" cultures of peasants'. Unlike in Africa, in Europe the traditions of non-ruling classes were also important. One of these traditions was the working-class tradition, which, with May Day celebrations and other new labour rituals, was halfway between 'political' and 'social' traditions, 'belonging to the first through their association with mass organizations and parties which could and indeed aimed to become regimes and states, to the second because they genuinely expressed the workers' consciousness' (Hobsbawm 1983: 286). These half-invented traditions were developed by social movements through the cultivation of a common dress code and common activities, such as in the case of the working class, football matches (Hobsbawm 1983: 293).

The performative nature of traditions, articulated somewhere between public and private representations, allows us to see how public representations join private ones. Examinations of various people's and groups' traditions provide insights into their relations to the past, and throw light on what is actually being preserved in the popular memory of the past and what was officially invented. The official management of the past through the invention of tradition aimed at concealing the balance of power and wealth was designed to reflect the dramatic changes of the period in such a way as to ensure the continuity of mass loyalty. The erection of new monuments, the invention of new symbols and the rewriting of history books can be seen as the state's responses to the insecurities of electoral politics.

The invention of tradition theory is applied by Hobsbawm and Ranger (1983) to explain changes in the nature of the state brought about by the emergence of mass politics. A question arises as to whether this theory's explanatory power is equally impressive in relation to other periods or other types of regime. In other words, in what kind of political cultures does the application of tradition theory tell us something interesting about social reality? Unfortunately, the application of this perspective to modern western societies has become 'somewhat predictable' and repetitive (Confino 1997: 1387). It suggests that the invention of tradition approach's relevance to open and democratic systems is questionable. Yet, an examination of public memories of the Nazis in postwar divided Germany shows that the presentist perspective still preserves some explanatory power in reference to undemocratic systems, which not only construct and control memory from above but also eliminate any potential challenges threatening the official version of the past. The comparison of West Germany's and East Germany's official ways of representing their Nazi past reveals not only how different political systems manipulate public memory but also variations in regimes' abilities to 'freeze' official memory. In both countries in the first 20 years after World War II public memories of the Nazis were constructed and implemented to justify the respective nations' political order. East Germany developed its own vision of the Nazi past, which marginalized the Jewish suffering and glorified the contribution of anti-fascists and communist resistance movements. West Germany's memory not only included the suffering of different groups (for example, German soldiers) and emphasized the courage of different groups (the upper class and Christian opponents of the Nazis), but was also marked by a recognition of Jewish suffering (as illustrated by the agreement to pay financial restitution to Jewish survivors), on the one hand, and by an unwillingness to confront the Nazi past, on the other (Herf 1997). However, in West Germany, in contrast to East Germany, the problem of coming to terms with the past became a focal point for public and highly controversial discussions. These debates, including voices calling for Germans to stop avoiding a confrontation with their Nazi past, as well as attempts to rewrite the past, started in the 1960s and accelerated from the mid-1980s onwards, with a series of public exchanges between prominent German scholars arguing for and against 'normalizing' the Nazi past (see Chapter 6). In contrast, in East Germany, as in all non-democratic systems where there is no counterbalance to state-party power and therefore no alternative versions of the past, the official memory remained stable and unchallenged. It seems, therefore, that the invention of tradition perspective preserves some relevance in reference to undemocratic systems, which tend to freeze memories and do not permit pluralistic debates.

It is an open question as to what degree the processes of the invention of the national consciousness and the organizing of forgetting imply nothing more than fabrication and falsity rather than 'imagining' and creation. Benedict Anderson (1983: 15), when discussing Gellner's (1965) observation that nationalism invented the nation, points out that Gellner equates 'invention' with fabrication. In other words, Gellner implies that somewhere 'true' communities exist but that some pasts are 'invented'. The invention of tradition theory likewise assumes that modern societies' traditions are quite recent in origin, which suggests that older traditions are the 'real' ones. For Anderson, all communities are imagined, and therefore they cannot be distinguished by 'their falsity/genuiness'. However, for many historians, not only for those aiming to describe the past as it 'actually had been', this equation presents a problem, since when talking about invention (e.g. the invention of Scotland) we overlook the problem of whether 'people [are] free to invent, any nation, any group, what they want? Are there no constraints?' (Burke 1998: 202). The presentist approach fails to acknowledge that the past endures in the present not only through self-conscious commemoration rituals 'but through psychological, social, linguistic and political processes that keep the past alive without necessarily intending to do so' (Schudson 1997: 3).

Moreover, it is not always possible, particularly in democratic countries, to impose on people totally invented or fabricated traditions. As numerous examples from many countries show, people tend to reject any vision of the past which contradicts their recollection and sense of truth. Some past events can be of such importance to people that they feel compelled to tell their stories, therefore a collective memory is not so easy to undermine or totally distort (Schudson 1997: 5). Even more importantly, if a central power denies the reality of any groups' memory and experience, it often discredits itself (Osiel 1997: 113). The invention of tradition approach also avoids the very interesting question of why some traditions but not others become popular and enjoy social support. What is remarkable about traditions is not that they are invented, as almost all of them, at least to some degree, are, but *why* so many of them work and are accepted as 'real'.

By treating memory and commemoration as sources of support for the exercise of power and authority, and instruments of élite manipulation used to control lower-class and minority groups, the invention of tradition perspective tends to reduce the concept of collective memory to the notion of ideology or 'false consciousness'. It further assumes that ideology is in opposition to the 'truth' (Layder 1994: 105). Consequently, while its social and cultural aspects are underplayed, memory 'becomes a prisoner of political reductionism and functionalism' (Confino 1997: 1395). The equation of ideology with memory is also misleading because the main function of ideology is to ensure cohesion, while collective memory can be both of the divisive and the solidifying kind. Even more importantly, the fact that the past is transmitted through lines of authority does not necessarily mean that all public commemorations are intended to include 'false consciousness' (Schwartz 2000: 16). The memory of a social group cannot always be reduced to the political aim of sustaining relations of power as it is not necessarily solely imposed from above. In this sense memory differs from custom, which dominates so-called traditional societies.

The growing recognition of the weaknesses of this approach is, however, accompanied by an increased comprehension that the essence of tradition is always to confer the legitimacy of continuity on what is in practice always changing; that there is no such thing as a completely pure tradition; that the appeal to the past has always been selective and often part of demagogy, and therefore traditions always incorporate power, whether they are constructed in deliberate ways or not (Luke 1996; Collini 1999; Giddens 1999). Such a new understanding led to the development of a more moderate version of the presentist approach. This modified restatement of the dominant ideology thesis, moreover, has further enhanced our understanding of how we remember.

The popular memory approach: confronting the dominant ideology

Like the previous approach, the popular memory perspective assumes that our recollection of the past is instrumental, influenced by present interests, and that the politics of memory is conflictual. However, in contrast to the previous theory, this approach is less deterministic and allows some space for other solutions to the conflict over memory than just its manipulation and control from above. In other words, unlike the presentist perspective, which assumes that conflict is the natural state of society and that memories are socially 'constituted' from above, the popular memory theory points to the possibility of the construction of memory from the 'bottom up', as it appreciates a way of remembering and forgetting that starts with the local and the particular and then builds outwards toward a total story.

In contrast to the invention of tradition approach, which argues that memory is imposed on a public that has no agency, this perspective assumes that groups (in some circumstances) are capable of asserting their own version of the past. The writers interested in the popular memory approach analyse the connection between the hegemonic order and local groups' memories and classify these particular rememberings as 'public memory', 'counter-memory', 'oppositional memory' or 'unofficial memory'. Although these researchers stress that the dominant vision of the past is linked to the techniques and practices of power, they tend to investigate a much richer spectrum of representations of the past than the invention of tradition approach. This type of memory studies took its earlier inspiration from Foucault's concepts of popular memory and counter-memory and later from the works of the British cultural studies theorists.

Even though the notion of popular memory does not play any essential role in Foucault's writing, it has been a significant step in the development of memory studies. His conceptualization of memory as discursive practice provides memory with 'discursive materiality' and therefore allows for its investigation 'in the different discursive formations' (Foucault 1978: 15). Such a definition of memory, together with Foucault's argument about the power and knowledge relationship, was intended to shed light on the process that determines which voices are heard in the public forum. Foucault views popular memory as 'actually a very important factor in struggle' because 'if one controls people's memory, one controls their dynamics' (Pearson 1999: 179). When people's memory is programmed and controlled, according to Foucault, we deal with 'popular memory' which is subordinated in its relations to the dominant ideologies and which therefore reproduces the established consensual view of the past.

According to Foucault, 'popular memory' is a form of collective knowledge possessed by people who are 'barred from writing, from producing their books themselves, from drawing up their own historical accounts – these people nevertheless do have a way of recording history, of remembering or of keeping it fresh and using it' (Pearson 1999: 179). The 'popular memory', seen in opposition to the dominant memory, is a political force of people marginalized by universal discourses, whose knowledges have been disqualified as inadequate to their task, located low down in the hierarchy. Since power relations always involve the possibility of resistance, Foucault assumes a connection between memory and popular resistance, particularly in the nineteenth century, where 'there was a whole tradition of struggles which were transmitted orally, or in writing or in songs, etc.' (Pearson 1999: 179).

Although Foucault argues that 'where there is power, there is resistance', his assertion that power plays the dominant role in the construction of memories seems to weaken this claim and leads him to a pessimistic conclusion that people are unable to liberate themselves from oppressive power (Baert 1998: 131). Consequently, despite his attention to otherness, and despite his pointing to the importance of links between memory and political struggle, Foucault undervalues the ability of popular memories to resist dominant control. His lack of interest in human agents and the fact that he delocalizes discourses results in his failure to analyse the actual consequences of popular memories (Friedland and Boden 1994: 25–7). Many writers have criticized Foucault's inability to account for the dialectic relationships between the popular memory and the dominant discourse (Bommes and Wright 1982; Harper 1997; Pearson 1999; Weissberg 1999). Foucault's notion of popular memory is blamed for assuming that popular memory is a 'wholly unified' and coherent construction as if it was entirely 'laid from above' (Bommes and Wright 1982: 256). Pearson (1999) rejects Foucault's assumption that mass media reprogrammes memory by representing the values of the dominant social formations. Harper (1997: 164) calls for a more historically and socially rooted analysis of collective memory because 'a fuzzy concept' of popular memory has become 'far too attached to a particular orthodoxy, which is usually fuelled by a sense of political disappointment'. This criticism translates itself into studies which attempt to analyse the content and precise location of alternative memories that exist beneath the dominant discourse, or into studies which illuminate the complexity of the connection between the hegemonic order and historical representations.

The first type of investigation has been developed since the early 1980s by the Popular Memory Group at the Centre for Contemporary Studies in Birmingham, while the second type often invokes Foucault's (1977) notion of counter-memory. The Popular Memory Group's studies have emerged as a result of the growing criticism of the presentist approach and as an attempt to further enhance the appeal of the popular memory approach. Research initiated by the Group adopted theories about narratives from literary criticism and its members, many of whom were particularly interested in the British memory of World War II, studied various forms in which people articulate their memories. The Popular Memory Group combined its criticism of oral historians' failure to account for many layers of individual memory and the plurality of versions of the past with its re-evaluation of Foucault's notion of popular memory. In its major book, *Making Histories* (1982), the Group outlined its position on the significance of the past and expressed its interest in the investigation of the construction of public histories and the interaction between private and public senses of the past.

The Popular Memory Group provided further negative reviews of the presentist approach as its members were critical of the invented tradition argument that memory is created solely from the 'top down'. The Group did not conceive of a dominant political order as monolithic, singular or totalizing, but rather as a dynamic, conflictual, fluid and unstable 'site of contestation between the dominant social formations in the ruling power bloc and those marginalized social formations seeking concessions from the dominant, and whom the dominant constantly strives to incorporate' (Pearson 1999: 180). The Group, in contrast to Foucault, stressed more directly and more consequently the dialectical interaction between 'popular' and 'hegemonic' discourses and between private memory and public memory. The interaction between these aspects of memory, understood as a hegemonic process of ideological domination and resistance, shapes the content of dominant memory. Popular memory is conceived here as a site of struggle between different voices seeking to construct versions of the past, while its connection with dominant institutions ensures its pervasiveness and domination in the public sphere.

The Popular Memory Group defined popular memory as a 'dimension of political practice' and saw it as a composite construct of various traces, influences and layers. Thus, its aim was to consider all the ways in which a sense of the past is produced: through public representations and through private memory (Popular Memory Group 1982: 205, 207). Although when referring to the representations which affect individual or group conceptions of the past, members of the Popular Memory Group speak about 'dominant memory', they do not mean to imply 'that conceptions of the past that acquire a dominance in the field of public representations are either monolithically installed or everywhere believed' (p. 207). The Group assumes that dominant memory is open to contestation, although they insist that we should not overlook the fact that there are 'real processes of domination in the historical field' which result in some memories being marginalized or excluded, while others, especially those which conform to the 'fattened stereotypes of myth' are successful (p. 208). Among institutions influencing the public construction of the popular memory, the state and various cultural and educational institutions are seen as the most influential.

The study initiated by the Popular Memory Group focused on the relation between dominant memory and oppositional forms across the whole public field and on 'the more privatized sense of the past which is generated within a lived culture' (1982: 211).

The international impact of the Group can be illustrated by such studies as Luisa Passerini's (1987) *Fascism in Popular Memory*, which analyses the cultural memory of the Turin working class, and Alistair Thomson's (1994) *Anzac Memories: Living with the Legend*, which explores the power of Australian legends in shaping individual memory and illustrates the complex entanglement of national and private memory. Such investigations are in many respects similar to research that invokes Foucault's (1977) notion of counter-memory.

The Foucault-inspired counter-memory strand offers an important critique of dominant ideology as it contains a suspicion of totalizing public narratives. The idea of counter-memory illuminates the connection between the hegemonic order and historical representations because it allows us to overcome the presentist approach's failure to differentiate between the 'truth' and ideology, and provides the possibility of accounting for subordinated voices from the past. Bouchard, in his introduction to Foucault's book *Language, Counter-memory, Practice*, refers to counter-memory as 'other voices which have remained silent for so long' (1977: 18). In Foucault's view the recovery of these other voices and traditions allows us to make visible the relationship of domination which 'is fixed, through its history, in rituals, in meticulous procedures that impose rights and obligations. It establishes marks of its power and engraves memories on things and even within bodies' (Foucault 1977: 150). Through counter-memory, we 'disinvest ourselves from the power that a particular constellation of meanings once held over us' (Clifford 2001: 133). According to Foucault, counter-memory 'must record the singularity of events outside of any monotonous finality' (1977: 144). It also has to 'cultivate the details and accidents that accompany every beginning' and it ought to describe 'the endlessly repeated play of dominations' (Foucault 1977: 150).

Researchers interested in counter-memories have found Foucault's general theory, and especially his interest in the plurality of forces, practices and regimes that exist within a society, as well as his assertion that all discourses are merely partial claims to truth, very attractive and well-suited to their objective of showing that power bends discourses to its needs and so revises our conception of the past. Foucault's shift of the focus from memory to counter-memory appeals to many contemporary historians interested in studying how commemoration and tradition serve political purposes: 'It was Foucault who showed historians the way in which discourse receives its shape and how in turn that shape frames our understanding of the past' (Hutton 1993: 123). Foucault's approach 'undermines the apparent coherence of present belief or normative system' (Baert 1998: 127) by confronting the present with the past, by demonstrating how new meanings coexist with old ones and by showing the mutlilayered nature of reality where the present and old belief systems create 'an unstable assemblage of faults, fissures and heterogeneous layers that threaten the fragile inheritor from within or from underneath' (Foucault 1977: 146). The discourse against power is 'the counter-discourse which ultimately matters' (Foucault 1977: 209) because it can confiscate, at least temporarily, power to speak on the specific issues. With the struggle against power aiming 'at revolving and undermining power where it is most invisible and insidious' (1977: 208), the discourse of struggle is not opposed to the unconscious, but to the secretive, hidden, repressed and unsaid.

Counter-memories, as discursive practices through which memories are continuously revised, illuminate the issue of the discontinuity of intellectual tradition as well as 'the process of differentiating ideas . . . integral to the production of discourse' (Hutton 1993: 114). Being the alternative narrative which challenges the dominant discourse, counter-memory has direct political implications. By challenging the hegemony of the political élite's construction of the past, counter-memory turns memory into a 'contested territory in which groups engaging in a political conflict promote competitive views of the past in order to gain control over the political center or to legitimize a separatist orientation' (Zerubavel 1997: 11). As the examples of the French and the Russian Revolutions demonstrate, where previous counter-memories became official memories used to support the new governments' order, counter-memory can be transformed, as it increases its popularity, into a dominant discourse.

Studies of counter-memories illustrate that collective memory constructed from the bottom up can exist in different relations to the dominant/official representation of the past, ranging from sharp contrast to close similarity. According to investigations of many different cases of oppositional memory quoted in the literature, from memories of minority nationalities, through memories of various social classes, we learn that memories of the same event can be formulated very differently by various groups, that images of past events and their participants change as time passes, that political actors replace one another and that political activism and its accompanying tensions stimulate interest in the past (Szacka 1997). An examination of various class-based memories suggests their importance as a source of class identity. For example, several studies demonstrate the use of imagery of resistance against the state as a representation of peasant collective identity (Connerton 1989; Fentress and Wickham 1992). Similar conclusions have been reached about working-class memories which include, along with recollections of the resistance to the state and employers, memories of the antagonistic relations between groups and categories, and of divisions within the labour movement (Samuel 1981; Bauman 1982). Workers' memory reveals their capacity for independent thinking and self-reliance as well as an independence from the influence of organizational leaders, and thus destroys 'mythologies about the role of organizations as all-powerful machines manipulating the passive masses' (Debouzy 1986: 276).

More recent studies of both popular and counter-memory have prepared the ground for the development of a more moderate version of the dominant ideology approach to studying memory. These new works (e.g. Bodnar 1992), assume that public memory can be simultaneously multivocal and hegemonic. Public memory is seen as being a form of ideological system, the function of which is to mediate the competing interests and competing meanings of the past and the present. So, it is concluded that even though public memory is not simply class or status politics, it is often distorted in a way which, in the final instance, reflects the main power relations. While it is true that memory's distortions take place not through simple coercion but through a more subtle process of communication, the point is that 'the sources of cultural and political power are not simply diffuse' (Bodnar 1992: 19).

However, even this moderate version of the dominant ideology has not avoided voices of criticism pointing to several weaknesses in this approach. First, critics suggest that the popular memory approach still conceptualizes the past as 'a political fact, made and remade in the service of new power arrangements' (Schwartz 2000: 16). Second, it is pointed out that historical facts do not support many conclusions formulated by this type of research. For example, Schwartz (2000) notes, while referring to Bodnar's (1992) investigation, that it was not the official national élite that taught various majority groups patriotism and used their wealth and privileges to make heroes in their own image, as the popular memory approach claims, but that those groups' patriotism was often a result of their own ethnic and religious leaders' efforts and visions. Furthermore, the popular memory approach not only avoids the reductionism and the predictability of the presentist perspective, but also fails to explain why some symbols, events and heroes, but not others, are incorporated into public memory. Finally, it does not have anything to say about cases where popular memory invokes not manipulated and conflictual sentiments but rather shared symbols. Since the popular memory perspective assumes that conflict is the natural state of society, it dismisses the possibility that the politics of memory can be consensual *and* conflictual. It is therefore unable to explain how it happened that, for example, some memories constituted common models for acting for the whole nation and as such 'embodied a universal cultural presence' (Schwartz 2000: 255).

In the light of the growing recognition of the assumption that the content of memory cannot be seen as only manipulated, and that official recollection and social experience are vital elements of memory, the popular memory approach has been modified. The acceptance that memory is always partly a 'given', that it is never purely a construction and that every community should be seen as partly a 'community of fate' and partly a 'community of will' (Booth 1999) are the starting points of the dynamics of memory approach, which will be our next subject of investigation.

The dynamics of memory approach: memory as a process of negotiation

In this section we examine theories of remembering that focus on the active production and mediation of temporal meanings of the past. In contrast to presentist theories, which show who controls or invents the content of social memories, the dynamics of memory perspective views collective memory as an ongoing process of negotiation and illustrates 'limits to the power of actors in the present to remake the past according to their own interests' (Schudson 1997: 4). While the invention of tradition approach argues that memory is constructed from above and does not conceptualize groups as active agents continuously attempting to assert their own version of the past, this alternative theory points to the possibility of the construction of memory from the 'bottom up' and argues that the past is neither a subjective nor a linguistic fabrication. It also assumes that people keep the past alive for not necessarily instrumental reasons as their memories reflect a respective group's not always coherent system of values and views. Arguing that distortion of memory can occur for various reasons and arguing against ascribing manipulative motives in advance, this approach questions the assertion that the maintenance of hegemonic control by dominant social groups is the sole factor responsible for memory content. Without denying instances of memory distortion caused by its manipulation by political élites, the dynamics of memory perspective nevertheless points out that in some cases (e.g. in post-colonial situations where the creation of national identity is necessary for functional reasons of political and cultural cohesion) 'the willful alternation of collective memory becomes a necessity for a valuable, progressive society' (Kammen 1995b: 340).

The dynamic perspective's definition of memory does not reduce remembering to an instrument of élite manipulation used to control the lower classes and minority groups. It locates memory in 'the space between an imposed ideology and the possibility of an alternative way of understanding experience' (Radstone 2000: 18). By not viewing memory as a hostage to political conditions of the present, this approach allows some space for progressive challenges to the status quo. At the heart of this broad dynamic of memory approach lies a belief in the relationship between remembering and transformation. Investigators of alternative memories, especially traumatic memories, do so not only to honour history's victims but in the hope that memory can prevent repetition of tragic events. In other words, in contrast to the invention of tradition approach, which views memory as a social group's experience that essentially sustains relations of power, the dynamics of memory perspective argues that memory is not solely constrained by the official narrative. It assumes a more 'complex view of relation between past and present in shaping collective memory', and sees collective memory as 'an active process of sense making through time' (Olick and Levy 1997: 922).

The dynamics of memory approach argues that 'the past is highly resistant to efforts to make it over' (Schudson 1989: 105). According to this perspective, although it cannot be denied that many groups use the past for instrumental reasons, nor that we should be grateful for all works done by 'interest theory', nonetheless, such a vision denies the past as purely a construction and insists that it has an inherent continuity. Not only do groups not have equal access to the materials available for the construction of the past, but the available materials are far from infinite. As Schudson (1989) argues, conflicts about the past among a variety of groups further limit our freedom to reconstruct the past according to our own interests. Finally, taking into account that groups can choose only from the available past and that the available past is limited, it can be asked: are they free to choose as they want? According to Schudson (1989: 109), they are not: 'Far from it. There are a variety of ways in which the freedom to choose is constrained'. Among the many factors constraining people's choices are traumatic events that make 'the past part of us' as their impact and importance *commit* us to remember them.

The dynamics of memory approach also tries to correct the Durkheimian insistence on the persistence of what is remembered by pointing to 'the fact that permanent and changing visions of the past are part of one another' (Schwartz 2000: 302). Likewise, this approach differs from Halbwachs' perspective because it argues for the need to historicize identities and meaning systems and tries to comprehend not only how people use the past but also how the past endures in the present. Although the dynamics of memory approach argues along the collective memory approach's line that collective memory is a record of resemblance, it does not assume that the group remains the same, and therefore can accommodate changes in the group's memory and account for its incoherence. Halbwachs, on the other hand, asserts the stability of a social group's memory because he assumes that the group's identity, which determines the content of collective memory, is stable and hitherto well established. In contrast, the dynamics of memory approach recognizes the temporal dimension of identities and argues for the need to analyse them in terms of constitutive and transforming moments. Seeing collective identities as historically constructed enables this perspective to account for changes in groups' identities and their aspirations for themselves and others. In other words, memory, as conceptualized by the dynamics of memory approach, is never solely manipulated or durable; instead, the role of agency and the temporal dimension of memory as well as the historicity of social identities are stressed and analysed.

While both the invention of tradition and the Halbwachs approach emphasize the impact of the present upon the past, they do not attempt to explain the use of historical knowledge in interpreting the present and do not see that the past endures in the present in ways other than invented acts of commemoration. In contrast, the dynamics of memory approach is interested in non-commemorative memory, which is distinct from recollection. Although commemoration and recollection are often intertwined, they nonetheless direct research attention to opposite areas: the recollection orientation aims to develop an interest in narrative representation of the past, and the commemoration orientation enhances an interest in performativity, which further focuses attention on habits and therefore on 'bodily automatisms' (Connerton 1989: 5). Until recently, the majority of studies of collective memory have focused on the activity of commemoration as serving 'the need of a community to resist change in its self-conceptions' (Hutton 1988: 315). Connerton's conceptualization of political commemorative rituals, which adopts Durkheim's idea of social memory as standing 'at the heart of a society's system of rituals' (Pickering 1998: 9), explains how social memory is transferred through commemorative ceremonies and bodily practice (see Chapter 4).

In contrast to investigations of commemorative practices and rituals, which emphasize studying those acts of transfer that make remembering in common possible, the investigations of recollection are interested in narrative reports of the past.

The new approach is less interested in commemorative practices as stabilizing memory and reproducing the group's cohesion; rather it focuses on activities of recollection as 'the act of establishing a relationship with some event issue, or entity of the past' (Zelizer 1995: 217). Narratization, which refers to both telling a story about the past and telling a story about the past's relations to the present, is an effort to comprehend and interpret while making a story intelligible and interesting (Schudson 1995: 357). The recollection of the past, from this perspective, focuses on the central products of narrative activity – namely on the construction of a narrative identity, both at the level of history (e.g. identity as a nation) and at the level of the individual (Wood 1991: 4). This makes identity less stable, as many stories can be woven from the same material, and it defines remembering as a processual action by which 'people constantly transform the recollections that they produce' (Zelizer 1995: 216). Seeing these transformations as collective memory's defining mark moves this approach away from the study of memories as encoded in habitual practices.

The dynamics of memory approach stresses the presence of the past in the present through psychological, social, linguistic and political processes (Schudson 1997). Thus, it allows for the perception of the past, which, as Mead (1932) argues (see Chapter 4), is not a result of its utility, but rather a result of the fact that the past matches and articulates present feelings. Although the dynamics of memory approach agrees with the two previous perspectives' rejection of the vision of the past as unchangeable and durable, it is less willing to reject without question the importance of the past in shaping the present. This qualification of the previous theories' assumptions is a result of the dynamics of memory approach's attempt to combine two visions of the past: the permanent and the changing. In addition, this point is helped by the new perspective's conceptualization of memory as being determined by a dialectic past-present relation and therefore constantly in a process of transformation. Above all, the previous perspectives assume the opposition between history and memory, with collective memory becoming a distorted version of history. Yet, the definition of collective memory as not rooted in historical knowledge does not allow, according to the dynamics perspective, for an examination of the reciprocal workings of history and memory. Hence, the dynamics of memory theory treats history and memory as highly interdependent; however, it does warn against assessing memory and history, since they perform differently in terms of each other. The writers interested in the dynamics of memory approach analyse how, when and why some social events are more likely to form part of collective memory. As they do not conceptualize the past as necessarily always linked to the techniques and practices of power, but view collective memory as a negotiation process that provides groups with identities, they investigate representations of the past embodied in historical evidence and symbolic structures. Researchers writing within this paradigm try to grasp the elusive memories which are not solely constructed from above, as well as the dialectic relationships between past and present. Although the dynamics of memory perspective is not yet a well established and coherent theory, all these studies share the view of culture as a repertoire which provides us with cognitive categories for remembering and elaborate on the issue of the temporality and context of remembering. They also further develop Halbwachs' idea of fluidity of memory by addressing the issue of how memory is transformed.

An interesting example of a study which focuses on how collective memory continuously negotiates between available historical records and current social and political agendas is Schudson's (1992) examination of Watergate memories. This investigation of how Americans remember Watergate demonstrates that we cannot freely alter the past to suit our own interest. Schudson's study illustrates that the past endures in the present not only in formal commemorative practices 'but also in fundamental processes of social life' that are not specifically or self-consciously dedicated to memory (1992: 65). The examination of Watergate was intended as an investigation of non-commemorative domains of collective memory, since the memory of Watergate is rehearsed mainly in congressional debates and institutionalized in legislation on governmental ethics. Schudson found that although Watergate does not function in popular memory, its legacy remains a powerful part of individual lives and is the essential element in shaping the functioning of many American institutions. Generalizing his discovery, Schudson states that the past 'continues into and shapes the present *personally*, as it is transmitted through individual lives; *socially*, as it is transmitted through law and other institutions; and *culturally*, as it is transmitted through language and other symbolic systems' (1997: 6). Schudson argues that previous theories of collective memory are 'incomplete, and oddly, inhumane' because the ways people 'make use of the past, and the reasons they seek to, are more devious and complex' than any of those strands allow (1992: 55). Criticizing various past approaches to collective memory for denying its historicity, Schudson points out that they portray people as 'unrestrained by their own pasts or by their own location in time' (1992: 55). According to him, people are neither solely rational actors who use history to their own ends, nor are they merely cultural dopes. Recognizing the importance of seeing human behaviour as framed within its temporal dimensions, Schudson examines the continuity of the Watergate framework and shows how the legacy of this experience 'imposed itself' on Americans' perception and understanding of yet another political scandal – the Iran-contra story: 'People did not choose the Watergate frame. It chose them' (Schudson 1997: 13). Since the language of Watergate created constraints in the handling of later scandals, it can be said that the past enters into American lives, laws, and language in ways that people and political élites can only marginally control: 'The past seeps into the present whether or not its commemoration is institutionalized' (Schudson 1997: 15). Paraphrasing Marx's famous quote about the historical agency of man, Schudson concludes that although people 'do indeed rewrite the texts of history', they 'do not choose which texts to work on' (p. 15).

This point is well illustrated in Barry Schwartz's works on changes to Lincoln's memory from one generation to the next. Schwartz (2000), in his examination of the reworking of the sixteenth American president's reputation, notes that although the quality of Lincoln's image is transformed (from that of a simple and accessible person to that of a remote figure), at the same time an essential continuity is maintained. He argues that Lincoln's reconstruction can be acknowledged without denying the real Lincoln and that 'memory comes into view as both a cumulative and episodic construction of the past' (Schwartz 1990: 104). Schwartz's study of how collective memories of Lincoln were used during World War II by American political élites shows that 'these image-makers', while on the one hand projecting what was meaningful to themselves onto the general public, on the other hand 'were socialized by the communities they endeavored to reach . . . their depictions reflected as well as shaped their audience's conception of Lincoln' (1990: 112). Because Protestant-inspired moralism shapes the way Americans have always gone to war, Lincoln's commemoration was used by élites to endorse the war, to formulate the war's meaning and make it comprehensible to the public.

In his most recent book, Schwartz tries to correct the main errors of the previous theories of collective memory and argues that memory is 'a cultural program that orients our intentions, sets our moods, and enables us to act' (2000: 251). Being critical of the politics of memory approach, he rejects conceiving memory as a political fact which is 'made and remade in the service of new arrangements', because such a conceptualization would lead to 'an atemporal concept of collective memory' (p. 16). Schwartz's focus on the correspondence between memory and historical fact results in his definition of collective memory as 'a representation of the past embodied in both historical evidence and commemorative symbolism' (p. 9). The fact that old beliefs coexist with new, as each generation modifies the beliefs presented by previous generations, illustrates that collective memory adapts to society's changing needs and tendencies. This observation forms the basis of

Schwartz's criticism of the Dukheimian strand's insistence of the continuity of memory. It also focuses his attention on how collective memory changes and continues at the same time, as well as on the issue of how culture's needs for stability and revision are reconciled with one another and with society (p. 302). Schwartz, in other words, conceptualizes collective memory as a unifying process that provides a framework of meaning through which society maintains stability and identity, while adapting to social change. Consequently, the investigation of Lincoln's changing and enduring images leads to the conclusion that while the present is constituted by the past, 'the past's retention, as well as its reconstruction, must be anchored in the present' (p. 302). However, Schwartz warns that we should not overestimate the carrying power of 'the present' by failing to recognize that the same present can sustain different memories and that different presents can sustain the same memory (2000: 303).

To sum up, the dynamics of memory perspective is a broad stream of investigations into collective memory, which – through the process of analysing and verifying the previous approaches – has been gaining in strength and coherence. Although still without a clear focus, this perspective avoids political reductionism and functionalism. It argues that history cannot be freely invented and reinvented and that suppression of alternative interpretations and coercion are insufficient to ensure that particular interpretations will be accepted. Its conceptualization of memory as a contingent product of social or political actions and as a ground or basis of further action, highlights memory's processual and interactive development as well as its unstable, multiple and fluctuating nature. Understood as the outcome of multiple and competing discourses, the contemporary collective memory is invoked to shed light on political culture. As this perspective manages not to reduce culture to social structures, while at the same time not downplaying it, it provides a more comprehensive view of culture and society and thus escapes the predictability of the presentist approach (Confino 1997). Studying remembering as 'a process that is constantly unfolding, changing and transforming' (Zelizer 1995: 218) demands that we capture memory's processual and unpredictable nature. This perspective runs a lower risk of reifying collective memory as it is aware of the flexibility and ambiguities of memory and because it incorporates conflict, contest and controversy as the hallmarks of memory.

This chapter's discussion of the four main theories of remembering shows the development in our understanding of memory. This development is characterized by both the continuation and the transformation of the conceptualization of the notion of memory. For example, the dynamics of memory approach – while recognizing that Halbwachs and presentist theory properly embed collective memory in the present, and accepting other perspectives' assertion about memory's selectivity – develops both points further. At the same time, while the previous approaches focus on rituals, rites and commemorations, the dynamics of memory perspective pays more attention to memory as a product of narrative activities. Yet, all these theories give insufficient attention to the interpreting self (Prager 1998) and none of them are particularly attentive to the level on which memory takes place (individual and social) nor to the context of memory, which is generative and constitutive of what we experience as memories. Nevertheless, the dynamics of memory perspective can be enriched by focusing on the ways in which individual experience is structured and understood through cultural narratives. Such a step requires more attention to be devoted to the complex entanglement of private and public memories as this can provide a means of showing the ways in which individual experience is always structured and understood through cultural narratives. In what follows we explore the relation between individual and social memory, and the importance of generational and wider cultural frameworks in producing collective memories.

Further reading

Bodnar, J. (1994) Public memory in an American city: commemoration in Cleveland, in J.R. Gillis (ed.) *Commemorations: The Politics of National Identity*, pp. 74–104. Princeton, NJ: Princeton University Press.

Coser, L.A. (ed.) (1992) Introduction, in *Maurice Halbwachs: On Collective Memory*, pp. 1–36. Chicago: University of Chicago Press.

Halbwachs, M. ([1926] 1950) *The Collective Memory*, trans. F.J. Ditter and V.Y. Ditter, London: Harper Colophon Books.

Hobsbawm, E. (1983) Introduction: inventing traditions, in E. Hobsbawm and T. Ranger (eds) *The Invention of Tradition*, pp. 1–14. Cambridge: Cambridge University Press.

Popular Memory Group (1982) Popular memory: theory, politics and method, in R. Johnson, G. Mclennan, B. Schwartz and D. Sutton (eds) *Making Histories: Studies in History Making and Politics*, pp. 205–52. London: Hutchinson.

Schudson, M. (1989) The present in the past versus the past in the present, *Communication*, 11: 105–13.

Schwartz, B., Zerubavel, Y. and Barnett, B. (1986) The recovery of Masada: A study in collective memory, *Sociological Quarterly*, 127(2): 164–74.

CHAPTER 4

THE REMEMBERING PROCESS

The previous chapter established that the four main sociological theories of remembering, while rightly insisting that memory and temporality cannot be detached from each other, do not sufficiently address the issue of the nature of remembering. In order to explore the remembering process it is not enough to explore collective memory as simply 'publicly available symbols and meaning systems not reducible to what is in people's heads' (Olick in Schuman and Corning 2000: 914). There is also a need to consider how collective consensus is connected with the actual thought processes of any particular person and how 'feeling states and bodily desires, inherited from the past but prevailing in the present, can rewrite the past in the service of the present' (Prager 1998: 83). Thus, in the first part of this chapter we discuss the embodiedness and embeddedness of memory. In order to further account for what makes an individual memory social, the following sections of the chapter will look at the role of generational memory and the significance of traditions in shaping processes of remembering.

The embodied self and frames of remembering

> *'The past is myself, my own history, the seed of my present*
> *thoughts, the mould of my present disposition'*
> *(R.L. Stevenson, quoted in Tonkin 1992: 1)*

Now that we are familiar with the problems and dilemmas faced by social theories of remembering, the difficulties involved in attempts to capture the essence of an individual remembrance will not surprise us. The complexity and variety of individual memory, ranging from long-term and short-term memory, through semantic memory and procedural knowledge, which allows us to learn new skills, to repressed memory, make inquiries into this subject a challenging task.

Most traditional laboratory-based memory research has attempted to understand memory as a context-free, isolated psychological process. In their effort to objectify and externalize memory, current clinical memory studies focus mainly on the brain, separated from the remembering mind, and on the past, distinct from an interpreting present. These studies can be seen as the continuation of the three sciences of memory from the nineteenth century, although technological advancement has changed their nature (e.g. neurological studies, which used to focus predominately on the brain, are now able to work at the level of cell biology). Moreover, new technologies are responsible for the emergence of a new branch of the science of memory – computer modelling of memory in artificial intelligence (Hacking 1995: 199). Experimental psychologists have been concerned to understand the phenomena of remembering and forgetting in order to gain a fundamental understanding of the brain and sensory apparatus, viewed as a system capable of selecting, organizing, storing and retrieving information. Modern cognitive psychology tries to construct a scientific understanding of memory's underlying mechanisms and researchers have constructed many empirical generalizations about short-term memory, flashbulb memory and recalling. However, despite the rapidly expanding accumulation of know-ledge about memory, and despite the growing consensus about the extent and importance of memory distortions (Tulving and Craik 2000), scientists dealing with memory from the perspective of experimental, developmental, cognitive and neuropsychology have not yet produced a new, interesting theory: 'In short, the results of a hundred years of the psychological study of memory are somewhat discouraging' (Neisser 1982: 11).

An individual remembering is a very complicated act, but even more importantly the relationship between public and personal memories is not a simple one. For example, there is an enormous difference between appropri-ated memories and personally acquired memories (Mannheim 1972: 296) while, at the same time, much of what we seem to 'remember' and what we assume to be our personal memories we have not actually experienced personally. For instance, many of our childhood 'memories' are actually recollections of stories told by our parents. Furthermore, while the avail-ability of personal information depends on the content of the remembered event, people experience these events not only in the context of public narra-tives but also within the compass of their own activities (Brown et al. 1988: 139–57). What we know of what happens in remembering is that we relive an earlier perception which is, as in every conscious perception, 'an act of recognition, a pairing in which an object (or an event, an act, an emotion) is identified by placing it against the background of an appropriate symbol' (Geertz 1973: 215). Thus, memory is produced by an individual but is always produced in relation to the larger interpersonal and cultural world in which that individual lives – for example, one remembers one's childhood as a part of a family. However, while recognizing that the cognitive process of remembering contains much that is social in origin, and thus also the importance of studying social contexts in which even the most personal memories are embedded, we want to avoid, as we have already mentioned in Chapter 1, an oversocialized conception of man. In other words, we attempt to overcome the valid criticism of Halbwachs' approach as neglecting the question of 'how individual consciousness might relate to those of the collectivities those individuals actually made up' (Fentress and Wickham 1992: ix). A very interesting example of how this can be achieved comes from Jeffrey Prager's study of 'false memory syndrome'.

Prager (1998) shows the complexity of the process of remembering by discussing the case of his psychoanalytical patient, Ms A, who developed a belief that she had been sexually abused as a child. Analysing her false memories over the course of numerous sessions, Prager suggests that major current discourses are the essential factor in producing memory. Ms A's misremembering of her childhood, argues Prager, needs to be placed within the context of the American national preoccupation with the themes of childhood abuse and victimization, fuelled by the popularity of the Recovered Memory Movement (see Chapter 6): 'The atmosphere was such that few people would not wonder whether they themselves, as children, had suffered abuse by an adult. The cultural milieu, I believe, was contributing to Ms. A.'s memories' (Prager 1998: 76). Arguing that memory is always embedded, Prager illustrates the intersubjectivity of memory by showing how the larger interpersonal and cultural worlds in which individuals live constitute their memories. Even more importantly, he asserts that not only is the reconstruction of the past always dependent on frames of meaning and contexts of significance generated in the present, but that it is also shaped by our emotional experiences.

The recovery of the past rests upon both memory's *embeddedness*, which encourages us to pay attention to the influence of the present on the recovery of the past, and its *embodiedness*, which alerts us to the ways in which our feelings and bodily sensations, generated in the past, help to interpret that past. When considering both, we cannot avoid, Prager argues, noting their connection with the notion of self. Memory is 'embedded because the self is a "socially constructed" or "socially constituted" entity' (1998: 71), while being 'embodied in a particular person, a person actively engaged in forging selfhood' (p. 81). Thus, Prager concludes that the conception of memory as both embedded and embodied does not explain the whole mystery of the human process of remembering, which can only be fully grasped if we take the role of the self into consideration. In short, for Prager, remembering is 'an active, interpretive process of a conscious mind situated in the world' (p. 215).

Arguing that the sociological focus on collective rituals, rites and commemorations of present symbols yields insufficient attention to the interpreting self, Prager examines the internal pressures driving the self to remember 'the past in the idiosyncratic ways that are required for one to situate oneself temporally in a past, a present and future' (1998: 70). By combining the conception of memory as embedded and embodied with the notion of the interactive self, Prager provides us with a sociology of memory which includes both 'a conception of mediating selves capable of resisting dominant cultural modes of thinking' (1998: 90) and a conception of how available schemata of understanding or cultural codes influence our desires and perceptions. Also of further note is his assertion that memories are not solely the product of an individual mind, but are also the result of an individual's relation both to self and to the outside world, and therefore cannot exist without input from the larger context. This claim introduces the third important factor in the consideration of memory, the self, which is seen as being 'able to symbolically mediate between possibilities and to exercise reasoned and reflective judgment' (Prager 1989: 90).

The concept of memory, seen as a vehicle of the embodied self which itself is embedded in the larger cultural world, helps Prager to explain Ms A's problems with her self-conception. Her effort to find a 'cure' for her pain, and in turn her search for a meaningful language in which to express her past feelings, can only be understood if we see memory not solely as a cultural product but also as the result of an individual's relation to self and to the outside world. Another argument supporting the view that any explanation of the remembering experience is not sufficient without the inclusion of the idea of the self points to the fact that individuals are able to resist dominant cultural frameworks. In other words, relying only on the concept of memory as embedded to account for how people construct their own memories is not satisfactory as it is not sensitive to the issue of how cultural symbols, discourses and images resonate with the individual. Prager concludes that memory, viewed as a process of remembering, 'necessarily constitutes and reconstitutes relationships, including one's relationship to oneself' (1998: 90). He understands memory as a necessarily intersubjective vehicle of self-constitution that always operates in relation to others, to the past and to a future. Consequently, memory is 'part of this unending work of selfhood, of organizing and locating oneself in relation to the cultural language of the cultural universe around one' (1998: 125).

The self, experienced as a product of a unique past, is the centre of auto-biographical memory. Autobiographical memory, or memory about the self, 'is the source of information about our lives, from which we are likely to make judgments about our own personalities and predictions of our own and, to some extent, others' behavior' (Rubin 1988: 7). Autobiographical memory also provides a sense of identity and of continuity. According to Barclay (1988), most autobiographical memories are reconstructions of past events that are driven by highly developed self-schemata. Consequently, the past is reconstructed to fit with personal 'self-theories' of how people consider they were likely to act, while their knowledge about themselves is acquired from routine life events – from what they do, think and feel every day. Commenting upon Barclay's findings, Rubin asserts that when 'we recall from our lives, we behave more like authors writing autobiographies than like videocassette recorders' (1988: 3). Although we 'convey in precise and honest terms a plausible and consistent record of our own intentions and actions', our recollection is never 'complete and accurate' (1988: 3). Instead we are involved in a never ending dialectical movement in which 'an individual's state when remembering can change the memory, and the memory can change the individual' (1988: 4).

Memories of most everyday life events are transformed, distorted or forgotten because autobiographical memory changes over time as we change (Barclay 1988: 82–9). The best illustration of how our acquired autobiographical self-knowledge and knowledge about others drives the reconstruction of plausible, yet often inaccurate, elaborations of previous experiences comes from Neisser's (1982) study of the testimony of John Dean in the Watergate investigation. The media at the time were so impressed by the depth and detail of Dean's apparent 'photographic' recollections that they described him as 'the man with the tape-recorder memory' (Baddeley 1989: 51). In his testimony Dean was able to recall prior meetings with the president, Richard Nixon, in astonishing detail. Later, however, the infamous Watergate tapes were discovered, including tapes of the meetings about which Dean testified, and their comparison revealed that his memory was rather selective. Analysis of the tape-recordings provided evidence that Dean had often distorted the scene so as to portray himself as more important than he actually was. It shows that Dean's recall of his conversations with Nixon during his Watergate testimony was accurate about the individuals' basic positions, but inaccurate with the respect to exactly what was said during a given conversation. It can therefore be argued, concludes Neisser (1982), that memory is often a reconstruction, not a reproduction, and that an egocentric bias is a normal element of remembering. Autobiographical information is remembered because the memory marks an intersection of personal and societal histories and as such it defines the person's self-identity (1982: 48). In the same vein, Barclay and DeCook (1988: 92) state that autobiographical recollections 'are not necessarily accurate, nor should they be; they are, however, mostly congruent with one's self-knowledge, life themes, or sense of self'.

Prager's (1998) argument that memories are embodied in a particular person's sensations, feelings, techniques and gestures, brings to our attention the importance of the body and its habitual and emotional experiences as both a reservoir of memories and a mechanism of generating them. The importance of bodies is further reinforced by the argument that the acceleration of change and the resulting alienation of the past leave us today 'with only one fixed point of reference' – the 'site' provided by our own bodies (Antze and Lambek 1996b: xiv). The body is the main 'container' of habitual memory, according to Connerton (1989), because the past is passed on to us in practices of the body or in the ways of doing and being. The nonverbal articulation of memory can be seen as a practice of representation that enacts and gives substance to the discourse of collective memory. If 'there is such a thing as social memory . . . we are likely to find it in commemorative ceremonies' because commemorative rituals are a means of transmitting social memory (Connerton 1989: 4). While examining the similarities and differences between commemorative rituals and other rituals (e.g. religious ones), Connerton discovered that commemorative ceremonies function effectively as mnemonic devices because of their formalism and performativity, two features that they share with all other rituals. Moreover, commemorative ceremonies are of cardinal importance for communal memory because of their ritual re-enactment of persons or events from the past (1989: 51–67). If, therefore, commemorative ceremonies prove to be commemorative only in so far as they are performative, we should examine bodily automatism and habitual enacting: the 'performativeness of rituals', seen as encoded in set postures, gestures and movements, send a simple and clear message (1989: 58); 'One kneels or one does not kneel', and to kneel in subordination is not to 'state subordination, nor is it just to communicate a message of submission. To kneel in subordination is to display it through the visible, present substance of the body' (1989: 59). Bodily practices of a culturally specific kind entail a combination of cognitive and habit memory, which is re-enacted through acts of performance that remind performers of a set of rules and principles of classification and distinction (1989: 88). So, we preserve versions of the past not only by representing it to ourselves in words or through storing and retrieving information, but also through commemorative ceremonies, in which we re-enact an image of the past through memorized culturally specific postures, gestures and practices.

The importance of bodies is reinforced further by the argument about the role of emotions in the process of remembering. Emotions play an essential role in any recollection because memories not tagged by ongoing social emotions tend to fade out, and because emotions are always 'in part about the past' (Nussbaum 2001: 177). Seeing memory as 'the child of both satisfaction and frustration' (Lowewald in Prager 1998: 187) places emotions at the core of memory, which in turn makes the body an important 'site' of memory, because experiencing intense emotions (both negative and positive) blurs the Cartesian mind-body distinction (Prager 1998: 183–7; Brison 1999: 42). Such strong sensations help to overcome memory distanciation and make the recalled memories vivid and somatic. The body as an important 'site' of memory is frequently discussed in studies of trauma (see Chapter 6). Emotional responses, as important affective states that screen out certain memories and allow for other memories to surface, are inscribed in the body. They invoke a particular personal history; within their expression in the present they bring memories of past experiences that contribute to the forming and experiencing of the present. Viewing emotions as essentially interpersonal communicative acts, Prager writes that the embeddedness of 'past experiences is written in bodily sensation and feelings, recording layer upon layer of experiences that have been made subjectively meaningful' (1998: 187).

A good deal of empirical evidence supports the view that emotions, whether positive or negative, tend to be socially shared and that the social sharing of emotions results in a strong emotional impact on the exposed person (Barbalet 1998). An emotional experience provokes a person to talk about it with others, as those affected attempt to understand and learn more about their experience. The more intense the personal emotions, the more likely it is that we will share them with others. Talking about an event is 'a form of rehearsal that may aid memory' because talking or translating an experience into language, seen as the social mechanism guiding memories, can help to organize and assimilate the event in people's minds (Pennebaker and Banasik 1997: 8). Language – as the primary symbol system that defines the framework for individuals' memories – is therefore 'the vehicle for important cognitive, and learning processes following an emotional upheaval' (Pennebaker and Banasik 1997: 8). The more an event provokes an emotion, the more it elicits social sharing and distinctly vivid, precise, concrete, long-lasting memories of the event. This type of memory, known as flashbulb memory, is seen as being qualitatively different from ordinary memories and as superior in terms of time because this type of memory is assumed to be clearer and less affected by time than other memories. Being a result of a surprising and emotionally intense event, a flashbulb memory is likely to be long-lasting (Finkenauer *et al.* 1997).

Flashbulb memories (e.g., connected with assassination of a public figure or with tragic public events, such as 11 September 2001) allow individuals to place themselves in a historical context because, when talking with others about an extraordinary public event, people are able to include themselves in the narrative. Thus, flashbulb memories, on the one hand 'are individual because they consist of people's memory for their personal discovery context' (Finkenauer *et al.* 1997: 192), and on the other hand, are social memories because they involve a collective shared recollection of the actual event, and because interpersonal rehearsal plays an important role in maintaining and consolidating such memories. Individual memories become social through interpersonal communication and collective remembering that locate events in the thematic-causal structures in which they occur. However, we also experience these events within the compass of our own activities. This directs our attention to the third and final assertion in Prager's explanation of the remembering process, which stresses the role of the social and cultural context.

The claim that individual memories are constructed from cultural forms leads Prager to argue that remembering is achieved 'not monologically but dialogically' (1998: 218). Because the way we remember is determined through a supra-individual cultural construction and because the act of remembering is itself interactive, promoted by cultural artefacts and cues employed for social purposes, and even enacted by cooperative activity, collective memory can be seen as a shared social framework of individual recollections. One of the first demonstrations of the reconstructive nature of our memories, and the first proof that remembering is shaped by our expectations and general knowledge regarding what should have happened as much as by the content of a specific event, was provided by Frederic Bartlett (1932). Bartlett conducted an experiment in which white American students read a Native American legend entitled 'The War of the Ghosts' and were then asked to recall the story as accurately as possible. He found that the resulting recollections seldom reflected the original story, as subjects tended to forget pieces of the narrative that didn't fit their cultural expectations. Bartlett concluded that we remember and think about the past through shared frames of understanding, which 'gives a persistent framework into which all delayed recall must fit and it very powerfully influences both the manner and matter of recall' (1932: 296). Frames of meaning, or ways in which we view the past, are generated in the present and usually match the group's common map of the world. Thus they usually change following major social shifts that affect entire mnemonic communities. We rely on them to supply us with what we should remember and what is taboo, and therefore must be forgotten. Such a conceptualization of frames of remembering as providing us with a 'menu' of what to recall suggests the possibility of the employment of Goffman's (1974) concept of frame as a means of advancing our understanding of memory's embeddedness. Goffman's notion is of enormous help here because it enables us to do justice to the collective side of memory without reducing the individual to a passive follower of an internalized collective order.

Framing, writes Goffman, is a result of our desire to organize our experiences into meaningful activities. Following the ancient Greek saying that the man who sees everything is blind, it can be claimed that frames, by directing our focus, make us notice what is important, therefore ensuring clarity and simplicity in the definition of a situation. Frames, as an element out of which definitions are built up, permeate all levels of ordinary social actions and as such provide a background understanding for events. In *Frame Analysis* Goffman argues that an agreement concerning the identity of a particular event is reached by implying one or more frameworks or schemata of interpretation, which renders 'what would otherwise be a meaningless aspect of the scene into something that is meaningful' (1974: 21).

Goffman stresses that the authorship of a definition of a situation does not ordinarily belong to the people in that situation but that social organization and social structure are responsible for framing people's experience. At the same time he claims that constructionist views fail to notice the multi-dimensional and layered nature of situations: 'It is not just that different people might have different definitions of the same situations, but that each participant can be in several complex layers of situational definition at the same time' (Collins 1988: 58). Goffman's avoidance of complete relativism (as seen in his recognition of the primary importance of the physical and social worlds, and his interest in analysing the organization of experience) parallels the dynamics of memory approach's insistence on the reality of the past while, at the same time, adding to it the assertion that people do indeed interpret the past (Schudson 1997: 15). Since people continuously project their expectations and perceptions, or frames of reference, into the past, and since they continuously build frames upon frames, the past is reconstructed in a more complicated way than the simple assertion that the present influences the past would suggest.

According to Goffman (1959: 247), the reality and sincerity of frames is protected by the use of various procedures that anchor frame activity and induce in us a belief that what appears to be real *is* real; yet it is the material world that is the ultimate grounding, while all transformations of it are secondary. His approach allows us to view forgetting as the result of the disappearance or change of frameworks due to shifts in social conventions. The fact that there can be many frames and that they are constructed upon each other, with primary frameworks at the beginning of the process, results in the multiple nature of reality. While engaging in the process of framing, people prove themselves to be capable of dealing with many frames without any problems. They are also capable of adjusting frames to 'fit' the actual occurrence itself in such a way that the definition of the event, as provided by the framework of shared memory, becomes confirmed. Such a construction of the social world ensures our conventional conduct, which in turn is understandable only in terms of the frame. When the fit is imperfect 'the past is at once an idealization and critique of the present world' (Schwartz 2000: 253). In other words, in order for collective memory to inspire and mobilize, the fit must be imperfect, leaving enough discrepancy to allow for the evaluation of the present. The workings of primary frameworks become most visible when discussing generational memories and groups traditions.

Generational memory: imprint of a 'spirit of the times'

The idea of generation is very old. It was used, for example, in ancient Greece and features in the Old Testament, where it is conceived in a genealogical sense as the measure of distance between parents and children. Despite its long history, the notion of generation has had a brief and not very successful career as a scientific concept. However, attempts to elaborate the idea are interesting because they tend to transcend the arbitrary limits of conventional academic disciplines. For example, Marias' (1970) formulation of the concept of generation, while relying on historical method and tracing the theory back to Ibn Khaldun's fourteenth-century writings, incorporates philosophical, literary and sociological insights. Seeing generation as 'the concrete unit of authentic historical chronology', Marias emphasizes that it requires more than merely biological or biographical information, since we 'must also know the structure of the world at that time' (p. 101). Following Ortega's idea of generation as 'the visual organ with which historical reality can be seen in its real and vibrant authenticity', Marias defines generation as 'systems of prevailing conventions' and therefore as 'a fundamental ingredient of each of us' (1970: 102, 101, 83). He points out that affinity between members of a given generation 'does not arise so much from themselves as from being obliged to live in a world of a certain and unique form' (p. 104). Since to live is something 'that happens in the form of coexistence' (p. 79) and since generation is our historical world, it is from this generational basis that we face reality in order to mould our lives.

Such assumptions about the importance of generation and a 'spirit of the times', which leaves its imprint on the collective memory of a given generation, have energized various perspectives, from ideas of generation as a way to explain the feeling of 'destiny' among a specific group of people, to perspectives arguing that generation 'alone could help to compose a dynamic portrait of a society'(Renouard in Nora 1996b: 505). The majority of these theories seem to stress the uniqueness of each generation and their mutual distance, yet in reality generations have much in common and tend to resemble each other (de Tocqueville 1968). In the same vein, Halbwachs ([1926] 1950) argues that there is a 'living link' between generations which ensures that the past is handed on via parents and grandparents and goes beyond the limits of individual experience. While the generational gap is perceived as providing a basis for changing the present, generational continuity is regarded as a source of stability and legitimacy. In other words, as generation follows generation, each receives an inheritance from its predecessor, and this intergenerational transmission, or tradition, is a foundation of societal continuity.

It was Mannheim who injected a more sociological perspective into the notion of generation. His classic essay on 'The Problem of Generation', originally published in 1928, is still the main point of reference for all the more recent contributions. By insisting that in order to share generational location in a sociologically meaningful sense an individual must be born within the same historical and cultural context and be exposed to experiences that occur during their formative adult years, Mannhein endorsed the conceptualization of generations as something more than merely collections of age cohorts. His description of links between the generations as a social category and memory suggests that theories of social memory should be a central part of the sociology of knowledge (Plicher 1994). Mannheim's theory of generation, designed as part of his theoretical strategy to understand 'the existential basis of knowledge' and develop an alternative approach from Marxism to social change, sees generation as 'one of the fundamental factors in the unfolding dynamic of history' (1972: 288–90). The specificity and uniqueness of each generation's experience results in the different character of their respective collective memories. Moreover, Mannheim uses this notion in 'a surprisingly contemporary way to encompass all types of knowledge a person might acquire, that is conceptual knowledge of words, world knowledge, skills as well as memories' (Conway 1997: 21).

Stressing the difference between appropriated and personally acquired memories, Mannheim argues that the memories we acquire for ourselves in the process of personal development are real memories which we really possess and which are the basis of our generational identity, since this type of knowledge is generally better preserved in our memory and has real binding power (1972: 296). He further specifies that it is the period of late adolescence and early adulthood which is the formative one for the constitution of a distinctive memory and personal outlook. The concept of 'the inventory experience', which is an experience absorbed from the environment in early youth, allows Mannheim to argue that young people's fresh encounters with the wider world in this critical stage of their lives become 'the historically oldest stratum of consciousness, which tends to stabilise itself as the natural view of the world' (p. 296). In this perspective, experience from adolescence and early adulthood is carried forward with self-awareness and contributes to differences in generational views of the world.

However, for a generation to be a key aspect of the existential determination of knowledge, its members need to share more than just demographic characteristics. Mannheim believed that belonging to the same generation becomes sociologically significant only when it involves participation in the same historical and social circumstances which 'endow the individuals sharing in them with . . . common mentality and sensitivity' (p. 291). A unique generational memory, a result of its members' common exposure to social and intellectual processes, is dependent on the tempo of social change. The quicker the pace of social and cultural change, the greater are the chances that a generation gap will emerge, resulting in older generations controlling the reigning conceptions of history, while the young quickly acquire 'new strategies of action' for coping with life in unsettled times (Swidler 1986).

The growing tempo of change, together with the spread of democracy, can be seen as responsible for today's new interest in the idea of generation. With the decline of the importance and visibility of old divisions, knowledges and bonds, generational identifications become more important and hence it can be said that the 'generation is the daughter of democracy and the acceleration of history' (Nora 1996b: 508). Furthermore, in this era of electronic communication, globalization of popular culture and the importance of mass media, it is predicted that 'generations will exist more easily across social space because they will be able to share more easily a collective culture' (Eyerman and Turner 1998: 97). Emerging generational links and solidarities simultaneously simplify and complicate the network of social allegiances, as recent developments impose new limits and enhance new types of connection. These new trends have shifted attention from previous studies of generations as a variable which can help to predict future behaviour, to current investigations of generation as a collectivity constituted by the historical dimensions of the social processes predominant in that generation's youth. This recent interest in generational memory has helped to clarify some uncertainties connected with attempts to identify a concrete 'generation'.

New investigations of the collective memories of generations has solved the problem of how to define a generational cohort, as this type of research assumes that memories will be structured along the age dimension in ways that allow us to identify various generations. Unlike the traditional approach, new research 'starts with memories and works backwards rather than forward from generations' (Schuman and Corning 2000: 915). The importance of links between generation and memory, so prominent in the new studies, can be seen as a result of researchers' realization that, in order to assume that members of a cohort in terms of age adopt a certain line of action, there is a need to identify what earlier experiences are carried forward in memory by that cohort.

Several studies examine the existence of generational differences in memory by comparing the meaning of adolescent memories with those that occur in other periods of life (e.g. Schuman and Scott 1989; Schuman and Corning 2000). In order to verify hypotheses extrapolated from Mannheim's theory, this type of research investigates intergenerational effects, seen as the result of the intersection of personal and national history, examines the role of various stages in individual lives for memory encoding, and analyses whether adolescence and early childhood are the primary sources of political and social memories. In one such study, following Mannheim's suggestions that adolescence and early adulthood are stages of life uniquely open to gaining knowledge about the wider world and that those from an older generation are likely to interpret events in terms of their previously well developed view of the world, Schuman and Scott (1989) asked a cross section of Americans to identify any two 'especially important national or world events or changes'. Their research results show that memories are structured by generational divisions and that attributions of importance to national and world events of the past half century tend to be a function of an individual having experienced an event during adolescence or early adulthood. By examining the existence of generational differences in memory, Schuman and Scott's study proves that knowledge personally gained is more important, as people do not tend to regard those events and changes that occur after their early adulthood as important. For example, older generations were significantly more likely to mention World War II as one of the major events in the last 50 years than younger people, who did not personally experience it.

In addition, the *meaning* of events differs for various cohorts, which confirms Manheim's position. However, some types of event, due to their 'objective' importance, are seen as significant by all generations, including those who were not adolescents at the time. That said even in cases where the surface memory of an event does not vary according to age, the '*meaning* of the event . . . will be different for different cohorts' (Schuman and Scott 1989: 361). For example, the Vietnam War generation, who experienced the distrust and divisions of the 1960s, viewed World War II, which they did not personally experience, as the 'good war', while older Americans' perception of World War II is constructed around its impact on the world.

Those who chose an event that happened during their adolescence showed a strong tendency to explain their choice in terms of straightforward personal experience during that time (Schuman and Scott 1989: 370–3). For example, even though most Americans over 50 shared a memory of John F. Kennedy's assassination, this was identified as an important event predominately by people who were in their teens to early mid-twenties in 1963, when the assassination took place, while older people mentioned the assassination less frequently and in less personal terms. The younger people clearly remembered Kennedy's assassination 'in terms of either a specific "flashbulb" image of hearing of the event itself or a more general report of its being memorable' (Schuman and Scott 1989: 373). For instance, a woman aged 33 at the time of the study said 'I remember it vividly. I was in my sixth grade class when the principle came in to announce it' (p. 373).

Also of interest at this point are the studies undertaken by cognitive psychologists, whose work on autobiographical memories revealed the existence of what they termed the 'reminiscence bump' or 'peak'. These investigations illustrate the importance of adolescence and early adulthood as the critical stages for memory encoding (Rubin *et al.* 1998). A recent study by Schuman *et al.* (1997) focuses on actual knowledge of the past, rather than on the spontaneous recollection of past events. By checking their respondents' knowledge related to 11 political, social and cultural events spread over the past 60 years (many of which occurred midway in the life cycle of present older adults) Schuman *et al.* confirmed Mannheim's general prediction that it is during adolescence that 'life's problems begin to be located in a "present" and are experienced as such' (1997: 47).

If we combine the discovery that youth experiences focus memories on the direct personal meaning of events with our previous observation that people tend to share their emotionally loaded experiences with others, we can say that it is the sharing of memories among young people which ensures the persistence of memories from the period of adolescence and early adulthood. At the same time, young people's sociability and their sharing of experiences produces an affective basis to their generational identity. Generational memory allows people to have a certain social identification, both on an individual and a societal level. As people remember sharing memories and remembering together, a generational identity is constructed. In other words, a generational identity is produced through collective practices, established in response to traumatic or formative events which demand the sharing of memories: 'Generational memory grows out of social interactions that are in the first place historical and collective and later internalised in a deeply visceral and unconscious way so as to dictate vital choices and control reflexes of loyalty' (Nora 1996b: 526).

The most important moments for a generation tend to be unusual historical events since the more an event generates emotions, the more it elicits social sharing and is hence better remembered. A generation is a product of memory because of the formative role of memories of historical events from adolescence and early adulthood in the creation of a generational culture. Memory of the past is always intersubjective, a recollection of a past time lived in relation to other people. However, generational memory is historical not only because it consists of remembrances of historical moments: 'It is historical above all because it is first imposed from without, then violently internalised' (Nora 1996b: 523). People remember special emotional experiences from when they were young adults because, in order to make sense and reflect on these experiences, they talk about them with others. In turn, this mnemonic socialization, through which we learn what we should remember and what we can forget, provides bases for generational culture and identity. Generations, while being products of memory, are at the same time the main relationship in the production of history. This argument comes from Davis' (1989) reflection on Lision-Tolosana's ethnographic account of generational relations in a small town in Spain in the period 1900–61. By demonstrating how each new generation takes its inheritance from its predecessor, reacts against it, and – in response to the particular historical situation – creates a new environment that again is the object of reaction, Lision-Tolosana establishes that each generation had substantial autonomy to remake history.

Generational identifications are constructed out of generational cultures that provide a set of embodied practices, tastes, attitudes, preferences and dispositions, which are sustained by collective memories and enforced by control, through rituals of exclusion, of access to collective resources (Eyerman and Turner 1998). Such a perspective, emphasizing the importance of collective cultural experiences, allows for the adoption of Pierre Bourdieu's notion of *habitus* to express the uniqueness of a given generational memory.

Using this concept, Eyerman and Turner modify Mannheim's original conceptualization and define a generation as 'a cohort of persons passing through time who come to share a common habitus'. Sharing a collective culture and habitus provides members of a generation 'with collective memory that serves to integrate the cohort over a finite period of time' (1998: 91). Habitus is a system of durable dispositions to act which are produced by objective structures and conditions but are also capable of producing and reproducing those structures (Bourdieu 1977: 72). Habitus comprises strategies and practices through which social order 'accomplishes itself' and makes itself 'self-evident' and 'meaningful' (Bourdieu and Wacquant 1992: 127–8), as the dispositions to act are incorporated in social interaction within a historically formed social context. Being made up of 'the cognitive structures which social agents implement in their practical knowledge of the social world' (Bourdieu 1984: 468), habitus organizes the way in which individuals see the world and act in it. As such, it is at the heart of the dialectic between the objective and the subjective, because dispositions and frames of perception are at once historical, social and individual. Although people internalize 'the immanent law of the structure in the form of habitus' (Bourdieu and Wacquant 1992: 140), they are still capable of creativity within the limits of the structure. In a similar vein, Marias (1970: 92) argues that prevailing conventions, which define generations, are imposed on us but our reactions to them are not. Recent studies of generational memory also suggest that people increasingly develop greater independence and sophistication in their thinking, frequently acquiring knowledge beyond officially available information, and this places limits on the kind of élite manipulation of collective memory visualized by the presentist approach (Schuman and Corning 2000).

The concept of habitus, as 'a past which survives in the present and tends to perpetuate itself into the future by making itself present in practices structured according to its principles' (Bourdieu 1977: 82), also allows us to identify the importance of collective memory in creating a generational culture. Being a 'principle of continuity and regularity' (1977: 82), habitus is a system of practice-generating schemes which expresses identities and memories constituted by structural differences. Bourdieu's main focus is on the role of class location in the structuring of habitus. However, while examining the construction of collective identity and memory in contemporary societies we should emphasize the structuring role of generation as a mode of distinction based on age differentiation. Other dimensions of classification, such as class, gender or ethnicity, are also important as structuring forces and, moreover, all four of them often overlap. Nevertheless, in modern society, as Eyerman and Turner (1998) observe, there is a shift in favour of generation. From the perspective of generational habitus, all significant social, political and cultural events that a given generation experiences at first hand can be perceived as part of the social space in which that generation defines its collective identity. Within this space the marks of generational distinction are realized and generational memory is constructed. Of course, while the main events provide a space for self-production of a generational identity, 'the commercial mass media amplified and, at the same time, commodified it' (Eyerman and Turner 1998: 103).

Thus, generational identity can be conceptualized as a social identity linked to cultural differentiation, based on age distinction. Generational habitus, which is the foundation of generational memory, and therefore identity, can be seen as a system of practice-generating schemes rooted in the uniqueness of the sociohistorical location of a particular generation. Generational memory is to some degree a question of understanding human variations by means of history since, as Nora (1996b: 528) notes, generation is the 'spontaneous horizon of individual historical objectification'. While any classification of those generational variations needs to start with habitus, it should be followed by attempts to grasp the nature of the 'secondary variation' or 'vital sensitivity' of a given generation (Ortega in Marias 1970: 93). As generations 'with greater or lesser activity, originality and energy' constantly fashion their world they apply their unique sensitivity, rooted in and carried forward by their habitus, to interpret and make sense of later developments (Mannheim 1972: 300). The uniqueness of generational memories and differences expresses itself through a given generation's choice of meaning from the past to interpret the present.

However, despite unquestionable distinctiveness, no generation creates its own beliefs, norms and perspectives. Moreover, some events are so important that no single generational cohort develops greater knowledge of them than another, while, on the other hand, some occurrences 'stick' in the memories of people of different ages but who are related by other social characteristics, such as race, gender, social status or occupation. The study by Schuman et al. (1997), while confirming that early adulthood is a stage of life uniquely open to gaining knowledge about the wider world and that knowledge of a past event decreases with cohort distance from that event, also discovered that some social characteristics interfere with demographic division in terms of what is remembered. For example, African Americans in all age groups tend to know more about the historical events significant in the history of race relations, while women of all ages attach more importance to memories of events related to women's rights movements. World War II is now not only widely recalled, but the generational effect is less sharp and less visible due to the saturation of popular culture with various recollections of the war and the emergence of many memories of the Holocaust (Schuman et al. 1997: 71).

Such wider national remembering as well as cases of more narrowly defined intergenerational communication focus our attention on the essence of the notion of tradition, understood as a process of handing down from one generation to the next a set of practices, beliefs and institutions.

Traditions, while referring to the social transmission of cultural inheritance within a group, and therefore resembling Halbwachs' notion of collective memory, allow us to grasp the complexity of the links between groups and their respective memories without assuming that the shared experiences directly imply shared memories. This allows us to analyse how traditions constitute groups and to examine how groups, ranging from occupational to national, reaffirm their identities by constructing their memories through rituals, celebrations and narratives. In what follows, we employ the notion of tradition to further explore how groups remember.

Tradition: a chain of memory

Writing about tradition as being eroded has itself become 'tradition' (Luke 1996). There is a well established tradition of thought according to which tradition is something static, backward and conservative, something impervious to change and devoid of reflection, as well as connected with ignorance, dogma and irrationalism. This perspective is a result of the eighteenth-century Enlightenment which proclaimed tradition to be 'merely the shadow side of modernity' (Giddens 1999: 2). As Enlightenment thinkers sought to destroy the authority of tradition, itself being a creation of modernity, they established yet another tradition – the classical tradition in sociology with its focus on the problem of social order (Nisbet 1966). Following widespread criticism of this classical approach, since the late 1960s sociology has become preoccupied with the uniqueness of modernity and its main feature: change'. As a result, it is now common for writings about tradition to start with an observation about the absence in sociological literature of any analysis of the nature and mechanism of tradition (Szacki 1971; Shils 1981; Thompson 1996; Giddens 1999).

Apart from sociology's preoccupation with modernity, the present lack of interest in tradition can also be seen as a result of the widespread treatment of the concept – on the one hand, as something of the past which, by its very nature, is homogeneous and unproblematic, and on the other as something inherently ambiguous, almost too difficult to conceptualize. Consequently, as the main approaches to tradition confuse facts with values and diagnoses with appraisals, the appeal of the notion suffers. This confusion is present, for example, in the two opposite attitudes towards tradition in the history of European thought: traditionalism, expressing itself in attachment to and the idealization of the past, and utopianism, advocating future orientation (Szacki 1971: 279). Further ambiguities connected with this notion are due to the fact that traditions can be tied to different interests. For instance, radical thought, on the one hand, views traditions as 'inextricably embroiled in the legitimation of the *status quo*', and therefore necessarily conservative, while on the other hand, it admits that 'to be really radical, i.e., to go back to the roots, presupposed a need to regain a grounding presumably lost in a corrupt present' (Piccone 1993: 3). The former, as illustrated by the invention of tradition approach (see Chapter 3), points to the fact that traditions serve as a source of support for the exercise of power and authority, and therefore have an overtly political character and are nothing more than a set of sociotechniques of integration or projects of social engineering. The latter perspective argues that traditions can also be responsible for change because they can offer a uniquely external viewpoint, illuminating the limitations of our own era. Such self-conscious ways of invoking the past seem to be particularly appealing in today's society, where many traditions become outdated and where, therefore, it may become possible to see the present from an entirely new perspective by 'juxtaposing rather than integrating the past and the present' (Gross 1993: 6).

The notion of tradition, apart from its complex emotional and political connotations, also causes dilemmas because of its implicitness and consequent flexibility in delineating past events: 'In the pure tradition, the actions are guided by precedent without this basis requiring any principled defence' (Collini 1999: 55). In this sense, tradition is seen as something that can easily be brought to an end by more explicit and reflexive attitudes to the past. At the same time, however, the assumed implicitness of the notion further contributes to the confusion surrounding the definition of tradition, with some writers referring to tradition as an object and others describing it as a process of transmission (Luke 1996: 115). By pointing to tradition's role in transmitting in a given community certain elements of culture from generation to generation, the latter approach does not necessarily rule out generation's ability to make its own tradition. On the other hand, the former perspective's emphasis on tradition's faithfulness to forefathers limits the scope of freedom on the part of a social group to create tradition at will. Consequently, although it is frequently admitted that in everyday language the intuitive use of the concept of tradition is widespread and that probably not all traditions have disappeared, the literature is divided in terms of its evaluation of the essence and role of tradition in modern life, as well as in terms of the perceived need for the preservation or recreation of traditions in the contemporary word.

Despite the above differences, there are at least six common assumptions in the literature addressing the topic of tradition. First, it is agreed, although to different extents, that today traditions are so eroded that they seem to pose no obstacle to anything. Second, the implications of tradition are contingent on the particular historical context. Third, in every society there are many traditions and generally speaking they are not impervious to change. Fourth, although tradition is thought of as a liability, heritage – seen as tradition drained of its content and commercialized – is gaining popularity (Halbwachs [1941] 1992; Shils 1981: 12; Thompson 1996; Lowenthal 1998; Giddens 1999: 4). Fifth, we need to study the existence of tradition in the present without searching for what is beneath it and without asking whether such memories are authentic. Apart from the invention of tradition approach, the theories of tradition do not see it as a project of social engineering but as a *tradium* – that is, anything which is transmitted or handed down from the past to the present (Shils 1981: 12). Arguing in opposition to Hobsbawm and Ranger's (1983) view of traditions as nothing more than fabrications of the ruling élite, the majority of researchers tend to assert that, in order to create a convincing representation of the nation, a worthy and distinctive past must be rediscovered and appropriated (Smith 1997). Yet these writers admit that traditions, authentic or not, are frequently used as a sufficient reason for accepting a specific identity or perspective. In this respect, Halbwachs argues that everything is tradition, while Giddens (1999: 2) notes that all traditions, to various degrees, are invented.

Finally, the sixth assumption is that none of the main theories of tradition limits itself to a narrow understanding of the concept, as they all seem to view tradition as being a broad notion, comprising many aspects. Although some theories shed more light on tradition's normative aspect, others are more interested in its hermeneutic aspect or its legitimation aspect, while yet others focus on its identity aspect. However, all these orientations acknowledge that tradition cannot be comprehended without accounting for its other aspects as well. All four aspects are essential for our understanding of the role of tradition in society, but due to changes in today's society the importance of some aspects has increased while the significance of others has declined. For example, today, as the Scottish Nationalist movement in the UK, the Catalan independence movement in Spain and calls for a free Quebec in Canada illustrate, the identity aspect of tradition is growing in importance. This can be seen as a result of the process of globalization, which creates new opportunities for regenerating local identities, as well as a result of the increase in migration, both processes contributing to 'the quest for roots' (Thompson 1996: 104).

The identity aspect of tradition seems to be gaining in importance as traditions are re-employed as a way of creating a sense of belonging and strengthening group identities. It was Halbwachs' assertion that even quite small groups define themselves partly in relation to the memories they share which established the connection between collective memory and tradition on the one hand, and the formation of identity on the other. For Halbwachs, whose notion of collective memory comes close to meaning the tradition of more narrowly defined groups, talking about tradition should start with family traditions and be followed by an examination of different classes' traditions. According to him, social classes differ from each other not only because each performs a different function, but because each has different traditions which serve to legitimatize their position in the social hierarchy. After calling the 'totality of traditions' belonging to social class 'collective memory', Halbwachs concludes that 'there are at least as many collective memories as social classes'. These memories are formed 'through the simple play of the professional activity' and are transmitted from generation to generation within class boundaries (Halbwachs [1941] 1992: 141). Halbwachs argues that for different classes, tradition has different, unequal meanings and significance for society. He writes that the aristocracy, due to the fact that 'through generations there continues a totality of well-linked traditions and remembrance' (1992: 138), was for a very long time the main supporter and transmitter of national traditions. Because noblemen's status was not defined by their function but rooted in the 'pastness' of their titles, their 'tradition' preserved its depth and scope (Halbwachs [1941] 1992: 129).

The normative aspect of tradition refers to sets of assumptions, norms and models of action handed down from the past that can serve as a normative guide for actions and beliefs in the present (Thompson 1996: 91). It is especially emphasized in the Durkheimian approach which views tradition's routinized practices as providing a set of beliefs and patterns of action. In this vein, tradition, as the morality of remembering and forgetting, is seen to be securing a normative justification for practices and beliefs and providing people with some kind of direction when they are aimless, offering them 'some kind of anchor when they are adrift' (Schudson 1992: 213). In the case of modern societies, where tradition is often explicitly factual or descriptive, religious memory is the main example of the normative aspect of tradition. Hervieu-Leger (2000), in her book *Religion as a Chain of Memory*, places tradition, seen as an 'authorized memory', at the heart of religious belief. The essentially normative character of religious memory is reinforced by the fact of the group defining itself, objectively and subjectively, as a lineage of belief (Hervieu-Leger 2000: 125). Religious traditions, seen as binding members of a believing community to one another and to the past generations, are entirely oriented towards the past. All religious groups strive to achieve a unified religious memory which they claim to be fixed once and for all. However, in reality religious traditions are neither coherent, united or free of tensions. Moreover, detraditionalization erodes the strength of belonging to a particular chain of belief, while enhancing small surrogate memories. In the condition of the decline of common sacred identity, efforts to 'reinvent' memory chains appears inconsequential (Hervieu-Leger 2000: 141).

According to Shils (1981: 15), there is an inherently normative element in any tradition of belief which is presented for acceptance. Most traditions are normative in this sense, in that they are intended to influence the conduct of the audience to which they are addressed. For Shils, who sees tradition 'as a guarantor of order and civilization' (1981: 15), tradition is more than the statistically frequent recurrence over a succession of generations of similar beliefs, practices, institutions and works. He points to the normative consequences of the presentation and acceptance of tradition in the name of the necessary continuity between the past and the present: 'It is this normative transmission which links the generations of the dead with the generations of the living in the constitution of a society' (Shils 1981: 24). Thus, tradition ensures the identity of a society through time and this continuation is achieved due to a consensus between living generations and generations of the dead. Shils, however, does not assume that the content of this consensus is static, nor that each generation creates its own system of beliefs, patterns of conduct and institutions. The consensus changes through interpretation by a new generation, whose reinterpretation, actions and beliefs, in order to become a tradition, must enter into memory, here seen as 'the vessel which retains in the present the record of the experiences undergone in the past and of knowledge gained through the recorded and remembered experiences of others, living or dead' (Shils 1981: 50). Thus, memory is more than an act of recollection, it 'leaves an objective deposit in tradition' (1981: 167). The consensus is maintained through the reinterpretation of what earlier generations believed, and is carried forward by a continuing chain of transmissions: 'It is this chain of memory and of the tradition which assimilates it that enables societies to go on reproducing themselves while also changing' (Shils 1981: 167).

However, in modern, fragmented, pluralistic societies which are no longer governed by reference to tradition, where change is valued for itself, and where the principle of continuity is no longer commonly accepted, one cannot, as Shils does, 'make tradition encompass the whole body of *traditia* of a society or group' (Hervieu-Leger 2000: 87). As the modern differentiation of social fields and institutions produces a differentiation of total social memory into a plurality of specialized circles of memory, the normative aspect of a societal tradition can no longer be taken for granted.

The last element of tradition, its hermeneutic aspect, brings to our attention the fact that tradition also presupposes a set of taken for granted assumptions which provide a framework for the interpretation of the world: 'For, as hermeneutic philosophers such as Heidegger and Gadamer have emphasized, all understanding is based on presuppositions, on some set of assumptions which we take for granted and which form part of tradition to which we belong' (Thompson 1996: 91). In this respect, tradition is an interpretive scheme transmitted from one generation to the next. Such an understanding of tradition emphasizes its knowledge-like quality as it is defined as a kind of truth (Giddens 1992) or tacit knowledge (Polanyi 1958; Shils 1981; Calhoun 1983). Here traditions are seen as being the 'tacit component' of rational, moral and cognitive actions (Shils 1981: 33), or as tacit knowledge which underlines interactions and essentially orders people's actions (Calhoun 1983: 896). Polanyi, who argues for the importance of tacit knowledge in general, views tradition as the tacit knowledge which, due to its characteristics (such as its flexibility and openness for interpretation) can be reshaped to fit the present situation. While arguing that 'we know more than we can tell', Polanyi (1967: 4) points out that tacit knowing provides coherence and integrity to our observations and that 'this act of integration' lends meaning to our knowledge and controls its uses.

Seeing tradition as tacit knowledge that provides presuppositions that we take for granted and helps us to understand and interpret the world comes close to Goffman's concept of the key. The notion of the key refers to the set of conventions by which a given activity, one already meaningful in terms of some primary framework, is transformed into something patterned on but independent of it (Goffman 1974: 44). It can be understood here as an invocation of the past that presupposes an affinity between the past and the present. Keying, when discussed in relation to a group tradition, can be seen as the articulation of social, political or spiritual boundaries and conflicts, which at the same time opens up possible channels of communication among members of the group. Keying 'transforms the meaning of the activities understood in terms of one event by comparing them with activities understood in terms of another' (Schwartz 2000: 226). If tradition is, as Nora (1996b) claims, memory that becomes historically aware of itself, keying can be seen as tradition's expression of this awareness. Thus, keying is more than a group's sensitivity or mentality, not only because it adds layers of reality over ordinary activities and provides them with meaning, but also because it transforms memory into a cultural system (Goffman 1974: 43–4). Keying, argues Schwartz (2000: 226), arranges cultural symbols into a publicly visible discourse that flows through the organizations and institutions of the social world. Keying plays a very important role in facilitating our understanding of the world because it transforms memory into cultural standards, which, as the established sources of representations, shape our conduct and role performances. Keying, by bringing together symbolic models of the past with the experience of the present (Schwartz 2000: 26), expresses the uniqueness of a given group's or nation's memory.

Studying tradition during a national emergency shows how keying works because it demonstrates how tradition makes dramatic events comprehensible by making 'tangible the values for which resources and armies are mobilized' (Schwartz 2000: 26). Keying's function of meaning-making expresses itself by connecting events of separate periods in such a way that the events of one period are appropriated as a means of interpreting the events of the other. For example, Protestant-inspired moralism has always determined the way Americans go to war: 'To endorse a war and call on people to kill others and die for their country, Americans must define their role in a conflict as being on God's side against Satan – for morality against evil' (Lipset 1996: 20). The invocation of this type of moralism is clearly seen in President Bush's rhetoric after 11 September 2001: 'Our responsibility to history is already clear – to answer these attacks and rid the world of evil . . . The freedom-loving nations of the world stand by our side. This will be a monumental struggle of good versus evil, but good will prevail. In parts of the Islamic world, the United States is the Great Satan or American snake' (quoted in Alcorn 2002: 6). The president's speech illustrates the workings of keying and shows how it presupposes the resemblance of the events it brings together. Americans now, as in the past, as 'freedom is threatened once again', albeit by a different 'Evil Empire' from the Soviet Union, are on the side of good against evil. President Bush's keying of the attack on 11 September as the 'war against evil' has provided a symbolic framework enabling the nation to make sense of the attacks and the 'war'. Connecting the present to past events, invoking the American moralist tradition, pointing out that 'our enemies would be a threat to every nation and eventually civilization itself' provides a unifying framework of meaning through which society comprehends recent events and prepares itself to face a new situation. In this respect, keying, is a cultural programme that orients our intentions and enables us to to adapt to social change. In other words, tradition can be a very important part of the process of change. Society does not proceed from one organizational structure to another by abandoning all of its old institutions and traditions because, as Halbwachs convincingly argues, when society 'becomes too different from what it had been in the past and from the conditions in which these traditions had arisen, it will no longer find within itself the elements necessary to reconstruct, consolidate, and repair these traditions' ([1941] 1992: 160). It is only within the framework of the old notions and under the pretext of traditional ideas that a new order of values is slowly elaborated.

Although the past is no longer the exclusive source of the present, tradition in some respects retains its significance in the modern world. It is still an important means of making sense of the world, a crucial way of creating a sense of belonging as well as a valid source of rethinking the present. However, with the process of transmission increasingly detached from social interaction in a shared locale, the growing importance of the media and the advancement of individualization and globalization, tradition's normative and legitimation aspects have declined in significance. While all these changes do not necessarily spell the demise of tradition or render traditions inauthentic, they suggest that in today's society it is impossible to assume either purely tradition-informed or purely autonomous modes of being (Heelas 1996). The complexity and diversity of our contemporary approach to tradition can be seen as a result of a number of factors: the uprooting of traditions from the social locale of everyday life, the decline in orally transmitted tradition, the increased role of the media, the deritualization of tradition and the growing contact between various traditions through the media and through the movements of migrant populations (Thompson 1996: 103–4). In order to understand this new cultural landscape we need to analyse the shift in the nature and role of the past in our lives.

By exploring the embodiedness and embeddedness of memory, this chapter has argued that the study of remembering should include the concept of self, and any such research should view emotions, gestures and the whole body as vehicles for memory. When attempting to account for what makes an individual memory social, following the argument that the past is seen through shared frames of understanding, we were led inevitably to Goffman's notion of 'frames' – the elements from which our definitions of individual situations are built.

The discussion of generational memories and their importance in the creation of generational culture focused attention on Bourdieu's concept of *habitus*: a system of practice-generating schemes which expresses the identities and memories constituted by structural differences. While defining 'tradition' as the social transmission of cultural inheritance within a larger group, it was suggested that Goffman's concept of the 'key' can help to enrich our understanding of the role of tradition in group memory.

Further reading

Connerton, P. (1989) *How Societies Remember*. Cambridge: Cambridge University Press.

Mannheim, K. (1952) *Ideology and Utopia*. New York: Harvest HBJ.

Neisser, U. (1982) Memory: what are the important questions?, in U. Neisser (ed.) *Memory Observed. Remembering in Natural Context*, pp. 3–19. San Francisco: W.H. Freman & Co.

Prager, J. (1998) *Presenting the Past: Psychoanalysis and the Sociology of Misremembering*. Cambridge MA: Harvard University Press.

Shils, E. (1981) *Tradition*. Chicago: University of Chicago Press.

CHAPTER 5

CONTESTED BOUNDARIES

Memory and history: ways of knowing the past

'Memory, on which history draws and which it nourishes in return, seeks to save the past in order to serve the present and the future. Let us act in such a way that collective memory may serve the liberation and not the enslavement of human beings'
(Le Goff 1992: 99)

Memory and history are two different 'routes to the past' (Lowenthal 1985). Yet, the ways in which these two orientations are interconnected cause a lot of confusion. Some scholars accept that memory and history are different, others strongly object, while still others overlook the distinction and write about 'remembered history' (Lewis 1975), or 'historical memory' (Bauman 1982), or even view the historian as a 'physician of memory' (Hartman 1986: 1). In order to clarify this confusion, we will now look closely at the difficulties in distinguishing between memory and history.

A memory orientation towards the past 'involves the invocation of the past through ritualized actions designed to create an atemporal sense of the past in the present' (Kartiel 1999: 99–100). A historical orientation implies 'a reflective exploration of past events considered along an axis of irreversibility' and is directed toward developing our understanding of these events' causes and consequences. The main difference between the two approaches is supposedly connected with the fact that memory tends to mythologize the past, to look for similarities and to appeal to emotions and is thus considered arbitrary, selective, lacking the legitimacy of history and ultimately subjective, while history calls for critical distance and documented explanation, and opposes memory's non-linear temporality and its indivisibility from imagination. Therefore memory studies, with their central questions concerning lived experience and subjectivity, are seen as bringing different methods of inquiry and different traditions of representation of the past than history. However, since history combines the objective as well as the subjective (as it means both: the things that happened and the narration of the things that happened), and because of the dilemmatic nature of memory's object of study (as memory marks the continuity in the preservation of the past and alters the past in terms of the concerns of the present), the relationship between the two is far from simple.

From antiquity, when Cicero declared history to be 'the life of memory' (Burke 1989: 97), the relationship between history and memory has reflected the importance of the question: *who* has the right to tell the story of the past? Ancient and medieval authors shared the assumptions that there is no history without its written preservation, that every event worthy of being remembered has certainly been put into writing by a witness and that this memory can be relied upon (Funkenstein 1993: 3–20). So, for example, Herodotus thought of historians 'as the guardians of memory, the memory of glorious deeds' (Burke 1989: 110). Until the nineteenth century, history traditionally told stories which relied on memories and it was assumed that 'memory reflects what actually happened, and history reflects memory' (Burke 1989: 97). Memory was seen as promising a kind of certainty about the existence of particular events in the past and as enabling people to believe in the persistence of that past. Because without memory of the past there is no history and because memory was not perceived as an alternative to history, the relationship between history and memory did not seem to be of any concern. In other words, it was assumed that history begins where memory ends and memory was perceived as 'a sort of limit on history that written sources, archives and increasingly sophisticated sources of criticism allowed one to get beyond' (Laqueur 2000: 1).

In the nineteenth century, historians attempted to advance history as an autonomous discipline by promoting the application of scientific methods and rejecting any connection with memory. The growing processes of the institutionalization and the professionalization of history also created a new distance from the past. Furthermore, as history increasingly dealt with the past absent from living memory (i.e. the past that had to be extracted from written records) its suspicion of memory also grew. Practitioners of the new 'scientific' history, such as Leopold von Ranke (1795–1886), rejected 'the fictionality of history' (Arnold 2000: 52) and called for objective historical analyses that could claim 'truth', as opposed to seemingly subjective and unreliable memory. They established the long-lasting definition of the boundary between memory and history, according to which memory, as 'partial and subjective' was organized by history which, due to its 'superior languages of objectivity', was capable of facing 'accounts of individuals with the truth of the archive' (Eley 1997: ix).

Demanding that history should ignore the present and its meaning as much as possible, nineteenth-century historians saw memory as completely insensitive to the differences between periods. They believed that historical narratives were a form of science and that history, as public and written, was verifiable and able to guide private memory (Weissberg 1999: 11). Paradoxically, great-nineteenth century historians, despite their insistence that history should only say 'how it really was', were themselves 'giving shape to the memory of a particular culture' (Connerton 1989: 16). Their selective focus on the history of politics, influenced by the rise of nationalism, found its way into society through their textbooks, speeches and lectures, and thus facilitated the construction of national memory. Moreover, nineteenth-century historians' thinking about history 'reflected the moods and sentiments of the community in which thinking took place' (Funkenstein 1993: 11). So, history and collective memory were never completely alien to each other, not even in nineteenth-century history-making practices.

Although the argument for the separation of history and memory achieved its apogee in the nineteenth century, its most forceful support in the social sciences came relatively late, when positivistic history was already leaving the stage. It was formulated by Maurice Halbwachs, whose theory of collective memory we discussed in the previous chapter. According to him, historians represent the past differently because history, which establishes the difference between past and present, 'starts only when tradition ends', while memory confirms similarities between past and present as it tends to simplify and to see events from a single, committed perspective ([1926] 1950: 78). Consequently, collective memory differs from history in two main respects. First, collective memory, as the 'repository of tradition', is a current of continuous thoughts, and therefore is marked by irregular and uncertain boundaries (Halbwachs [1926] 1950: 78). History, in contrast, divides the sequence of centuries into fixed periods and reconstructs the past from a critical distance. Second, while there are as many memories as groups, history is unitary: 'History can be represented as the universal memory of the human species' (Halbwachs [1926] 1950: 84). History is an intellectual, critical and impersonal activity, which emerges as the primary mode of knowledge about the past when tradition weakens and social memory is fading. Memory, on the other hand, is always relative, as every collective memory requires the support of a group, and to be rooted in the concrete: in space, gesture, image or object. Written history examines groups from the outside, while collective memory, which a group knows from within, 'allows the group to recognize itself through the total succession of images' (Halbwachs [1926] 1950: 84). Thus, the group feels 'strongly that it has remained the same and becomes conscious of its identity through time' ([1926] 1950: 84). Such a memory rests not on *learned* history but on *lived* history, which is less impersonal, less schematizing and provides a more complete picture of specific periods and their uniqueness ([1926] 1950: 57).

Halbwachs' conceptualization of the core difference between memory and history, as connected with the fact that memory permits social groups to become aware of their identity through time while history stresses discontinuities and is situated outside and above groups, has initiated a long debate about the nature of this relationship. Today, Halbwachs' old-fashioned positivist concept of history is abandoned, with many critics rejecting his narrow definition of history as 'naïve' and pointing out that history cannot 'literally' construct the past (Schwartz 1982: 3876), while a historical narrative may itself become an integral part of the collective memory (Hutton 1993: 129). Others criticize Halbwachs for undermining the notion of historical continuity by detaching it from history and for overlooking the fact that the relationship between memory and history is as underlined by conflict as it is by interdependence (Zerubavel 1997: 5). Even Halbwachs' contemporaries, as the example of the French *Annales* school's interest in collective mentalities illustrates, adopted a more conciliatory view of the relationship between memory and history than his demarcation of history and memory.

Prior to and following World War II, less traditional historians rejected the focus on the history of events and slowly shifted the study of history towards the examination of past rituals, practices and ways of thinking. Their interest in the history of civilizations and cultural histories, which can be seen as an equivalent to collective memory, gradually undermined the distinction between historical and memory studies. This new fluidity in the relationship between history and memory created conditions for the development of memory studies (Zelizer 1995). One of the first studies of 'popular memory' initiated by social historians and historical anthropologists was linked to a Marxist-inspired focus on class and dissident voices (Fentress and Wickham 1992). The 1960s saw the development of oral history, which was marked by ideas of the social movements of the time and was connected with 'history from the bottom up'. However, the professional practitioners of oral history, who 'left their ivory tower, mingled with people and democratized the practice of their trade' have been faced with questions about the 'objectivity' of such scientific discourse, its political bias and its attempt to integrate all cultural differences into a single institutionalized discourse (Debouzy 1986: 262–4). Such doubts about the 'truthfulness' of oral accounts and the validity of a reliance of on oral records, have encouraged a rethinking of how representations of the past should be constructed and reproduced (Tonkin 1992).

The traditional perspective was further undermined by the crisis of historicism, which was contemporaneous with growing critical self-reflection in academic history and the development of a new interest in memory. The criticism of history, as developed by Whyte (1978) and Foucault (1977), pointed to the hidden ideological biases built into any model of representation. It presented historical narratives as irrevocably tainted with the language of power and control, and demonstrated that history privileged the experiences of those in a position to leave behind documentary evidence and silenced those without access to the printed word. With neither memories nor histories seen as objective, 'Remembering the past and writing about it no longer seem to be the innocent activities they were once taken to be' (Burke 1989: 98). Seeing collective memory as the creative imaging of the past in the service of the present and an imagined future, studying the fluidity of images, the commodification of memory and the acceptance of the debatability of the past have introduced a new dynamic to the interaction between memory and historiography in the representation of the past.

From the 1980s memory studies has been challenging history's monopoly over the past. History's redefinition of its subject from 'past politics' to 'past everything' (Wrightson 2001: 34), the growing power of interdisciplinarity and the expanding visibility of cultural studies have also provided the impetus for historians' interest in memory. As the wider domain of ideas and assumptions about the past has been claimed for historical study, the traditional conceptualization of the boundary between memory and history has been destabilized. This current process of redefinition has led to 'an extremely fruitful indeterminacy' (Eley 1997: ix), with history being freed of disciplinary constraints and becoming 'an organic form of knowledge' (Samuel 1994: 442–4). The increasing attention paid to the memory narratives of marginalized groups and the rise of interest in the politics of memory have resulted in studies of history that closely resemble Halbwachs' treatment of memory – i.e., as the product of a social group (Hutton 1993; Olick and Robbins 1998; Weissberg 1999). Followed by successive waves of interest in commemorative politics during the 1990s, these new reformulations of the relationship between memory and history have led some to argue that 'history and collective memory can be complementary, identical, oppositional or antithetical' (Zelizer 1995: 16). However, the voices of historians who claim that there is a fundamental difference between memory and history are still influential. One of these belongs to Lowenthal (1985), who sets history and memory apart because he views historical knowledge as being collectively produced and shared, while memory, according to him, does not imply group activity. Another voice belongs to Pierre Nora who also insists, although for different reasons, that memory and history are two different orientations towards the past.

According to Nora, the organizer and inspiration behind the seven-volume *Les Lieux de Memoire,* published in France between 1984 and 1993, memory has moved into the core of historical understanding as we no longer live in a world overflowing with living memory. An English three-volume edition of this work, published in 1996 under the title *Realms of Memory* consists of 134 essays by over 100 historians and provides a catalogue of those places of memory which now form the basis of French national identity. The order of the three volumes (the Republic, the Nation, and France) represents a historical progression from unity, through uncertainty to multiplicity and illustrates the way in which institutions or symbols which are sectarian in their origins can become, in time, national possessions.

This ambitious study, conceived as rethinking the French experience, maps the mnemonic symbols of French cultural identity – from impressionist paintings and gastronomy to the Vichy Regime – and produces a catalogue of the realms of remembrance from which contemporary French identities are forged. Nora's focus on 'realms of memory', which are seen as a cultural support for a particular collective memory, explicitly refers to the art of memory with its technique of using places and images to facilitate remembering. This devotion to the tradition of memory also manifests itself in the similarities between Nora's insistence that there are as many memories as groups and Halbwachs' idea of social frameworks of memory. Moreover, there is a clear resemblance between Nora's way of opposing history and memory, according to which 'memory attaches itself to sites, whereas history attaches itself to events' (Nora 1989: 22), and Halbwachs' conceptualization of history as universal, abstract, and in contrast to relative and particularistic memory. For both Nora and Halbwachs, memory, being reduced to commemoration, is a distorted version of history. This means that they cannot examine collective memory 'as the reciprocal working of history and commemoration' (Schwartz 2000: 11).

Nora, like Halbwachs, sees memory and history as 'in many respects opposed' and describes natural memory as spontaneous, singular and filled with gesture and emotion, while pointing out that history is reflective and universal (1996a: 4). Living memory, which is 'subject to the dialectic of remembering and forgetting' as well as censorship and projections of all kinds, is rather unpredictable because it is 'capable of lying dormant for long periods only to be suddenly reawakened' (Nora 1996a: 3). History, on the other hand, is always incomplete, critical and 'suspicious of memory'. In this respect, Nora's conceptualization of history differs from Halbwachs' view. While Halbwachs' aspiration was to keep memory and history apart, Nora is interested in exposing their changing relationship to each other. Over the past century, history, which always distrusts memory and desires to 'surpass and destroy it', has aimed to equip itself with a 'critical method whose purpose is to establish true memory' (1996a: 4).

Nora's insistence that we are 'obsessed with memory' at the same time as we have destroyed it with historical consciousness, resembles the paradoxes of late nineteenth-century Europe's memory discourses. Today, as at the end of the nineteenth century, it is the acceleration of history which is seen as destroying familiarity and tradition and as being responsible for the renouncement of memory in contemporary societies. The current causes of this acceleration (i.e. globalization, democratization and the advent of mass culture) have undermined society's anchoring in the past and have brought about an age of historical forms of representation (Nora 1996a: 6). In the past, 'history was holy because the nation was holy' (1996a: 5) and historians, as pillars of national continuity, provided legitimization to the nation. However, with the state divorced from the nation, memory as a living presence vanished and history gave way to the legitimization of society in terms of the future. In other words, today we live with memory constantly on our lips but in societies without living memory. While historians' critical self-awareness and self-reflection destroyed all assumptions about the truth in their presentation of the past, remembering becomes a matter of reconstruction of memory and the responsibility for remembering is passed to the archives: 'Now that historians have abandoned the cult of the document, society as a whole has acquired the religion of preservation and archivalisation' (Nora 1996a: 8). The scale of collecting expands in inverse proportion to our depth perception, so as the importance attached to artificial and symbolic substitutes for memory increases, historians have 'less and less to say about more and more' (Nora 1996a: 13).

Prior to the nineteenth century, memory was such a pervasive part of life that people were hardly aware of its existence. Now, as the consequence of the expulsion of rituals from modern life, memory is no longer authentically lived and specific places of memory do not simply arise out of lived experience – instead they have to be created. Hence, history can claim a victory as we collect, exhibit and catalogue the form but not the substance of memory: 'The trace negates the sacred but retains its aura' (Nora 1996a: 9). This transition from the first immediate form of memory, which was in less rapidly changing societies taken for granted, to indirect, archival memory, leaves us with realms of memory which, as moments of history are 'no longer alive but not yet entirely dead, like shells left on the shore when the sea of living memory has receded' (1996a: 7). Memory has become a matter of explicit signs, not of implicit meanings; in this sense, it is more a matter of associations, allusions and symbols. Nora distinguishes four types of realm or site of memory: symbolic sites (commemorations, pilgrimages, anniversaries, emblems); functional (manuals, autobiographies, associations); monumental (cemeteries, buildings); and topographic (archives, libraries, museums). These realms are the last remaining places where we can still read our own past and history. Their exploration helps to refill 'our depleted fund of collective memory'; however, they invoke not so much a sense of identity with those remembered, but rather a sense that we should remember them precisely so as not to be like them (Nora 1996a: 20).

Nora's contribution to the debates over modes of inquiry into the past is connected with his reformulation of Maurice Halbwachs' distinction between memory and history in the context of modern conditions, where history is 'no more than the official memory a society chooses to honor' (Hutton 1993: 9). Stressing the influence of place and time on the direction of historical pursuit, he argues that now, as society has lost its anchoring in the past and as the state has lost its control over national memory, history can only study yesterday's places of memory as the remaining points of intersection between memory and history. In Nora's study of 'the historical present' memory is an essential medium and 'an object of study for its own sake' (Carrier 2000: 43–4). Memory, seen as plural, mediated and fluid, is an instrument of both construction and deconstruction of symbols and their meanings. However, such an examination of the evolution of the representation of events and cultural traditions reduces memory to a history of the past's images (Hutton 1993: 22).

Some critics have strongly objected to Nora's concept of history as highly nostalgic and have rejected his idea that memory and history are different and that the latter is superior to the former (Tonkin 1992; Sturken 1997). Nora is perceived as 'a cultural conservative' because his analysis is understood to be a backward-looking lament over the diminution of our commitment to the past (Schwartz 2000: 313). His idea of memory is rejected as solely consisting of an inventory of 'official' places of memory, and thus as being an expression of coercive national memory (Samuel 1994: 11). Nora's argument is also criticized for not having relevance beyond France, while the Frenchness of his position is seen as responsible for his cultural pessimism (Winter and Sivan 1999b: 2). Moreover, Nora's presentation of the French symbiotic relationship between memory and the country's most fundamental social cleavages can be criticized for reducing the explanation of the uniqueness of France's lack of excitement over memory to one factor: the decline of the importance of sectarian divisions in this nation's politics (Collini 1999).

With much evidence that rituals, which Nora sees as vanished from modern societies, are still alive, critics insist on the continuity and significance of collective memory in contemporary nations (Noyes and Abrahams 1999). Arguing that difficulties faced by migrants trying to enter the French culture can be seen as an indication of the continuous importance of a popular memory, Winter and Sivan (1999b: 2) suggest that collective memory's obituary, as written by Nora, is premature and misleading. Also, the scope of various recent celebrations and initiatives seems to be indicative of the continuity of interest in memory. The bicentenary of the Revolution in 1989, after all, was a highly charged and politically contested event. Moreover, with the French government spending more on museums and cultural activities per capita than does any other western country (Winter and Sivan 1999b: 2), it seems that France continues to be engaged with the celebration of the past. So, Nora's anxiety over the fate of living memory, resulting from his devotion to the national culture, is a classic case of Minerva taking flight at dusk.

Nora's work has inspired many new studies of memory. Dramatic growth in this area over the two last decades has also been enhanced by the acceptance and inclusion of particularistic memories into history narrative, due to 'a healthy result of decolonisation' (Klein 2000: 138). This revival of interest in collective memory, in turn, remakes 'historical imagination' (Klein 2000: 128) and leads to the blurring of boundaries between history and memory. The recent challenge to theories assuming the split between history and memory reveals how complex, tense and politically charged the relationship between history and memory can be and shows that for each memory there is a counter-memory, while works addressing the issue of the politics of memory illustrate the political nature of the relationship between memory and history (Laqueur 2000: 1).

The interdependence of history and memory has been enhanced by a cultural turn in history, which has highlighted the importance of cultural narrative. This cultural turn proposes that history, as another form of narration, does not have any particular claim to truth. Its interest in imaginative representations of the past restores the significance of memories for historical inquiry and legitimizes methodological pluralism. Now, 'memories continue to be memories, and it is their relation to lived historical experience that constitutes their specificity' (Radstone 2000: 11), while historians are 'consumed by epistemological doubt and are not sure if they can find out what actually happened in the past' (Reynolds 2000: 5). As history becomes one among many types of narrative and memory is appreciated for its authenticity and truthfulness, the boundary between memory and history is becoming fluid (Anzte and Lambek 1996b).

Today's transformation of the relationship between these two orientations makes some 'sort of reconciliation' between memory and history possible (Laqueur 2000: 2). Habermas (1997), for example, rejects the simple dichotomy between memory and history and argues that 'a historical consciousness ideally performs critical work on memory in order to undo repression, counter ideological lures, and determine what aspects of the past justifiably merit being passed on as living heritage' (LaCapra 1997: 99). On the other hand, memory which can 'sometimes [be] retreating, sometimes overflowing' in its relationship to history (Le Goff 1992: 54) helps to delineate significant problems for historical research. This more conciliatory approach conceptualizes history's links to memory in a very flexible way and allows us to talk about the representation of the past as a continuum: 'the constructs of public-collective memory find their place at one pole and the "dispassionate" historical inquiries at the opposite pole' (Friedlander 1993: viii). It will likewise view conflicts between memory and history as a manifestation of 'the tension between the isolating, intellectual stance of critical reflection' (history) and 'the all-consuming moment of ritual, communal bonding' (memory) (Katriel 1999: 127). In other words, rather than insisting on an opposition between memory and history, any attempt at a general interpretation of the past has to accept the interrelations of history and memory and has to rely on both their methods of inquiry. Memory is a special kind of knowledge about the past, which stresses the continuity, the personal and the unmediated (Warnock 1987: 37). To comprehend the nature of memory requires the clarification of the type of causal connection between the present recollection and past events. Only by understanding that what memory supplies 'is not an itemized past but a continuity of conscience in which I recognize myself as a continuity of identity and my present experiences and engagements as my own' (Oakeshott 1983: 15), will our remembering of the past not be confused with our historical understanding of it.

Memory and time: the continuity of the past

'situated outside time, why should he fear the future?'
(Proust [1922] 1989)

Since Hobbes' observation that without memory we would have no idea of time, the notion that there is a connection between memory and time has been a common feature of various conceptualizations of memory (Warnock 1987: 18). These approaches assume that time, being constitutive of human experience, is captured in memory as it provides links between the past and the present. However, memory also problematizes our relation to time since its working suggests that in the social realm the past is not a fixed entity and that there are two ways of speaking about the past: as something that is no longer there but has been there, and as something that was once there (Baert 1992; Hacking 1995; Ricoeur 1999).

Memory's non-linear temporality poses difficulties for history as it replaces history's quest for the truth of the past with a revision of the past promoted by later events. It makes the past problematic because in memory 'the time line becomes tangled and folds back on itself. The complex of practices and means by which the past invests the present is memory: memory is the present past' (Terdiman 1993: 8). Furthermore, while history focuses on the historicity of past events, memory, by contrast, is seen as not having a sense of the passage of time; it denies the 'pastness' of its objects and insists on their continuing presence (Novick 1999: 3–4). Time is also a problem for memory because there is no single time but a variety of times as there is no common frame of time to which all humans continually relate (Adam 1990; Hutton 1993). Moreover, an indeterminacy of the past, as exemplified by continuous changes in retroactive rediscriptions of past people and their actions means that the past is not fixed (Hacking 1995). Today, even more importantly, one of the main problems connected with the relationship between memory and time is the replacement of the past by the extended present and the blurring of the relations between public time and private time.

These complex relations between time and memory suggest that the temporal dimension cannot be captured by accepting the closed linear view of time, which assumes that there is a steady gradual movement in one direction and which does not take into account dialectical relationships between social reality and its past and future. Social scientists, who until recently have neglected the issue of time, now insist that people should be conceived in relation to their representation of the past. They emphasize the distinction between natural and social time and a need to grasp the nature of people's experience and use of the past (Baert 1992). Moreover, there is a necessity to account for time as a historical concept and for the changing role of time in culture and society, which brings with it changing attitudes to, and the role of, memory in social life. A short survey of the main ways of conceptualizing the relationship between memory and time will show different perspectives on the nature of the past and on people's representation of their own past. These positions vary from insisting on the pastness of the past, through approaches regarding the past as being continuously recreated and reformulated into the emergent present, to positions stressing the timelessness of the past.

Time has always puzzled people, as the numerous metaphors and myths of its divine image illustrate. However, time was not a central philosophical concept until the demise of metaphysics (Heller 1999). There were, of course, famous doctrines of time – for example, Aristotle's definition of time as the measure of motion, which could be contrasted with Augustine's idea of internal time as the measure of both motion and rest (Funkenstein 1993). However, in ancient metaphysics, 'the concept of time is not really a concept of time' but is the accomplishment of the circular motion, the constant repetition of the same (Heller 1999: 174). The modern understanding of time, initially helped by the Jewish-Christian tradition's conceptualization of historical time, dates from the arrival of modernity (Baert 1992). The shift in our approach to time is seen as the bookmark dividing premodernity from modernity. In the former period, the Christian tradition dictated thinking about time mainly in terms of the future, presented statically and spatially as the time of the Last Judgment. Modernity has introduced the concept of linear historical time and the notion of secular future as well as the concepts of progress and truth as offsprings of modern temporality. Time plays a central role in facilitating the dichotomization of the universe into sacred and profane. It also serves to keep the private and public spheres of life apart, while the relations between temporal arrangements and group formation are essential in solidifying in-group sentiments as well as establishing inter-group boundaries to separate group members from 'outsiders' (Zerubavel 1981; Adam 1990; Baert 1992).

It was Henri Bergson (1859–1941), the most celebrated French philosopher of his day, who introduced the notion of time into the very core of philosophical reflection. Arguing that it is memory that makes time relative, he declared that 'the moment has come to reinstate memory in perception'

(Bergson [1896] 1996: 42). He placed our persistence through time at the centre of his conceptualization of memory as subjective experience (Warnock 1987: 55). Seeing memory and time as the most fundamental philosophical problems, Bergson argued that memory brings the past into the present and therefore the past 'might act and will act by inserting itself into a present sensation from which it borrows the vitality' ([1896] 1996: 44). As memory binds perceptions into a continuum, ensuring, by the same token, the unity of the self experienced, a flow of inner life which reveals our true nature counters the distinction between a past and a present self and makes time relative.

Bergson introduces two different concepts of time. The first is temporal duration, *durre*, or 'inner time' which is 'defined less by succession than by coexistence' ([1896] 1996: 44). Our intuitive perception of this time is the source of knowledge about the self. As pure duration is fluid, without boundaries, without a beginning and without an end, the subjective insight into inner time is constituted in continuous emergence (Bergson [1896] 1996). In contrast to the richness and variety of inner subjective time, which ensures human creativity and spontaneity, and provides access to philosophical and spiritual knowledge, the second type of time, *temps*, belongs to the material, practical world. It is objective, reversible, quantitative and divisible into spatial units. The quantitative type of time, measured by the mechanistic clock, answers the needs of ordinary life where there is little scope for human intuition and where a spatial concept of time is essential. This homogeneous and mathematical time is a category imposed on experience by the conscious and practical mind. It ensures that the flow of experience is turned into a manageable and spatially separate set of things (Bergson [1896] 1996; Warnock 1987: 18–29; Adam 1990; Coser 1992: 7–9).

Memory, seen as preserving our own awareness of inner time, overcomes the dualism of body and mind because while being informed by sense impressions it is not absolutely dependent upon the matter of the brain. It is never a simple representation of the past, as it is perceived as linking together the past, present and future. Memory is viewed as temporally prolonging 'the past into the present' (Bergson [1896] 1996: 210) by animating all past perceptions that are alike. Bergson divides the mnemonic realm into two distinctive forms of memory: 'habit' memory (used daily to tell us what things are) and 'representational' memory, which is a 'pure', involuntary and spontaneous form through which we know ourselves and in which we are aware of 'pure duration' (Bergson [1896] 1996: 213).

According to Bergson, the whole of past experience is always present at the level of the unconscious, where all experiences exist timelessly. The unity and completeness of past experience stored up in the unconscious ensures that, as nothing is forgotten, nothing is destroyed. The notion that memory retains everything was the essential element of Bergson's theory of intuition and human creativity which argues that it is not science or reason but rather

intuition and contemplation that 'can unravel the riddles of human existence' (Coser 1992: 7). His concept of spontaneous memory, which brings to
our attention the importance of feelings, emotions, intuition and people's
ability to unify duration, has been very influential in modern philosophy,
with Sartre and Heidegger, for example, arguing that time expresses the very
nature of human subjectivity and that the past is not existentially finished,
while the future is already existentially present. Bergson's ideas have also
found their way into literature, with Proust's famous novel *Remembrance of
Things Past* [1922] 1989) being the prime example.

Proust, like Bergson, privileges memory as the means for transcending
subjectivity and perceives time as consisting of a series of moments. He, like
Bergson, also believed that our memory preserves the past. As 'each day of
our past has remained deposited in us' (Proust [1922] 1989, Part 1: 844), we
cannot escape involuntary remembering, which is famously illustrated by
the narrator's memory of childhood that comes to him with the taste of a
madeleine (a cookie) dipped in hot tea. When he unconsciously recognizes
the taste of the madeleine, the past is reborn and lived again. Thus, he
becomes 'an extra-temporal being and therefore unalarmed by the vicissi-
tudes of the future', and even anxiety on the subject of his death ceases (Part
3: 904). With this 'escape from the present', at moments when the past is
reborn in him, the narrator is able to 'rediscover days that were long past,
the Time that was Lost' (Part 3: 904).

Bergson and Proust also shared the idea of the unreliability of the data
provided by consciousness as they both distrusted the overt content of
mental representations. They both saw remembrance as an unpredictable
adventure and both were suspicious of consciousness because its practical
orientations, interests and workings of habit can conceal the nature of
reality and lead to self-deception (Terdiman 1993: 200–9). When speaking
of the reality of life which the hero of his novel *Jean Santeuil* is unable to
perceive, Proust explains: 'we cannot experience [reality] while we are living
its moments, because we subordinate them to a self-interested purpose, but
these sudden returns of disinterested memory [make] us float between the
present and the past in their common essence' (quoted in Terdiman 1993:
209).

However, Proust's involuntary memory, although it cannot be deliberately sought, is not experienced on the level of unconsciousness since we
can only emotionally experience the past when the power of present sensations to call up memories is followed by the deliberate recollection of the
past. What was given to the narrator through an involuntary association
generated by the taste of a madeleine was not a feeling of the past but rather
a feeling of the authenticity of reality: 'something that, common both to the
past and the present, is more essential than either both of them' (Proust
[1922] 1989, Part 3: 905). Thus, according to Proust, the meaning of our
experience materializes in memory and what we call reality is a certain

relationship between sensations and memories which surround us at the same time. Our ability to grasp 'a fragment of time in the pure state' (Part 3: 905) means that we have achieved 'a universal and timeless understanding of what things are alike' (Warnock 1987: 95). For Proust, time 'is no fugitive, it remains present', while memory, by overcoming the gap between past and present, 'suppresses the mighty dimension of Time which is the dimension in which life is lived' (Part 3: 1087). Being free from 'the order of time' is to be miraculously liberated and brings joy as the word of 'death becomes meaningless: situated outside time, why should he fear the future?' (Part 3: 906).

Bergson's emphasis on subjective time and individualistic consciousness lower the attractiveness of his ideas to social scientists, although many of his concepts have been debated as phenomenologists continue to draw attention to the lived quality of experience and to the inner duration of action. Halbwachs, Durkheim and Mead, although accepting the importance of many of Bergson's ideas, actively criticized them. Durkheim, who conceptualizes time not as intuition but as social construction, was the first to say that all time is social time. He saw time not as inner time or duration, but rather as an attribute of a social group which is fixed by the rhythms of collective life and which, in turn, ensures the group's regularity and stability: 'A calendar expresses the rhythm of the collective activities, while at the same time its function is to assure their regularities' (Durkheim [1912] 1965: 10–11). According to Durkheim, time is abstract and impersonal, while its collective character, seen as a result of the fact that there 'is a time common to the group', makes social time 'a veritable social institution' ([1912] 1965: 23). As Durkheim notes, observation 'proves that the indispensable guidelines, in relation to which all things are temporally located, are taken from social life' (p. 10). Time, as an objectively given social category of thought produced within societies, varies from society to society.

A similar argument was developed by Halbwachs ([1926] 1950: 84), who rejected Bergson's individualism and his concept of inner time and instead, accepted Durkheim's perspective and argued that 'human time is defined by chronological frameworks on which social groups agree' ([1926] 1950: 126). Seeing time as 'real only in so far as it has content, in so far as it offers events as material for thought', Halbwachs pointed out that 'each group immobilizes time in its own way' and that this recall depends on the power of the group that frames the memory ([1926] 1950: 127, 126). Halbwachs also questioned Bergson's insistence on the significance of intuition and dreams as not reflecting the essence of human experiences which are always taking place in a social context and are characterized by continuity and regularity. Criticizing the French philosopher's view that nothing is forgotten, Halbwachs pointed out that when memories do not find some form of externalization they wither. Rejecting the idea that the whole of past experience is always present to us 'like the printed pages of a book' and that remembering is a removal of obstacles causing forgetting, Halbwachs ([1926] 1950: 75) noted that forgetting is not necessarily an individual failure, but rather a deformation of recollections due to 'vague and piece-meal impressions and remembering a process of fitting them together under suitable stimuli'.

Mead (1929, 1932), who was among the first to demonstrate systematic-ally the importance of time in social reality, also objected to Bergson's idea of the primacy of the introspective experience of time (Joas 1997). For him, time is embedded within actions, reality existed in the present and the pres-ent implied the past and the future. He understood all past as reconstructed in a present and argued that the past itself is not a past at all – only its relation to the present is the grounds for its pastness. Thus, according to him, the past is continuously recreated and reformulated into different pasts from the standpoint of the emergent present. Although the pasts are empir-ical in their consequences for current conduct, the only test of the truth of what we have discovered about the past is this past's continuity in our shared consciousness.

Mead's idea of collective memory and his insistence on the discontinuity, adjustment and selectivity of the past are in many aspects similar to Halbwachs approach. Both men stress that people use the past to give mean-ing to the present and to exercise the full spread of power across time and space. Moreover, Mead, like Halbwachs, believed that society's understand-ing of its past is always instrumental to the maintenance of present beliefs and values. However, while Halbwachs sought to show how the present situation affects our perception of the past, Mead's aim was to understand the use of historical knowledge in interpreting the present, and therefore he placed accents differently. Schwartz et al. (1986), in their analyses of the role the story of Masada – the case of 'recovered history' – played in Jewish culture, convincingly illustrate that for Mead collective memory can be selected not for its value in promoting legitimization of power but for its capacity to give meaning and assistance in interpreting the past.

The story of Masada, an unsuccessful battle in AD 73 when 960 Jewish patriots killed themselves rather than surrender to Roman troops, fascinated Jews living in interwar Palestine not because of its heroic message but because it explained the precariousness of their situation and because it articulated the ambiguity of their feelings. Consequently, it provided them with a chance to rethink and define in a new way their destiny and solidarity. The content of collective memory reflects its objective fit with reality, not its utility: 'collective memory is drawn not to that which is useful but to that which is appropriate' (Schwartz et al. 1986: 160). We tend to accept as valid stories that are appropriate as objects of collective identification in a given context, so in times of crisis or insecurity, different stories present them-selves to us as appropriate from those articulated in times of prosperity. Mead believed that pasts are remembered and constructed in ways that meet group needs and that the kind of past events most invaluable in a given stage of a group's life are those able to enhance a group's survival (Schwartz *et al.* 1986). The example of Masada, which 'is both a complex of uncontested historical facts and a powerful component of modern Israel's national mythology', illustrates that its mythological function 'does not in the least invalidate its historicity, nor would its demythicization enlarge our historical knowledge' (Assmann 1997: 14). In other words, the validity of a given perception of the past is not a result of its utility and has nothing to do with its truth values, but is rather a result of the fact that the past matches and articulates present feelings.

Another important point developed by Mead's dialectic approach is his suggestion that the reconstruction of the past occurs when people realize, through self-reflection and awareness, the inadequacy of the old presentation of the past. New pasts are most likely to emerge during periods of rapid change. In the context of change, conditions of insecurity and destabilization can be routinized by the reconstruction of the past in such a way as to assimilate it into a meaningful flow of events: 'The past which we construct for the standpoint of the new problems of today is based upon continuity which we discover in that which has arisen and it serves us until the rising novelty of tomorrow necessitates a new history' (Mead 1929: 235). Mead's theory can be interpreted as the conceptualization of memory, if not as a motor of change, as Baert (1992: 141) suggests, then at least as an instrument of normalization, as a means of reconstructing a disturbed societal pattern of living into its normal condition.

Mead was a constructive pragmatist who believed that the past arose in such a way as to enable 'intelligent conduct to proceed' against situational problems (Mead 1932: xiii, 29). Baert (1992: 86) summarizes the role that the past plays in Mead's theory by pointing out that the presentation of the past can be either a *past-in-now* or a *past-for-now*. The former, past-in-now, refer to the use of the past in the present, when people adopt passive attitudes towards the past which experiences its power through practical consciousness and tacit knowledge. The latter, past-for-now, refers to the symbolic reconstruction of the past in the present, when people are active in respect of their past as they reflect upon underlying structures.

The sociology of time has recently become a distinct field of research illuminating its social construction, the temporal aspects of societies and the present specificity and transformation of time (Zerubavel 1981; Adam 1990; Baert 1992). Following Heidegger's and Schutz's focus on the problem of being and becoming, many writers analyse ways in which body, action and space merge across a time horizon. Researchers from a wide range of disciplines suggest that there are various senses of time and point to the changing role of time in culture and society, and changing attitudes to time, including changes in our relationships to the past. Overall, new studies of time show that contemporary societies question the neutrality of time and its linearity, while proclaiming the death of time, the end of the future and the globalization of time (Young 1988; Hassard 1990; Novotny 1994; Adam 1998). The breakdown of the previous temporal order into an extended present came first with the discovery of a global simultaneity, which can be dated to the *Titanic* catastrophe of 1912, of which – thanks to new means of communication – people in various countries could read in the morning newspapers. It was followed by the arrival of the timeless global culture of the computer era. With the collapse of the old temporal order, as the past and the future are replaced by an extended present, where instantaneous time replaces linear time, memory seems to be unimportant. The acceleration of change, with constant changes in work, life situations, social and material conditions, makes memory of the previous generation irrelevant for younger people. As more people participate simultaneously in more events, and as more experience a faster pace and fluidity of time, people's need for their own private time and their desire to regain control over their time is also growing. The consequences of constant change, striving for innovation, the increasing pressure and speed of time lead to a call for the development of new mechanisms of balance between novelty, repetition and the past.

This new paradoxical situation creates new challenges for sociology, which now needs to reflect upon time in such a way as to see how 'nature, society and individuals are embedded in each other and are interdependent' (Ellias 1992: 16). These challenges can be addressed by the conceptualization of people as not only living in time, but also as having 'an awareness of the passing time which is incorporated in the nature of their social institutions' (Giddens 1981: 36), by placing them in relation to their representation of the past and by seeing the self as articulated in time. It is here that collective memory proves most useful as it allows us to conceptualize the link between groups and time in a fruitful way.

Memory and imagination: the meaning of the past

> '*I told you the truth . . . Memory's truth, because memory has its own special kind. It selects, eliminates, alters, exaggerates, minimizes, glorifies, and vilifies also; but in the end it creates its own reality; it is a heterogeneous but usually coherent version of events; and no sane human being ever trusts someone else's version more than his own*'
>
> *(Rushdie 1980: 253)*

For the Greeks, Mnemosyne, the goddess of memory, was not only the mother of history but also of poetry. The connection between memory and poetry's illuminative power of imagination has been appreciated by many artists, and many of them express it explicitly. From the poet Simonides, who is credited with the invention of the art of memory, to contemporary writers of memoirs, this association between memory and imagination has been perceived as central to telling a story. In an earlier form of memoir-novel, such as Defoe's *Robinson Crusoe* or *Moll Flanders*, the conceit was that the story told is true. Balzac and Flaubert still believed that they were writing 'history', but by the late nineteenth century such conceit had become convention and the genre of the novel proclaimed memory's fictional nature. Thus memory's relationship to the notion of 'truth' or factual evidence had become complex. Proust was interested in memory, not history, as he assumed that memory gives reality to the past and that we construct the past through an act of imagination. Another great twentieth-century master of memory, Nabokov, asserted that it is an act of will and that 'writing true stories is the product of a fascinating struggle between imagination and evidence' (quoted in Modejska 2000: 6). C. Letty Fox, in her novel *Her Luck* (1946), plays with the blurred line between memory and imagination: 'I don't know what imagination is, if not an unpruned tangled kind of memory' (quoted in Parks 2001: 90).

At the beginning of the twentieth century, Virginia Woolf still warned that 'fact and fiction can't go together' (quoted in Modejska 2000: 5), but since then the relationship between imagination and memory has become closer, although less clear-cut. With new forms of writing blurring the lines between memories and facts, between the clearly autobiographical and the strictly fictional, memory and imagination seem to be intimately bound together. In recent years it has become 'fashionable to blur the distinction between novels and history by emphasizing the fictional element in both of them' (Ginzburg 1994: 388). Of particular relevance here are novels by Toni Morrison (1990), who compares memory and fiction, and the work of A.S. Byatt who concludes her exploration of the differences and similarities between memory and fiction by saying: 'We need to make images to try to understand the relation of our images to our lives and death. That is where art comes from' (1998: 71). Historians adopting this approach (e.g. Natalie Zemon Davis in her book *Fiction in the Archives: Pardon Tales and their Tellers in Sixteenth Century France* (1987) combine literature and history. Davis' script for the film *The Return of Martin Guerre* is even closer to fiction. On the other hand, some fiction is closer to history. For instance, novelist Thomas Keneally, after historical research, wrote 'a piece of non-fiction which gets a prize for fiction' (Burke 1998: 229) and which was made into the film *Schindler's List*.

This lack of separation between memory and imagination and history and fiction is of course nothing new – Thucydides invented all the speeches in his *History of the Peloponnesian War*, while Walter Scott's great novels made people wonder whether they were reading history or fiction. What is probably new today is the postmodernist writers' claim that we cannot know the past and therefore we may as well invent it (Byatt 2001). At the beginning of the twenty-first century, with history gone, there is a view that writers should explore the past using their imagination which can possess 'the past even if we can't know the truth about it, even if the past did not exist except in the form we choose to make it' (Bayley 2001: 16). Moreover, now, when readers are seen to be sophisticated enough 'to hold several layers of reading at once, and to enjoy the interplay between conceit, the fiction and the authorial stake in the story told', a new form of writing is emerging which further clouds the distinction between fiction and non-fiction (Modejska 2000: 26).

There is also no shortage of evidence for the connection between imagination and memory outside of literature. Philosophers – for example, Spinoza, Montaigne and Pascal – have always been interested in the powers of these two phenomena, and they often thought of memory in terms of images. Hobbes thought that memory and imagination were the same in essence, since both dealt with the absent or unreal, except for the fact that 'memory supposeth time past, as fancy does not' (quoted in Warnock 1987: 18). Hume, who recognized this difference, pointed out that ideas presented by memory are much more lively and stronger than those presented by imagination. Imagination, according to him, offers a great deal more free play than memory because in memory our ideas are bound to occur to us in the temporal and spatial order in which we actually experienced them (Warnock 1987).

The argument that memory is the same as imagination was brought forward by Giambattista Vico, a seventeenth-century scholar and teacher of rhetoric. He argued that memory is virtually synonymous with imagination because memory originates in the ontological act of creating images in order to give meaning to the phenomena of the world (Hutton 1993: 34). According to Vico, memory has three different aspects: *memoria* (memory, when it remembers things), *fantasia* (imagination, when it alters or imitates them), and *ingegno* (invention, when it gives them a new turn or puts them into a proper arrangement and relationship) (Price 1999: 13–16). Vico's definition of the threefold nature of memory suggests that a creative memory 'makes' the truth of the past by interpreting, altering and producing a coherent version of events. Thus, Vico's theory of memory, as 'an act of interpretation that enables us to establish connections between the familiar images of the present and the unfamiliar ones of the past' anticipated the modern science of hermeneutics (Hutton 1993: 34).

In modern times, viewing historical interpretation as a task of reconstructing the collective mentalities of the past was carried further by Dilthey and Heidegger. The most influential contemporary representative of this strand, Gadamer, also shares Vico's view of history as based on imaginative reconstruction of the past. For Gadamer (1975) there is no uninterpreted mode of experience, while life acquires its significance in so far as it is interpretation, since to perceive is to interpret. In Gadamer's hermeneutic perspective, memory is conceptualized not as a kind of knowledge to which images are not essential, but in terms of images. Bergson also suggested that memory is virtual and enters the field of consciousness as an image, however his theory is criticized by Sartre (1972), for whom memory is one way in which we are conscious of reality.

For Sartre, any theory of imagination must satisfy two requirements: 'It must account for the spontaneous discrimination made by the mind between images and its perceptions; and it must explain the role that images play in the operation of thinking' (1972: 117). Since there are three kinds of images (of purely invented, past and anticipated things) memory and anticipation are two different problems which are, moreover, radically different from the problem of imagination. For Sartre, the main difference between imagination and memory is that imagination is about the unreal, while memory is about the real, the past: 'If I recall an incident of my past life, I do not imagine it, I recall it' (1972: 210). According to Sartre, memory is determined by the nature of reality itself and is on the side of perception, while imagination is on the side of fiction. However, his effort to rule imagination out of perception of all kinds, so that we can distinguish between memory and imagination, is not totally successful as he finally realizes that we cannot give a simple description of recalling without reference to images (Warnock 1976).

Generally, the relationship between memory and imagination is conceptualized in two different ways. On the one hand, there is the hermeneutic perspective of thinking about memory in terms of images and pointing to narrative imagination as a principle of identity and memory. On the other hand, there is a strand of thought which stresses the social reproduction of memory and that tends to insist on the limited scope of our freedom in the process of recall. According to the latter approach, memory is seen as a part of patterned practices, which reduces the complexity and restricts the uncertainty of our social environment. The past is seen to be known not through imaginative stories but rather through the rationalization and the conventionalization of experience: 'Thus the memories of the majority of people come to resemble increasingly the stereotype answers to a questionnaire, residence, educational degree, job, marriage, number and birthdays of children, income, sickness and death' (Schachtel 1982: 193). As mentioned in the previous chapter, Bartlett (1932), who argued that people's memories reflect their groups' standards and patterns of thinking, carried out a series of psychological experiments in which people were given a brief but rather ambiguous story to read and after a period of time were asked to recall it. As they tried to remember the story, they engaged in 'effort after meaning' – i.e. they rationalized its less intelligible aspects and reinterpreted it in light of their world knowledge. Bartlett's conclusion that people always justify their statements by employing existing schematas and remember what 'everybody else remembers too' suggests that it is not imagination but rather conventional schematas that organize our remembering.

The importance of the process of rationalization rather than imagination in our thinking about the past is particularly true in the case of collective memory, whose higher level of articulation, necessary for its transmission, makes it more schematized, conceptualized, simplified and conventionalized. While any individual's memory also includes unarticulated experiences, and is therefore highly complex, collective memory is more schematic as images can be 'transmitted socially only if they are conventionalized and simplified; conventionalized, because the image has to be meaningful for an entire group; simplified, because in order to be generally meaningful and capable of transmission, the complexity of the image must be reduced' (Fentress and Wickham 1992: 49). Yet, imagination is important because the powers of memory and imagination are impossible to separate (as shown by the systematic errors in our remembering which are evidence of memory's imaginative reconstruction) (Bartlett 1932: 213), and because there is nothing in remembered images themselves that allows us to tell if they refer to something real or imaginary (Fentress and Wickham 1992: 49).

Memory is the experience of the past mediated by representation, so it is the construction of images that puts memories before our eyes and which reveals what experience means. Although imagination is perhaps not essential to all types of memory (e.g. habitual memory, which incorporates practical and usable knowledge of the world and does not rely on the deployment of images), exploring something imaginatively requires memory (Warnock 1987: 76). Memory and imagination are interconnected through their respective roles in assigning and reading meanings, as memory is crucial to our ability to sustain a continuity of experience, and this sense of continuity is essential for understanding the world, while our imaginative thinking is based on our ability to make the world intelligible and meaningful. It was Oretga y Gasset ([1926] 1960) who claimed that modern people are empty because of their lack of memory, and since without memory they cannot understand the present, they lack imagination and an inner desire to excel. Also, Bauman (1982), who defines historical memory as an acquired set of narratives embedded in everyday consciousness, stresses that such historical narratives serve to make sense of the present world. Thus, we need to cultivate both memory and imagination because memory is central in the process of assigning meaning, which, in turn, is necessary if we are to cope with today's overabundance of images and information.

Memory and imagination are also brought together in testimony 'because the witness says I was a part of the story, I was there', while at the same time they use their imagination to retell the story (Ricoeur 1999: 16). In testimony, memory is recalled in such a way that others can imagine being there – this imaginative narratization helps them to imagine a true experience.

However, when imagination reveals meanings of the past and makes the past visible as if it were present, it sometimes resembles fiction more than historical narrative. Thus, in the final analysis, in our search for the truth or what really happened, we rely on trust: 'When I testify to something, I am asking the others to trust what I am saying is true. To share testimony is to exchange trust. Beyond this we cannot go. Most institutions rely fundamentally on the trust they place in the word of the other' (Ricoeur 1999: 16). Thus, while aiming to achieve a balance between imagination and an objective and critical recall, we depend in the last instance on the trustworthiness of others.

When discussing memory and imagination, therefore, we need to realize not only that it is very difficult to separate them but also that we tend to accept various shapes of their relationship in different genres and in different contexts. Fact, fiction, memory and imagination, speculation and invention are all parts of telling the story of the past, and this story will carry us forward, will become the crucial condition of social harmonious coexistence, only if it does not undermine social trust. The extension of trust in any particular setting depends in part on 'the actors' reinterpreting their collective past in such a way that trusting cooperation comes to be a natural feature of their common heritage' (Sabel 1993: 107). Therefore, in order to ensure such trust and avoid conflicts, there is a need for a critical evaluation of one's traditions, which can only be achieved if we fully understand the contested nature of the past.

Contested memories

Because memory is a field of the articulation of public and private interests, values and aspirations, it is also the site where contradictions of identities are often contested. As memory discourse has established itself as the language through which modern societies express their dilemmas and controversies, battles over memory are not uncommon. Such controversies indicate that past events have not yet 'passed to history' (Hartman 1986: 1) and that memory is open, fluid and contestable. Arguments over memory are frequently strengthened by reference to numerous remarks about the power of remembrance which are abstract and ambiguous enough to become rhetorical weapons. One of the most famous quotations is Orwell's saying, 'Whoever controls the past controls the future. Whoever controls the present controls the past'. A quote from Santayana, which says that those who refuse to learn from history are bound to repeat it, and the words of an eighteenth-century Hasidic rabbi, Ball Shem Tov, 'The secret of redemption is remembrance', are often mentioned. The use of rhetorical arguments in battles over memory is important because they tend to sharpen our knowledge of what should be remembered and acted upon, while at the same time covering up the fact that memory is often lost to interests, politics and emotions.

As monuments replace the real site of memory (Nora 1996a), they increasingly provoke discussions which are interesting examples of contested memories. There is a restrictive relation between monuments and memory. Monuments seeking to honour collective memory can be 'forgetful' of some elements of the past (Young 2000). Whose vision of the past is 'put into a monument' can be the result of protracted struggle and often has lasting political implications. For example, one of the most publicized controversies was a conflict over the form and content of Washington's Vietnam War memorial. Conflict arose when the official state authorities' vision of the monument, as a symbol of patriotism and glory of the nation, did not match with ordinary people's desire to commemorate pain, grief and suffering. The clash of these two interests shows that 'the shaping of a past worthy of public monuments and commemoration is contested and involves a struggle for supremacy between advocates of various political ideas and sentiments' (Bodnar 1992: 9)

Memory is also contested when different groups of people declare equally passionate attachments to the same place, city, or site. Recently the controversy between Poles and Jews over Auschwitz's site provoked strong reactions because Auschwitz, the Nazi concentration camp located in Poland, is a sacred place for both involved groups. This controversy has also attracted international attention because of its very sensitive nature and moral implications. The site of Auschwitz camp, where German Nazis murdered 1.6 million people, the vast majority being Jews (1.35 million) from across Europe, has been the subject of continuous contention since the mid-1980s. The controversy was sparked when a Carmelite convent appropriated a camp building in 1984 and was further fueled by the erection of more than 100 crosses on the site in the mid-1990s (although the first one was placed at the site earlier, in 1979 to commemorate Pope John Paul's visit to Auschwitz). The Polish presentation of the site's history has until relatively recently tended to marginalize Jews – for example, the 1986 guidebook to the Auschwitz-Birekanu museum had nothing to say about Jews at all! Thus, for Poles, Auschwitz has become a symbol of its nation's martyrdom, yet, as the largest Jewish cemetery, for Jews it is the most prominent symbol of the Holocaust (Bartoszewski 1991). Consequently, the Poles saw the nuns' decision to locate convent near the martyrdom site as a means of extending prayers for Poles killed at the camp, while the Jews saw it as a sign of the Polish Catholic Church's aspiration to impose its own symbols on the site.

The first phase of the conflict involved numerous charges and counter charges, and the involvement of both religious and political organizations (including the Polish and Israeli governments) was only resolved by the intervention of the Vatican, causing the nuns to leave the site (Rittner and

Roth 1993). The end of communism, which 'unfreezed' Polish memory and opened it to new voices and pressures, initially reignited the conflict over how to commemorate the victims of the Holocaust. The unauthorized construction of crosses by nationalistic and radical Catholics in an adjoining field added fresh fuel to the controversy, as Jewish groups objected to them and to the Church's role as the guardian of the spirituality of the victims. As the international demands for the protection of Auschwitz made the controversy into a diplomatic incident, the Polish authorities again became involved. Although in 1998 the Polish government lost its legal challenge to take over the property where the crosses stood, they were all removed apart from the original one. The debate about the 'Papal Cross' still continues, but the conciliatory solution to this long-lasting controversy is now, due to the more open and democratic nature of the Polish system, closer to a resolution than ever before.

The convent controversy can be described as a conflict over who should commemorate the victims of Auschwitz, and in what way. An example of a battle over what actually happened in Auschwitz is the court confrontation between David Irving and Deborah Lipstadt. Irving's libel suit against Penguin Books accused Lipstadt's book, *Denying the Holocaust* (1993) of falsely labelling him as a Holocaust denier, or revisionist. The suit was tried in the British High Court in London from 1996 to 2000, where Irving argued that his reputation as a historian had been harmed by the alleged libellous words in Lipstadt's book, which brands him as 'one of the most dangerous spokespersons for Holocaust denial' and as somebody for whom the problem with the gas chambers in Auschwitz was that they were 'a myth that would not die easily'(Lipstadt 1993: 181, 179).

In *Denying the Holocaust*, Lipstadt examines deliberate misrepresentation and manipulation of historical evidence about Nazi crimes and argues that, while Holocaust denial is not a new phenomenon, it has increased in scope and intensity since the mid-1970s, and that one of the most essential claims the deniers make is about the evidence of Auschwitz as a death camp. Because Auschwitz has become central to Holocaust denial and since Lipstadt had to prove the accuracy of the statements in her book, the Auschwitz question played a central role in the court proceedings. An expert witness analysed the historical evidence for the gas chambers at Auschwitz and refuted revisionist claims to the contrary. The demolition of the arguments of Holocaust deniers against Auschwitz resulted in a judgment that destroyed Irving's reputation as a historian and discredited Holocaust revisionism. Lipstadt remarks in her book that if 'Holocaust denial has demonstrated anything, it is the fragility of memory, truth and history' (p. 216), yet her victory in court shows the importance of vital historical documents. If there is a lesson for memory from the trial, it is that it 'cannot be validated as a historical source without being checked against "objective evidence" ' (Assmann 1997: 9).

The conflict between revisionists and Lipstadt illustrates the issue of memory's role as a source of historical truth, while the convent controversy was a conflict over rights to symbolic representation of the past. Memory is also a subject of dispute when sides in a conflict accuse each other of exploitation and abuse of memory. At least three different arguments are put forward in such battles over memory. First, it is argued that memory is misused because it is assigned a sacred status. Novick's protest against the sacrilization of the Holocaust memory is a good illustration of such a stand. Second, it is argued, (e.g. by Finkelstein in reference to Holocaust memory) that memory is abused when it becomes an ideology. Third, the commercial exploitation of memory, leading to its banalization and sentimentalization, is perceived as lowering memory's status and value.

Novick's book, *The Holocaust in American Life* shows the evolution of Jewish memory of the Holocaust and illustrates that changes in what we remember depend upon political and sociocultural contexts. It presents collective memory as always and inevitably grounded in current concerns, understandings and needs and asserts that it is 'in crucial senses ahistorical, even anti-historical' because it tends to simplify and does not allow for sufficient and multiple perspectives (1999: 3–4). The book tells the story of how in the aftermath of World War II the Holocaust was first marginalized and not cast as a uniquely Jewish event, and then came to be centred in American life. It asserts that current interest in the Holocaust comes close to 'fetishism' or a 'cult' and that this process of sacrilization establishes the Holocaust as a 'mystery' that cannot be explained and comprehended. Fifty years after the war, the Holocaust has become 'virtually the only common denominator of American Jewish identity' (Novick 1999: 7).

Like Novick, Finkelstein (2000) also argues against the sacrilization of memory by making it into a kind of 'mystery religion' and shows how memory, when it is used to serve some specific interest, can easily become indifferent to historical facts and inner contradictions. Both writers also note the reluctance of the American Jewish community of the 1950s to discuss the Nazi extermination. However, Novick's book is more balanced, while Finkelstein's approach is more schematic and polemical as he, in a rather reductive way, accuses the American Jewish establishment of using the Holocaust to defend Israel and uplift its own standing with American élites. Thus Finkelstein asserts that the Holocaust is not merely a religion but an ideology which serves a whole new industry. Building on, but going beyond, the insight of Novick's book, Finkelstein says that the Holocaust 'has proven to be an indispensable ideological weapon' (2000: 3). According to him, in the modern world when such notions as power, interest and ideology are no longer used, 'all that remains is the bland, depoliticized language of "concerns" and "memory" ' (2000: 5). Thus, the Holocaust memory is 'an ideological construct of vested interests', exploited by organized American

Jewry to deflect criticism of Israel and its own morally indefensible polices (2000: 6, 149).

Opposition to the process of memory commercialization, trivialization and banalization is behind the third type of contested memories. Following again our Holocaust case study, we can illustrate this type of contested memories with attempts to rescue the Holocaust memory from being commercially and emotionally exploited by media and business. Fights against publishers' trivialization and exploitation of the topic in all possible contexts are instigated in order to preserve the integrity of the historical record. Today's overabundance of information about the Holocaust, it is argued, can lead to the 'banalization of the Holocaust' rather than to a more profound understanding of it (Silverman 1999: 38). The 'Holocaust industry', 'the marketization of the Holocaust' and 'the Americanization of the Holocaust', are seen as a danger, as these trends can condition the way we receive any account of the destruction of European Jewry (Bartov 2000).

Yet, it is worth emphasizing that collective memory is not necessarily manipulated and can be a source of historical truth. Even more importantly, we should note that when memory functions as myth its evaluation from the point of view of the historical truth is irrelevant. Thus, to understand why contestations over memory take place and how such battles function in national cultures, memory needs to be seen as being 'located in a contested terrain on which mythical and rational images of the past sometimes work together and sometimes do battle, but these images always shape identity and its transformation' (Olick and Levy 1997: 934). This, in turn, can only be developed, as this chapter has argued, if we comprehend the complexity of the relationships between memory and history, memory and time and memory and imagination.

To sum up, the discussion of the relationships between memory and history, memory and time, and memory and imagination showed the transformation of these realtionships and their new-found openness, flexibility and dynamic nature. Today, rather than insisting on an opposition between memory and history, we are inclined to accept an interrelationship between the two, and to rely upon both their methods of inquiry. At the same time, we stress that our remembering of the past will not be confused with our historical understanding of it. In addition, the acceleration of change, as more and more people participate simultaneously in more and more events and experience a faster pace of life, leads to an apparent increase in the speed of time, which in turn reorganizes the relationship between time and memory.

Because memory involves the construction of mental images to 'place the past before our eyes', the interconnection between memory and imagination was also discussed by looking at their respective roles in assigning and reading meaning. It was argued that in order to achieve a balance between imagination and objective, critical recall, we depend on the trustworthiness of others. In the final analysis, the result is the frequently contested nature of the past.

Further reading

Adam, B. (1990) *Time and Social Theory*. Oxford: Polity Press.

Burke, P. (1989) History as social memory, in T. Butler (ed.) *Memory: Culture and the Mind*, pp. 1–32. Cambridge: Blackwell.

Hutton, P. (1993) *History as an Art of Memory*. Hanover, VT: University Press of New England.

Klein, K. (2000) On the emergence of memory in historical discourse, *Representations*, Winter: 127–53.

Lowenthal, D. (1985) *The Past is a Foreign Country*. Cambridge: Cambridge University Press.

Nora, P. (1989) Between memory and history, *Representations*, 26 (Spring): 7–25.

CHAPTER 6

STUDYING MEMORY

'*Memory is a powerful tool in the quest for understanding, justice and knowledge. It raises consciousness. It heals some wounds, restores dignity, and prompts uprisings*'

(Hacking 1995: 3)

Memory has always been a large and multilayered field of study, increasingly attracting researchers from various disciplines. The rapid expansion of the notion of memory in scholarly discourse means, however, that it would be impossible to survey the interest of all disciplines in any detail. Thus, in what follows we will discuss only four fields of studying memory: investigations of commemorative actions, investigations of the links between memory and identity, studies of traumatic memory, and research on connections between memory and justice.

Memory and commemorative activities

'*Commemoration is a way of claiming that the past has something to offer the present, be it a warning or a model*'

(Olick 1999: 381)

The recent growth of research into commemorative practices has been an international phenomenon. The surge of social scientists' interest in commemorative rituals and ceremonies cannot be seen in isolation from the major political upheavals of the late twentieth century, which have made the issue of memory central to political discourse and practice. It has been advanced by various international anniversaries and celebrations, with the celebrations of the fiftieth anniversary of World War II being the most important. As the rise of 'the age of commemoration', which can be attributed to the acceleration and democratization of history, has imposed on us a 'duty to remember' (Nora 1996a: 3), war has proved to be one of the most productive and compelling subjects in memory studies (Ashplant *et al.* 2000b: 6).

Commemoration celebrations are studied within many paradigms, although since the publication of Eric Hobsbawm and Terence Ranger's *The Invention of Tradition* (1983), which describes the constructed commemorative representations and rituals staged by the modern state, this approach has been the most popular. Within this paradigm researchers have been asking questions about the power of such commemorations to draw upon war sacrifices and loss as a means of re-establishing social cohesion and the legitimacy of authority. The popularity of this perspective is connected with the fact that it still captures the main objectives of commemorations, which always involve the construction or a unitary and coherent version of the past that still provides comforting collective scripts capable of replacing a lost sense of community. Furthermore, this type of investigation, by focusing on the uses of the past in monuments, museums, theme parks, historical films, textbooks, public oratory and other domains, highlights the role played by the media in refashioning tradition and framing acts of commemoration. Finally, the approach is still seen as providing the relevant theoretical framework for the exploration of commemorations and rituals imposed by authoritarian regimes, which shows how this type of state enforces a monolithic mode of war commemoration. Generally, the invention of tradition type of commemoration studies illustrates the significance of rituals for solidarity and the acquisition of shared forms of seeing and experiencing.

However, in today's democratic societies, with many new emancipatory opportunities and expanded individual choices, it has become increasingly difficult to construct a unified public memory. Thus, recent studies of commemoration, as they research different agencies' and collectivities' initiatives and responses to past traumas, talk about a multiplicity of invented traditions or a plurality of memories. This second perspective studies various groups and collectives of civil society, but not states. It sees commemoration as a struggle or negotiation between competing narratives, and stresses that the dynamic of commemorative rituals involves a constant tension between creating, preserving and destroying memories. The shift from the presentist perspective's concern with the memory of war, as practiced by the state, to the study of commemorative rituals as representations of war memories within a national culture (and in particular cultural forms) has been accompanied by a growing interest in the exploration of personal memories of war. Collective remembrance is conceptualized as 'the product of individuals and groups, who come together not at the behest of the state or any of its subsidiary organizations, but because they have to speak out' (Winter and Sivan

1999b: 9). Within this third approach to the study of commemoration and war memory, commemoration is analysed as an attempt at mourning and an effort to repair the psychological and physical damage of war.

Many recent works try to overcome the polarization between these three theoretical perspectives, not least because it has had 'a deleterious effect on the study of war remembrance' (Ashplant *et al.* 2000b: 9). They propose to eliminate this division by recognizing the complexity of the relationships between the various agencies, namely between 'those of individual memory, remembrance in civil society and national commemorative practices organized by the state' (Ashplant *et al.* 2000b: 10). Instead of being preoccupied with 'unmasking' the ways in which ideas and symbols of national identity represent ideological forms designed to shore up the position of the dominant class, social scientists' contribution to the study of memory is now more flexible and sensitive. Communities of memories are not seen as being exclusively based on national principles, as rituals of commemoration for AIDS victims, for example, illustrate (Sturken 1997). The ability to differentiate between the memory of various groups (e.g. national memory, class memory, individual memory) brings Halbwachs' theories back into the mainstream of sociological debate. Such new investigations of memory, supplemented with analyses of individual mourning and personal memory, have been further enhanced by inspirations coming from the work of Nora's team which shows the plurality of meanings and uses involved. This group's argument, that specific places of memory do not simply arise out of lived experience but instead have to be created, has been tested in investigations of how various nations resort to commemorative practices in order to give symbolic meaning to their past.

Studies of war have been contributing to our understanding of the traumas of military conflicts for a long time. This type of inquiry provides us with well documented evidence that the public memory of war has undergone significant modification in the last two centuries. From the pioneering work of Paul Fussel's *The Great War and Modern Memory* (1975), Mosse's *Fallen Soldiers: Reshaping the Memory of the World Wars* (1990), Jay Winter's *Sites of Memory, Sites of Mourning* (1995), through *War and Memory in the Twentieth Century* (1997) edited by Martin Evans and Ken Lunn, to *European Memories of the Second World War* (1999) edited by Peitsch, Burdett and Gorrara, many writers have analysed how wars have been inscribed in their respective societies' memory and culture. They explore the ways in which the search for a language of mourning went on during and after both world wars and how the imagery of war entered art, film, literature and poetry. They show how nations, due to massive losses in the two world wars, not only resorted to erecting so-called tombs of unknown soldiers, but also focused on mass mortality and mass suffering in their art. We learn from such studies that war, even in victorious states, was not represented in glorious terms. Memory of this terrible period was reflected in apocalyptic themes in prose and in a poetic language of communication about or with the dead (Winter 1995). Works such as *War and Remembrance in the Twentieth Century* (Winter and Sivan 1999a), look at how war has been remembered by various groups, from soldiers to the mothers of the dead, and Sherman's (1999) *The Construction of Memory in Interwar France*, or the collection edited by Ashplant *et al.* (2000a), called *The Politics of War Memory and Commemoration*, describe the ways in which communities respond to the unprecedented traumas of war.

The growing number of publications also focuses on the issue of the history and politics of commemoration. As images of past wars are constantly reproduced, revised and replaced, many studies 'trace the history of the representations of the past over time' (Olick 1999). This type of work illustrates the expansion of commemorative practices, their process of democratization and the conflicts and politics behind those practices, as well as their evolution. Such work shows how the state's interest in giving collective bereavement some concrete political meaning, together with public pressure for its acknowledgment, has resulted in the construction of war memorials and the development of new commemorative practices. For example, the spread of World War I monuments in France is attributed both to towns and villages' sense of loss and need to leave traces of all their dead, as well as to the state's interest in signifying national unity through commemorative activities and sites (Laqueur 1994; Sherman 1994). In his book, which shows how the French commemorations were actively shaped by this country's social and political life, Sherman (1999) provides evidence of how debated and contested the issue of how to remember was in the interwar period. Viewing the construction of memory as a social and political process, Sherman explores the types of experience contributing to French memories of World War I, such as war narratives, tourism and visual imagery, analyses what kinds of 'contestation' the commemoration produced, and how commemoration simultaneously reinforced and questioned existing distinctions within French society.

Much research in this area is interested in the meaning of war memorials. Noticing changes in the way wars are remembered and in the interpretation of monuments, various authors argue that the meaning of monuments is not fixed because 'like memory' it is profoundly unstable (Sherman 1994: 206). This will continue to be contested because commemorative practices operate within larger political and economic structures which mould the condition of a practice and mediate both the experience and the representation of memory (Evans and Lunn 1997). Discussions of the transformation of memorials to unknown soldiers illustrate the shift in the meaning of war memorials from justifying death and war to demonstrating, after World War II, the imperative 'Never again' (Koselleck 2001). Studies of the history of memorials and commemoration not only document war memories, but also decode ways in which the remembrance of wars has assisted the emergence of a rhetoric of national identity. For instance, Inglis' (2002) study of war memorials in Australia demonstrates how public rituals of mourning established the cult of the Great War at the heart of the Australian identity. Such investigations additionally examine which groups are acknowledged and which are not visible in national celebrations. For example, Koshar's (1994) presentation of the evolution of German remembrance of the Nazi period shows how different political interests shaped Germany's collective memory of World War II. Similarly, Savage (1994: 141) describes American Civil War memorials as being 'ultimately a story of systematic cultural repression, carried out in the guise of reconciliation and harmony'.

After World War II the nature of commemorative practices changed, becoming more democratic and local as well as less prone to manipulation by nationalist leaders (Mosse 1990; Young 1993; Gillis 1994b; Koonz 1994). An important point in the history of public commemoration, and not only in the USA, was the 1980s controversy surrounding the Vietnam memorial, which is commonly seen as 'a decisive departure from the anonymity of the Tomb of the Unknown Soldier and a growing acknowledgment that everyone now deserves equal recognition' (Gillis 1994b: 13). This, together with the proliferation in the 1990s of anniversaries, memorial services and ethnic celebrations, as well as the growing number of diverse and competing interest groups seeking to use constructions of the past to advance their agenda in the present, has established a new way of explaining commemorative practices, now seen as emerging from 'the intersection of official and vernacular cultural expressions' (Bodnar 1994: 75). This type of study, when arguing that beneath official memories, fashioned by the dominant discourse there are alternative memories, often invokes Foucault's (1977) notion of counter-memory, which illuminates the connection between the hegemonic order and historical representations.

Collective memory is conceptualized in a similar manner in cultural studies, which over the last two decades has expanded our perception of the past by analysing various ways and media through which remembering occurs in the public sphere. Memory, from this point of view, is defined as being at least to some degree independent from dominant structures or even as a counter-culture in itself, capable of resisting the dominant order. Here, cultural attempts to remember events that seem to defy the official representation are areas of particular scrutiny. By subjecting the process of producing sites of memory to critical analysis, researchers explore the forms cultural production takes in the dual context of the commercial management of public memory by the state and the increased articulation of memory by various agencies from within civil society. This type of research often conceptualizes collective memory as cultural memory, as it is argued that we are currently in a phase of transition from 'communicative memory' (or the memory of people who have first-hand knowledge of events) to 'cultural memory', in which memory becomes institutionalized through cultural means, such as commemorative rituals, memorials and museums (Assmann 1995).

This shift toward the study of cultural memory manifests itself in contemporary debates about modes of representation of war, where discussions of the aesthetic forms of commemoration introduce alternative understandings of war. Using the term 'cultural memory' opens the inquiry to the question of how popular culture has produced memories of wars and other catastrophes and disasters. The first wave of popular commemorative studies focused on the institutions of public remembering formed around the nexus of some physical memorial or commemorative. It showed a deep ambivalence in modern societies with respect to their attitudes towards the past (Sider and Smith 1997: 8). The second wave examined how films and TV images, photographs and advertisements, songs, theatres, museums, exhibits, tourist spots, fictions, school curricula and political speeches have shaped memory and commemorative activities, seen as important vectors of personal, local and national identity. In other words, cultural memories are studied as a reservoir of images which are socially and politically mediated as well as historically and culturally embedded.

Numerous examples of such studies suggest that there is an increasing interest in exploring how media and aesthetic forms question national narratives. Winter's *Sites of Memory, Sites of Mourning* (1995) surveys modernist genres of commemoration as adopted by survivors during the interwar period. Discussion of postwar films from different countries shows that these created 'spaces for the representation of otherwise hidden dimensions' (Ashplant *et al.* 2000a: 37). Sturken (1997), while examining how cultural memories of the Vietnam War are produced through objects, images and representations, explores how cultural memory can form an arena of resistance to dominant forms of national culture. Rejecting the assumption that the mass media reprogramme memory by representing the values of the dominant social formation, this orientation sees cultural memory as shaped and mediated by many factors, with the media being only one of them.

Some researchers in cultural studies conceptualize cultural memory as coming close to being an ideology or a form of collective (often false) consciousness, a position in which remembering is merely a political tool. Yet, many of those writing in this field are interested in commemorative symbols that do not necessarily invoke a sense of identity with those remembered. Moreover they view memorial sites as competing for our attention rather than for our memory and investigate the largely discursive 'work' that goes into the production of sites of memory (Katiel 1999: 103). This new approach is well illustrated by Sandage's (1993) study which shows how African-American civil rights groups appropriated the Lincoln Memorial to bring their demands to public attention. Such studies also observe that commemoration images often express neither the past nor the present but changing interactions between past and present: 'Past meanings are malleable to varying degrees, and present circumstances exploit these potentials more or less' (Olick 1999: 381). In other words, the complex reflexivity of commemoration can only be grasped by adopting a dialogical model. The study of the history, politics and memory of West German commemoration of the anniversary of 8 May 1945 allows Olick to explain the differences between commemorations not only as a function of the history to which they refer or the politics of the present, but also as shaped by the forms and media available at different moments. Seeing commemoration as 'an ongoing dynamic process involving social and political contexts and genres of memories' provides an interesting model for further studies.

Finally, turning to the most recent development in commemoration studies, we should notice the impact of the collapse of the Soviet Union, which resulted in a proliferation of investigations that examine 'organized forgetting', characteristic of state-sponsored representations of the past (Wanner 1998; Wingfield 2000), counter-memories, which survived despite official propaganda (Irwin-Zarecka 1994; Mason 2000), or new hybrid forms of identity emerging in the postcommunist era (Berdahl 1999). Studies looking at the Balkan region point to a connection between the eruption of identities constructed in conflict and violence and identities rooted in the claim to a common past (Jedlecki 1999). These investigations illustrate that as overarching structures such as nation state and ideology are further eroded, the past acquires new significance and meaning in terms of a ruptured and tragic present. Hence, memory and commemorative activities become more important as sources of individual and collective identity.

Memory and identity

> 'We choose to center certain memories because they seem to us to express what are central to our collective identity. Those memories, once brought to the fore, reinforce that form of identity'
>
> (Novick 1999: 5)

Identity is a key word of contemporary society. People use it to make sense of themselves, of their activities, of what they share with others and how they differ from them. It is also used by politicians to persuade people to understand themselves, their interests and predicaments, as well as to persuade them that they are 'identical' with one another. Social cognition and symbolic interaction, two prevalent perspectives in social psychology, provide the theoretical underpinning of the traditional understanding of identity. In the past few decades, the concept of identity has been taken up more broadly, both within sociology and in other disciplines. Many recent social theorists have extended the concept of identity to include social identity, which is defined by the extent to which individuals identify themselves in terms of group membership (Cerulo 1997). Collective identities are seen as implying notions of group boundedness and homogeneity, and an emotional sense of belonging to a distinctive, bounded group, involving both a felt solidarity with fellow group members and a felt difference from outsiders.

Today, memory is widely called upon to legitimate identity because the core meaning of any individual or group identity is seen as sustained by remembering. Memory, as a collective belief in some vision of the past as being 'the true' one in a specific moment of the group's life, is assumed to be the essential anchor of particularistic identities. Social memory, according to this perspective, is an expression of collective experience which 'identifies a group, giving it a sense of its past and defining its aspirations for the future' (Fentress and Wickham 1992: 25). Thus memory, when 'organized into patterns so that they make some kind of continuing sense in an everchanging present' (Young 1988: 98), becomes the main source of a group or a personal identity. Moreover, memory and identity depend upon each other since not only is identity rooted in memory but also what is remembered is defined by the assumed identity (Gillis 1994b: 3).

The idea that identity is rooted in the persistence of the subject through time is a very old one. Both philosophy and psychology claim that memory is a highly important element in the account of what it is to be a person (Warnock 1987). It was John Locke who posed the classical philosophical problem of identity by claiming that it is consciousness and remembering that make us who we are. In *An Essay Concerning Human Understanding* ([1690] 1975) Locke sees memory as the criterion of personal identity, and equates it with a collection of experiences which are laid away for later retrieval in their original form. He asserts that one's identity is constituted by one's psychological continuity: I am what I remember. For Locke, persons were primarily legal subjects who were responsible for their past actions, not merely because they could remember them but because in remembering them they identified themselves with the persons who performed them. So, an individual remains the same person over time for as long as they are able to summon into consciousness events from their past.

Memory's links with identity were also a frequent topic of nineteenth-century novels, while in sociology it is commonly assumed that telling stories about our past and making sense of that past is the main source of the self (Giddens 1991). Among the many modern political discourses which seek to establish the sameness and continuity of a group across time by referring to the role of the past in the construction of political identities, nationalism, liberalism and constitutional patriotism are the most popular (Booth 1999). Nationalism, which sees identity as rooted in some notion of shared traits (ethnicity, culture, religion, language), argues that nations, as communities of memory, protect remembrance of the past and use memory as a political instrument. For liberals, who contend that political life does not need to be rooted in a shared past and common experience, only a narrow band of continuity and shared common memory is needed. Constitutional patriotism, which occupies a middle position, seeks a reconciliation between the universalist demands of liberal principles and the need for a robust political identity, including a shared history (Habermas 1996).

The relationship between memory and identity is historical, with groups' identities and their memories being social and political constructs. At earlier historical moments, identity was not so much an issue; when societies were more stable, identity was to a great extent assigned, rather than selected or adopted. However, recently the nature of the links between identity and memory has become more problematized with the decline in theoretical and practical importance of theological and religious assumptions as stable sources of identity (Taylor 1989). Now, identity is seen as the product of multiple and competing discourses, and is thus unstable, multiple, fluctuating and fragmentary. The postmodern conception of identities as fluid, multidimensional and personalized constructions, together with the politics of identity, seen as a central aspect of postmodern politics and communities in which the legitimization of a unitary identity or an overarching sense of self has diminished, has highlighted the links between memory and identity. When groups based on the previously private identities of citizens (race, ethnicity, sexual preferences) compete for public recognition and legitimization, their claims are rooted in their common memory of suffering, victimization or exclusion. The dilemma of a post-national, post-traditional political identity is connected with the tension between the vision of a 'rational identity' centred around universal norms and an identity laden with the responsibility of remembrance, the legacy of the past. This friction between openness and diversity (an imperative placed on the agenda by immigration) on the one hand and the ethics of remembering and responsibility on the other is indicative of the most important dynamic of modernity. As the emphasis on individual choice and cultural identities grows, the tension between the particularism of 'realms of memory' and the openness of the universal democratic has become the focus of much new research.

This type of research illustrates that the openness of modern identity to critical revision, coupled with increased pluralism and the separation of national identity and political membership, means that particularistic differences and pluralistic memories have gained in importance. On the other hand, these investigations also show that, as the contemporary world evolves in the direction of greater homogeneity and uniformity (with the new role of media and globalization), this evolution not only strikes a blow at traditional identities but also increases the need for some kind of belonging. In other words, modern trends have both problematized identity and created a desire, as well as a space, for a new search for identity (Touriane 2000).

The conjunction of these two conditions – the need for collective identity and the destruction of traditional identities – is an additional factor responsible in part for the new cult of memory. Thus, 'the memory craze and uncertainty concerning identity go together' (Megill 1999: 43). We witness the growing plurality of memory seen as a stabilizer of and justification for the self-designation that people claim (Terdiman 1993). The statement 'I am an A' is now supplemented with: 'I have always been an A'. Here the memory of having 'always been an A' serves as a support for identity that might otherwise be seen as insufficiently justified (Megill 1999). This new link between memory and identity, seen as 'a sacred object, an "ultimate concern", worth fighting and even dying for' (Gillis 1994b: 4), has granted a new status to memory. Additionally, the increasing diversification and fragmentation of social interests in contemporary societies, together with globalization, migrations and demographic shifts, have provided the basis for a new politics of identity. The growing importance of the politics of identity, both as a defensive reaction against globalization and a prolongation of communal resistance (Castells 1997), has further enhanced the status of memory, now seen as 'an authentic mode of discourse among people of color' (Klein 2000: 138). As struggles for minority rights are organized around questions of memory, debates over the notion of identity, often employing the language of memory become increasingly politicized (Huyssen 1995: 4–5).

Today, despite the fact that the past seems to be lending dignity to the identity of many groups, a common past is more about the duty to remember rather than real memories. For example, being Jewish increasingly means only 'to remember being Jewish' (Nora 1996a: 12). With the decline of living memory, identity ceases to be based on a shared experience of past events and is, instead, rooted in a common heritage which 'distills the past into icons of identity, bonding us with procurers and progenitors, with our own earlier selves, and with our promised successors' (Lowenthal 1994: 43). In the shift from memory to heritage, certain aspects of the group past will be prioritized over others, 'sometimes leading to a sanitized or romanticized vision of the past' (Noakes 1997: 93). The self-congratulatory nature of the relationship between identity and heritage is often criticized for bland emptiness and escapist nostalgia. Since the further one moves from the past, the less one recalls its power dimension (Halbwachs [1941] 1992), heritage often offers sentimentalized and romanticized sources of identity. Yet heritage is closely connected with our need for a sense of the past, belonging and identity, and therefore can also be seen as a creative act, one in which we learn from each other's efforts and experiences (Lowenthal 1994: 43).

There are many important case studies concerning the connection between memory and particular national identities (e.g. Maier 1988; Russo 1991). One of the most interesting is Lyn Spillman's (1997) comparative study of the celebrations of national centennials and bicentennials in

Australia and the USA. Illustrating the process of creating national identities in both countries in the late nineteenth century and 100 years later, Spillman examines how the USA and Australia adapted to changes in their political situations. She argues, following Benedict Anderson, that a sense of shared experience through time is an important dimension of national identity and that this sense of past, progress and future is an important feature of imagined national community: 'When people in both countries imagined shared qualities which bound their communities, they also thought frequently of their political values and institutions and prosperity' (1997: 82). Moving away from the dominant ideology thesis, Spillman assumes that there are many possible alternatives for a version of the past and a vision of the future which people develop to represent the nation and its unity. While demonstrating that contemporary Australians and Americans articulate their identities through symbols of egalitarian democracy, she suggests that behind the different possibilities in which a nation might be 'imagined' lies 'a cultural process of great complexity, contingency and specificity' (1997: 150). Spillman's analysis reveals that the process of identity formation is illuminated if we examine symbolic repertoires, cultural production in the dynamics of centre/periphery relations, and the discursive field within which national identities are constructed.

The issue of the link between memory and particular national identities has been further problematized by the emergence of new postcommunist states. Wanner, in her book *Burden of Dreams* (1998), asks how, given the hybrid forms of identity created by the Soviet regime, does a new postcommunist Ukraine forge a sense of nationality? She looks at 'the representation of historical events as embedded in a process of identity reformation where power relations and the ability of various groups to advance their interest is revealed' (Wanner 1998: 32). One of the most powerful legacies of the past is the memory of the Chernobyl accident as it symbolizes the exploitative nature of the system and the victimization of Ukraine under the Soviet regime. As the Chernobyl memory reveals contestation and competing cultural claims, and thus actualizes the past in the present, Wanner asserts that the present acquires meaning only in terms of a ruptured and tragic past.

Studies of ethnic memories have been even more popular, which can be explained by the wide acceptance of memory as a means of the legitimization of group identity, by the growing problematization and fragmentation of national identities as well as by the acknowledgment that respect for the Other implies acceptance of 'difference of memory' (Ricoeur 1999: 12–16). Many contemporary studies of ethnic identities cast ethnicity as fluid and ethnic boundaries as continually changing. The issue of race and ethnicity is also frequently discussed through the examination of collective memory, which 'often becomes a form of mourning and a paradoxical sign of loss' (Weissberg 1999: 22). In one such study, Comaroff and Stern (1994) argue that ethnic consciousness can be viewed as a universal potentiality that is objectified as a political identity when a population recognizes a common threat. In this process of crafting political identities, individual memories are shaped by representations of the past in the public sphere, which take on various forms in response to specific circumstances.

In another study of the link between memory and collective identity, Fortier (2000) investigates identity formation among Italian migrants in Britain. She traces the identity narratives through which migrants' identities are constructed and stabilized, and describes written histories, politics of identity and popular religion as three areas where Italians create a new cultural identity grounded in memory. Living in diaspora brings liberation from the necessary rootedness of origins in a single territory, or a single place, and it means that identities are shaped from remembrance and un-forgetting. Thus, the investigation of diaspora, which places the meaning of 'home', 'origins' and 'tradition' in the context of migration, and where memories 'may be place based', yet are not 'necessarily place bound' (Fortier 2000: 159), assumes that the project of identity formation is a practice of remembering places. Fortier, following Connerton's (1989) assertion that collective forms of remembrance are performative, assumes that performative memory is essential for groups' identity. For example, the commemorations and rituals at St Peter's Italian church in London are presented as deeply performative, thus enhancing the cohesion and identity of the Italian migrant community: 'Activities at St Peter's are essentially about remembering; the formation of individual and collective bodies, which are called upon to inhabit the church and its surroundings' (Fortier 2000: 13).

There are also many case studies of the connections between memory and the identities of various social groups which show the construction of collective identities, as constituted through shared memories, as always involving groups defining themselves against their respective others (whether elders in the case of generational groups or employers in the case of employees). Groups have different criteria for judging the importance of past events, as well as different conceptions of time and of legitimization. Yet, in all collectivities' recollections of their respective past, the group is always positioned in relation to the outside world. Such memory is the most effective recourse any social group has to reinforce its social identity with regard to that of others. For example, Fentress and Wickham's (1992) examination of how working-class communities remember the past leads them to conclude that these communities (e.g. British mining communities) use the heroic imagery of a strike, whether won or lost, as a representation of community identity in opposition to the outside world.

In the 1990s, concern with memory went far beyond the studies of working-class or national identities. With memories occupying the foreground in identity debates over gender, sexuality and race, and with a new pressure on social and cultural memory, public debates about identities have now become intensely political. The new relationship between identity, memory and politics means that a notion of identity which is 'often shaped by defensiveness or victimology, clashes with the conviction that identities, national or otherwise, are always heterogeneous and in need of such heterogeneity to remain viable politically and existentially' (Huyssen 1995: 5). In other words, the preoccupation with memory as a basis for collective identity could lead to dangerous consequences, as the bloody conflicts between different groups across Europe attest. The ethical burden brought by the acceptance of the past in political identity results in many ambiguities and in difficulties of weighing claims that cannot be objectively balanced. Recent developments, such as conflicts in the former Yugoslavia, suggest that there is a short passage from the passions of identity politics to vengeance and vindictiveness (Melling 1997). According to Umberto Eco (quoted in Melling 1997: 259), 'ghosts of particularism' in a new invigorated 'cult of tradition' that sprang up as a source of hope for ethnic and national communities in the 1990s may now bring new conflicts. Groups that turn towards their past in order to glorify specific aspects of it use memory to foster pride in some of their communal traditions and to demand a recognition of suffering. When memory becomes the basis of 'the collective narcissism of minor differences' (Block 1998: 33), defenders of such groups' uniqueness almost inevitably develop hostile attitudes towards each other, and this can run a danger of allowing memory to be used as a political instrument that legitimizes nationalist myths and propaganda. Thus, some writers have warned that remembrance which is not accompanied by knowledge and thought is emptied of all responsibility and may endanger others (Megill 1999).

Even more importantly, today's fascination with memory may undermine liberal universalism because the reliance on memory to legitimate collective identity can question the universalistic principle. In addition, as argued by Maier (1993), it can act as an obstacle to democracy because focusing such group memories on narrow ethnicity may result in groups competing for the recognition of suffering, thus undermining the democratic spirit of co-operation. Such conflicts can, likewise, harm the advancement of a particular group's interest because the systematic neglect of causes of group disadvantage other than distinctive memory may result in a group suffering material deprivation, lack of education opportunities or discrimination (Barry 2001: 5, 305).

To sum up, while until recently it was assumed that it is history which provides groups with their identity, 'just as memory does for an individual' (Arnold 2000: 118), today various groups rely on their collective memory to claim their group identity. The current popularity of memory studies, and their acceptance into the history project, is based on the assumption that 'to rob us of memory is to destroy a part of us, something essential to who we are, something arguably as crucial to our identity as our physical person' (Booth 1999: 258). In other words, memory has established itself as a category of academic discourse and political rhetoric due to its growing acceptance as a criterion of authenticity of the self. However, scholars also turn to memory for a different reason. With the growing recognition that tragic past events, like the Holocaust, 'may defy any historical explanation' (Weissberg 1999: 12), witnesses' memories are appreciated for their explanatory power.

Memory and trauma

Traumas, representing the extremities of human experience, are the occasions on which collective identities are most intensively engaged. Therefore, memories of trauma are of interest to researchers of culture and society as well as of the individual psyche. Studies of trauma memories owe a great deal to medical discourse and psychoanalysis, although they are not just psychologically oriented. Many of these works analyse the cultural shaping of trauma memories or study culturally institutionalized memories of past traumas. The growing visibility of studies of trauma can be seen as a result of postmodernist theory's fascination with psychoanalysis and its interest in cultural studies. Both these factors have helped to establish memory as a therapeutic discourse which provides an authentic link to the past (Klein 2000: 138–40).

At the end of the nineteenth century, psychoanalysis started 'not with memory but with forgetting' (Mitchell 1998: 100). This interest in the absence of memory, combined with the prevailing explanation of mental problems, particularly hysteria, as being related to an earlier trauma, resulted in the assumption that painful experiences are constituted as repressed memories. The conflictual disturbance caused by repressed memories was seen as responsible for a patient's mental problems. Trauma came into focus again during World War I, when shell-shocked men produced the same symptoms as hysterics. In 1980, as the numbers of veterans of the Vietnam War diagnosed with psychological problems kept growing, the American Psychiatric Association established a new diagnostic category, called post-traumatic stress disorder (Prager 1998: 127). From the early 1990s the Recovered Memory Movement, popular mainly in the USA, has claimed that 'true' recollection of memory requires outside intervention to overcome an individual's tendency to repress traumatic experiences (Mitchell 1998). As the number of recovered memories of childhood abuse brought to the courtroom increase, the controversy over 'repressed memory syndrome' continues to grow. It is now evident that many cases of 'repressed memories' uncovered during therapy were inaccurate and were in fact ideas influenced by the movement's main message.

Trauma entered psychoanalysis and psychology via medicine, where it meant wounds, and later travelled from psychology to physiology (Hacking

1996; Young 1996). However, the most significant role in the history of the conceptualization of trauma has been played by psychoanalysis, which was developed by Freud as a way of curing troubled minds by recovering suppressed memories. His notion of the unconscious as a repository of repressed memories has shaped trauma studies by introducing the idea that it is precisely what cannot be remembered that is decisive for the subject (Hacking 1995). Freud, by defining sickness as a particular kind of failure of memory, made memory a clue to the human condition. However, for him memory is 'not a passive receiver whose performance can be measured quantitatively; it embodies a moral choice, a sequence of acceptance and rejection' (Rieff 1979: 38). Arguing that much of a person's traumatic past is shielded by amnesia, Freud suggests that such repression involves active forgetting of threatening memories by pushing them into the unconscious. Moreover, repressed memories, unlike forgotten ones, can acquire dangerous power over the personality, as partial leakage of painful memories can lead to neurosis.

Freud asserts that the events of a person's life are all recorded somewhere in the mind, ready to be accessed if only the memories can be released from repression. The observation of connections between hysterical symptoms and various cases of repressed memory related to childhood traumas led Freud to formulate the therapeutic aim of the science of psychoanalysis as the interpretation of memory, seen as constituting the essential link between two realms of psyche: its unconscious and conscious side. Memories are to be analysed for their associations, seen as displacements or defences constructed by the unconscious mind which performs the function of the guardian of memory. However, even memory fragments transmitted to the conscious mind are not transparent representations of past realities: 'They always surface in disguise. Revised and distorted by the psyche's conflicting needs, they are consciously rendered as a composite of truth and fiction' (Hutton 1993: 64). 'Screen memories' block access to more disturbing memories, and since they are not 'recollections of actual events, but reconstructions of those memories through the grid of contemporary feelings' (Isbister 1985: 130) the operation of our memories does not depend exclusively on past events, but also on present interpretations of those events.

Because of its attempts to cure traumatized people, psychoanalysis is essentially a technique of retrieving lost memories through 'memory and mourning which work together in the fight for the acceptance of memories and reconciliation' (Ricoeur 1999: 12–14). According to this psychoanalytic approach, the work of memory should not be separated from that of grief. If psychoanalysis is an art of memory, as both Terdiman (1993) and Hutton (1993) argue, it reveals a reverse mnemonic since it is concerned with forgetting rather than remembering, and with the unconscious mind rather than conscious psychical intent. In other words, screen memories, as mnemonic images that displace hidden memories, protect us from traumatic experiences: 'As an art of memory, therefore, Freud's psychoanalysis employs a technique for deciphering the unconscious intentions encoded in screen memories' (Hutton 1993: 68). Freud's focus on forgetting, or the selective omission of events, as an example of the reconstructive labour of memory, is in some respects similar to Halbwachs' emphasis on the normative nature of collective memory, seen as biased towards a positive image of the past (Igartua and Paez 1997). Because of the normative nature of collective memory aimed at defending a group identity, a common response to a traumatic past is silence and inhibition. Studies suggest that forgetting and silence is a very frequent reaction as groups organize forgetting, reconstruction and positive distortion of the past in order to defend group values and their own image (Frijda 1997; Paez *et al.* 1997).

Trauma studies have become central within both the humanities and the politics of social movements. In these fields, Freud's notion of 'memory work' and his idea of mourning as a form of 'working through' which is necessary in the process of acceptance of traumatic memories are conceptualized as types of reconciliation with the loss of objects of love. According to the culturalist version of psychoanalysis, nations – like individuals – must work through grief and trauma. Giving voice to one's traumatic past and recognizing it as part of one's history is a necessary step in escaping from patterns of suffering. Cultural studies' interest in trauma has been further advanced by its attraction to the concept of melancholia, a form of mourning where the loss is continually revisited. By investigating changes in the rhetoric of loss, the role of mourning and the transformation of the vocabulary of mourning, such studies testify to the importance of expressing grief in the process of recovery and the struggle to retain human decency (Damousi 2002). This confirms Benjamin's suggestion that we should not try to avoid returning to past traumas as people can only prevent the 'violence of amnesia' by conducting themselves like 'a man digging' who 'must not be afraid to return again and again to the same matter' or to the same 'buried past' (quoted in Sherman 1999: 229).

Trauma theories' consonance 'with a linear, historical model of temporality' and their 'prioritization of the event in their understandings of memory formation' offer us the possibility of overcoming a memory/history opposition (Radstone 2000: 89). Such studies of memories of trauma examine links between the inner world of memory and the external world of historical events by focusing on the experience of pain. By placing trauma at the heart of memory, these investigations view the body as an important 'site' of memory and therefore question the traditionally privileged position of vision in recalling the past. In other words, they concentrate on corporeal memory, which is memory 'inscribed into body in the form of permanent traces which structure, in response to certain perceptions, the repetition of affects and mental images associated with them, whereby this repetition is never the repetition of the same, but always another return' (Weigl 1996: 153).

Trauma changes the nature of remembering as it makes such memories particularly vivid, intrusive, uncontrollable, persistent and somatic. Traumatic bodily experiences are a powerful exception to the usual diminishing intensity of memory with the passage of time (Schudson 1995: 351). For Nietzsche, memory is a bodily phenomenon which operates on the principle that 'if something is to stay in the memory it must be burned in' (1969: 61). He saw experience of pain as the 'most powerful aid to mnemonics' and argued that 'whenever mankind has found it necessary to make memory for itself, it has never come off without blood, torment and sacrifices' (Nietzsche 1980: 802).

Culbertson (1995) and Brison (1999) assert that traumatic memory is a kind of somatic memory, as the nature and frequency of sensory, emotional and physiological flashbacks is determined by past trauma. Frequent involuntary renewals of traumatic memories, as they are more dependent on sensory representations than narrative memories, overcome emotional and psychological distanciation and assert the moral character of the self and memory: 'Traumatic memory blurs the Cartesian mind-body distinction that continues to inform our cultural narrative about the nature of the self' (Brison 1999: 42). The assumption that memory recollection is helped by the body is accepted in investigations of the traumatic subjective experiences of major personal disasters, such as abuse, rape or incest. Traumatic memories are also seen as factors that not only shape the destiny of individuals but also that of human civilization. Experience of trauma has, however, only recently become an essential element of public memory.

In the nineteenth and the first part of the twentieth century, memories of trauma, painful experiences and past wrongdoings were banished to the private realm and only 'official history' was made public. With nation states rarely confessing to their past wrongdoings, and with some governments (as, for example, the Nazi one) engaged in a war 'against memory' (Levi 1988: 31), it was not until the second part of the twentieth century, that people were given space to retrieve traumatic memories and allowed to prevent painful pasts from fading into the oblivion of history. With a general recognition of the emotional and social value of memories of the Holocaust and Nazi atrocities, a public space for trauma was created. This public space 'provides a consensual reality and collective memory through which the fragments of personal memory can be assembled, reconstructed, and displayed with a tacit assumption of validity' (Kirmayer 1996: 195). From the 1980s, personal narratives of the Holocaust brought issues of memory to public attention. The growing realization that the Nazi past 'is too massive to be forgotten and too repellent to be integrated into the "normal" narrative of history' (Friendlander 1993: 2) has established memory as 'the belated response to the great trauma of modernity' (Klein 2000: 140), while 'speaking the unspeakable' (as the subtitle of Leak and Paizis' 1999 book expresses it) has become a source of insights into the *Shoah* (the Hebrew name for the Holocaust).

The rediscovery of Holocaust memories is therefore seen not so much as a question of the return of the repressed but rather as being indicative of the crisis of western modernity. Historians' interest in the Holocaust is viewed as a result of the fact that 'our epoch has been uniquely structured by trauma' (Klein 2000: 138). It was Adorno's remark that in 'the concentration camps it was no longer the individual who died, but the specimen' (1973: 362) that transformed the Holocaust into a metaphor for the end of modernity. For Lyotard (1988), Auschwitz also symbolizes the end of universalism, the beginning of 'small narratives' and the end of the Enlightenment idea of progress. Lyotard argues that the *Shoah* signifies the end of history, as it demands that the distinctions between history and memory be overcome in order to narrate what cannot be presented within the traditional historical perspective. In other words, the Holocaust requires historians to be 'both a scientist and an artist at one and the same time' (Vidal-Naquet 1992: 208). With witnesses' faith in the adequacy of language and the reliability of memory eroded, the issue of how to explore the Holocaust, the founding moment in the contemporary crisis of testimony, becomes central to academic work.

The recovery of Holocaust memories has also had a massive impact on historiography, the humanities and social sciences because it has introduced these disciplines to the psychoanalytical approach and its effort to confront and 'work through' the memories of catastrophe and trauma. Researchers exploring memories of trauma, by adopting Freudian methods, study the testimony of survivors of Nazi atrocities for whom the past is not a problem of working back but 'working through'. They try to answer questions about the degree to which 'deep memories' can be recovered, and how the past can be represented 'in a way that the truth of its deep memory will not be forgotten for posterity' (Hutton 1993: 71–2). As academics realize that 'a history of the Nazi crime which did not integrate memory – or rather, diverse memories – and which failed to account for the transformation of memories would be a poor history indeed' (Vidial-Naquet 1992: xxiii), testimonies of survivors enter into history narratives. The appreciation of testimonies of traumatic memories as a valuable resource has not only undermined the distinction between truth and the oral testimony but has also stressed the urgency of the task because, as a prisoner of Buchenwald says, 'One day soon, no one will any longer have the real memory of that smell . . . the smell of the crematorium: flat, sickening . . . the smell of burnt flesh' (Semprun quoted in Gordon 1999: 140,134). When there are no longer survivors left to testify, when memories are no longer guaranteed and anchored by a body that lived through the Holocaust, a body that is marked by it – with a tattooed number being the most literal evidence of this – it must be asked 'How does one remember?' (Wiesel quoted in Landsberg 1997: 64). Without the sensory and mechanical memories which haunt the survivors, the transmission of the Holocaust memory becomes problematic as we cannot really understand and explore its atrocity.

The issue, however, is not to recall and reconstruct feelings but to give evidence to truth in order to preserve the moral order: 'The moral order requires memory and memory in turn demands certain narrative forms' (Kugelmass 1996: 195). Therefore, the enormity of the Holocaust cannot be forgotten and the forms in which it is given expression are important historical phenomena in their own right. The dominant rhetoric of Primo Levi's testimonial writing supports this argument. His phrase 'the duty to remember' means that remembering the Holocaust is an ethico-political problem because it has to do with the construction of the future: 'the duty to remember consists not only in having a deep concern for the past but in transmitting the meaning of the past events to the next generation' (Ricouer 1999: 9). The duty to remember is a duty to keep alive the memory of suffering by the persistent pursuit of an ethical response to the Holocaust experience. Levi, a prisoner of Auschwitz, tries to understand not 'only what we are prepared to admit to our imaginations, but also that which we cannot erase from them' (Gordon 1999: 133). In other words, the ethical dimension of his work is more important than the historical one, as the involuntary memory of the prisoner and the survivor blurs the boundary between the past and the present, the subconscious and the conscious. The moral duty to remember and to assign to the memory of the Holocaust an ethical value underlines Levi's turn from memories as historical testimony to memories as an 'ethics of testimony'. Yet after this ethical turn, after the loss of testimonial, Levi reinvents the historical consciousness of the Holocaust because he understands the importance of clear distinctions between truth and falsehood, as he knows that there can be no good use of memory if there are no truth claims. So, in this sense ' history returns as itself prone to trauma and loss, to fading along with memory' (Gordon 1999: 140).

With the memory of traumas and catastrophes now constituting a major field of intellectual inquiry, debates about the past in the public sphere are currently dominated by discussions of the meaning of traumatic events (Gray and Oliver 2001: 10). Studies of disruptive events, such as Neal's (1998) investigation of wars, depressions and political assassinations in *National Traumas and Collective Memory: Major Events in the American Century*, demonstrate how traumas become a part of the national narrative, as well as their importance in restoring a sense of moral community. The memory of the destruction of European Jewry, as a particularly compelling example of a more general point about history and memory, also calls into question the validity of memory and its use as testimony in relation to the judicial process as well as the desirability of retrospective punishment.

Today, with many newly democratized societies trying to solve their past traumas by quasi-legal procedures, studying the memory of trauma has gained a new significance and has become an important focus of research about collective memory. Hence, the issues of retrospective justice and the problems connected with attempts to dispose of painful memories will be our next topic.

Memory and justice

The topic of memory and justice has recently received a lot of attention, not only from social scientists generally but also from political scientists and legal theorists. This reorientation of research is connected with the fact that today many nations, and some international organizations, are deciding more consciously than ever what they should do about their respective past wrongdoings. The growing interest of newly democratized societies in addressing their past wrongdoings, as well as the increased recognition of the role of the legal system in shaping collective memory have focused research efforts on new questions concerning the relationship between memory and justice.

The dilemma as to how and what we should remember to ensure a good and just society has been long discussed. However, today's human rights language, the politics of identity and the spread of democracy facilitate the forging of a new connection between memory and justice. Assigning a new value to traumatic memory in a society that opens the space and desire for a search for new identities and encourages people to stay in touch with their authentic culture enhances remembering. New attitudes to the past and changes in remembering the past cannot be comprehended in the light of previous theories' explanations of the role of past injustices in the construction of a nation. Renan's insistence on forgetting, as an essential element in the creation and reproduction of a nation (see Chapter 1) is in defiance of the present focus on remembering past pathologies. Present attempts to confront the past are, however, in line with Adorno's argument that the culture of forgetting ultimately threatens democracy, because democracy requires a self-critical 'working through' of the past. While writing on the meaning of coming to terms with the Nazi past, Adorno stresses that 'the effacement of memory is more the achievement of an all-too-wakeful consciousness than it is the result of its weakness in the face of the superiority of unconscious processes' (1986: 1117). Ricoeur (1999: 9–12) also argues that, apart from the duty to forget, we also have a duty to remember. Moreover, there is no symmetry between the duty to remember and the duty to forget, as only by remembering can we construct the future, transmit the meaning of past events to the next generation and become heirs of the past. Whereas the duty to forget is a duty to go beyond anger and hatred, the duty to remember keeps 'alive the memory of suffering over against the general tendency of history to celebrate victors' (1999: 9).

While for Ricoeur both memory and forgetting contribute in their respective ways to the continuation of societies, for liberals, from Hobbes to Rawls, social amnesia has been the foundation of society as it allows it to start afresh without inherited resentments. To accomplish political and legal equality, through contract or convenant, the individual has to forget past injustices and the social categories that were the marks of inequality (Wolin 1989: 38). This trade-off is rejected by Habermas (1997), who is aware of the limits to what an 'ethics of forgetting' can achieve and emphasizes a communty's responsibility for a shared history and its moral accountability for its past. While liberalism is relatively uninterested in the link between memory and justice, Habermas (1997) emphasizes the responsibility for a shared history, although within the limits of the past of the constitutional order. According to him, we must accept the presence of the past as a 'burden' on moral accountability; the Holocaust must never be forgotten or 'normalized'.

The main reason for the recent increase in awareness of, and attempts to deal with, past wrongdoings is connected with the changed experiences of modern societies. Following Mead's argument that no society would go to the trouble of reconstructing its past had not some significant problems disrupted its normal patterns of living (see Chapter 5), it can be argued that today's interest in retrospective justice is a result of the new challenges faced by modern nations. We assume that it is healthier for a society to remember its collective wrongs because on the one hand we are not afraid that national unity is threatened by the experience of injustice recollected, and on the other hand due to the processes of globalization (particularly the globalization of the language of human rights) and democratization (including the 'democratization of history') every group of people strives to rehabilitate its past as a part of, and an affirmation of, its identity (Misztal 2001; Nora 2001). The growing importance of many nations' attempts to address their respective past wrongdoings is, thus on the one hand a result of a global spread of the language of human rights and on the other a consequence of the growing valorization of memory as the essential element of collective identity. In other words, the growing recognition that nations need to undertake the difficult task of working through their past pathologies is seen as an indispensable element of peaceful coexistence in the interconnected world.

The last decade of the twentieth century provided us with much evidence of attempts to address past injustices and, by the same token, to improve mutual understanding and relations between countries. There have also been numerous efforts at retroactive justice, which deals with the issues of how and why democratic regimes settle wrongs that were committed during an authoritarian era by the state and its agents (Elster 1998). We have witnessed a proliferation of apologies for past wrongdoings (e.g. the Pope's apologies to Jews and Aboriginals, 'sorry' from Japan's prime minster for his country's crimes during World War II, 'sorry' from the Canadian prime minster to his country's indigenous population), various attempts at retribution (e.g. compensation for the Nazi's slave workers or the US government's compensation to American citizens of Japanese descent for their treatment during World War II), and many efforts to discover the truth about the past. (More than 15 truth commissions were set up during the 1990s to investigate certain aspects of human rights violations under authoritarian rule, with the Guatemalan Historical Clarification Commission being the first and the South African Truth and Reconciliation Commission being the most recent.) Also, the criminal law has increasingly been used with a view to teaching a particular interpretation of a country's history. This is illustrated by many trials for past crimes (e.g. the trials of the Nazi collaborators Laval, Touvier, Bousquet, Barbie and Fauvisson in France and the arrest of Pinochet, the former Chilean dictator, for human rights violations), and the criminalization of denial of certain past events (e.g. denial of the Holocaust is a criminal offence in Germany). Recent developments, such as the creation of the Hague International Tribunal, set to try crimes of war committed in Bosnia-Herzegovina, which was followed by the establishment of the tribunal on the genocidal civil war in Rwanda and the creation of the permanent international criminal court, which from 2002 has been a tribunal with worldwide jurisdiction over atrocities and genocide, signal a growing interest on the part of the international community in addressing past injustices. As a result of the growing popularity of an approach to the past that assumes that it should be deliberately remembered, researchers' attention has been focused on the way in which countries have been dealing with the Nazi past, the role of the memory of the communist past in the reconstruction of the new democracies in Eastern Europe, discourses of retribution and reconciliation in post-authoritarian regimes, the processes of reconciliation through truth-telling, the healing of nations through confronting lies and crimes of apartheid and the role of both remembering and forgetting in enhancing a national unity. It can therefore be said that coming to terms with the past has emerged as the grand narrative of recent times.

The importance of dealing with the past is, of course, not a new preoccupation. As several authors have recently suggested, while pointing to the linguistic affinity between 'amnesty' and 'amnesia', many issues connected with dealing with past wrongdoings on the way to democracy were experienced in Athens after the civil war of 404 BC (Elster 1998; Ricoeur 1999; Cohen 2001). In the process of restoring Athenian democracy after the oligarchic coup the democrats ruled that in order to live together again as a political community and to ensure reconciliation, individual citizens were forbidden to recall the past. As amnesia became the legal rule, remembering past injustices bacame a punishable offence. After analysing in detail this first case of transitional justice in history, Cohen (2001: 342) concludes that while it was not an example of total amnesia or complete social harmony, supporters of the oligarchy remained immune from prosecution and the 'amnesty' was for the most part respected. Consequently, the reconstruction and restoration of democracy, as well as the rules of law, ensured a long period of political stability for the Athenian state.

This approach, which argues that every nation must first fill its internal fissures and 'forget' the antagonism that historically tore it apart, and which advises the forgetting of past pathologies and crimes, was first questioned by the Nuremberg Trials (1945–6). Yet this international tribunal, due to the long list of its shortcomings and an unfavourable political climate for international cooperation (Taylor 1971; Luban 1987) has had no imitators for almost 50 years. Moreover, after World War II a need to reintegrate societies restricted nations' desires to expose their past and the political climate of the postwar period favoured forgiving and forgetting. In many countries, after the initial punishment of leading figures, there was a long period of silence. In nations like France and Italy, after initial attempts to account for past wrongdoings and the initial stigmatization of collaborators, myths were constructed to gloss over the extent and depth of collaboration with the Nazi regime. In postwar France the complex readjustments that were designed to defuse political discord by denying the ideological reasons for the conflict ensured that for many years the truth was sacrificed to national unity. After World War II, both Gaullists and Communists offered a heroic reworking of the war in which Vichy was presented as an aberration involving only a few Frenchmen. The myth of resistance and the need for reconciliation dictated the vision of this remembered past (Rousso 1991; Bernstein 1992; Gross 2000). Italian politicians in the immediate postwar decades were also quick to define themselves in terms of a defeated enemy against whom all Italians could unite. Annual national celebrations of the end of the war focus upon the German atrocities and the unity of the Italian nation in the struggle leading to postwar democracy.

Recent studies have reopened debates about many countries' past by highlighting the political factors behind postwar forgetting. With the publication of the works of independent and foreign historians revealing French responsibility for the persecution, exclusion and martyrdom of 70,000 French Jews, France has been involved in coping with what is now known as 'Vichy Syndrome' (Rousso 1991). Controversy over the Vichy regime became especially visible following the 1991 dismissal of charges against Paul Touvier for crimes against humanity. Following the fiftieth anniversary of the deportation by French police during the Vichy regime of more than 10,000 non-French Jews from unoccupied areas of France to Auschwitz, 16 July was established as the Day of Remembrance of the racist and anti-Semitic persecution under the Vichy regime. Now, even countries that were more involved than others in the process of denial of their war past experience constant reinterpretation of their historical past.

After World War II, the Holocaust was a source of taboo and prohibition in West and East Germany. However, while East Germany marginalized Jewish suffering, and therefore rejected the relationship between memory and justice, West German political culture was constrained by shifts in the dominant interpretations of the Nazi era (Olick and Levy 1997). In the early postwar period West German democracy 'did not foster either memory and justice or democracy' (Herf 1997: 7–9), yet in the following years the inherent tension between memory and justice on the one hand and democracy on the other was one of the central themes of the country's postwar history. The initial period – in which the government was reluctant to embrace the example of Allied tribunals at Nuremberg, the courts were slow to prosecute Nazi war criminals, the process of de-Nazification was undermined and important public positions were taken by former National Socialist officials – was characterized by social amnesia and a weakening of memory. The policy and practice of the first West German chancellor was based on the assumption that for the transition of West Germany to a stable democracy it was a political necessity to adopt silence about the crimes of the past: 'Memory and justice might produce, it was argued, a right-wing revolt that would undermine a still fragile democracy' (Herf 1997: 7).

However, even during the initial period of reconstruction not everybody accepted this strategy. Despite the dominant practice of 'the defusing the past' (Habermas 1996: 45) and putting the past behind, there were calls for recall and reflection on the Nazi past. The political impact of such leaders as Heuss (who used his presidency to increase Germans' awareness of Nazi crimes and to criticize the delay and denial of justice) and Brandt (who fell to his knees before the Warsaw Ghetto memorial during a visit in the 1970s) slowly helped to establish more space for discussion and a new understanding that a policy of memory and justice does not have to lead to conflict (Herf 1997: 7–9).

The Holocaust received more attention in the 1970s (for instance, the screening of the television series *Holocaust* sparked the first public discussion of the past), and in the 1980s. Yet, generally it can be said that the Cold War era 'brought more democracy at a price of less justice and self-serving feeble memory' (Herf 1997: 400). The period was, moreover, not free from attempts to rewrite history. The most famous was an episode in 1985, when Chancellor Kohl invited President Regan to participate in a wreath-laying ceremony at a German military cemetery at Bitburg in a spirit of reconciliation. Regan's gesture, understood commonly as an attempt to suggest that the fallen German soldiers and the murdered Jews were both 'victims' of Nazi oppression (Hartman 1986: 6) was widely criticized as an attempt to 'consolidate the move away from any destabilizing effort to achieve mastery of the past' (Habermas 1996: 44). It also had unintended consequences as it accelerated a series of public exchanges between many prominent German scholars arguing for and against 'normalizing' the Nazi past. The famous 'Historians' Debate', which started in 1986, brought to public attention hidden meanings in the trend towards normalization, which was seen as a process involving the marginalization of the Holocaust in German consciousness, weakening the relationship between memory and justice. Habermas was one of the main protagonists in this debate and opposed questioning the uniqueness of the Holocaust and calls for forgetting by showing the importance of the relationship between the public role of memory and national responsibility: 'The . . . obligation that we in Germany have – even if no one else longer assumes it – to keep alive the memory of suffering of those murdered by German hands, and to keep it alive quite openly and not just in our mind' (quoted in LaCapra 1997: 97).

The fiftieth anniversary of the end of the war was accompanied by open, widespread and extensive discussions of Germany's recent past. The most recent developments, such as the opening of a Holocaust memorial in the centre of Berlin in 2001, and the repatriation payments made by German industry and banks to forced labourers from the Nazi era signal further changes in the relationship between memory and justice.

Since the collapse of the Berlin Wall in 1990, unified Germany has been called upon to engage with German history and acknowledge the burden of the past as part of the process of normalization. Habermas (1997) continues to argue for a critical evaluation of memory in order to exclude a particularistic nationalism and advance constitutional patriotism. United Germany has also had to wrestle with the issue of its communist past and act on the former East Germany's offences in the name of communism (Rosenberg 1995). McAdams (2001), in his survey of Germany's most recent experiment with retrospective justice, argues that East Germany's past, although not really masterable, has at least turned out to be a manageable burden. The new Germany has taken all possible steps to address past injustices as the government has decided to draw on multiple options, such as retribution, disqualifications and various forms of corrective justice. Thus Germany has had 'trials and purges and truth commissions and has systemically opened the secret police files to each and every individual' (Ash 1997: 195).

By all accounts, concludes McAdams (2001) Germany's recent experiment offers an illuminating lesson of what can be accomplished when governments seriously deal with a fractured past. The German case also shows the challenges a regime faces in helping citizens to confront the wrongdoings of the past. It provides evidence, according to Habermas (1997), that the issues of fairness and balance require a wide public debate on how to interpret the country's past. It demands that the former West Germany uphold its action to the same high moral standards that were applied to its eastern counterparts, and that all citizens engage in discussions of the nation's history. Habermas' argument, that without public debates on how to interpret the country's history, the normalcy of post-unification Germany will be not secured is reinforced in Sa'dah's (1998) study of strategies of reconciliation in Germany. She identifies the attitude of Germans towards their past and examines attempts to procure a democratic consensus and overcome a crisis of German democracy. Sa'dah links collective memory to the broader concept of political culture as her argument about reconciliation brings together the ideas of truth, trust and democracy.

Studies of postcommunist countries' strategies for dealing with a complex past contribute to our understanding of the complexity of the links between memory and justice in the context of fragile democracy. They show that, regardless of adopted strategies (ranging from decisions to ignore the past, through searching for a middle way to achieve a 'subtle blend of memory and forgetting', to dealing with the past with the help of all possible strategies), policies of readdressing past injustice are confusing and costly and, moreover, always raise as many objections as supportive voices (Huntington 1991; Holmes 1995; Los 1995; Elster 1998; Misztal 1999).

Research into postcommunist attempts to deal with the traumatic past also identifies the conditions which shape the nature of policy towards past wrongdoings, such as the nature of the previous system and its mode of collapse. The scope of freedom enjoyed by various countries in their use of the past to construct new postcommunist identities depends, it is argued, upon the type of transition to democracy and the credibility of the main actors. Studies of strategies for dealing with the past in newly democratized countries also show that, on the one hand, meeting people's demands for justice and information about the past is a very essential step in the further democratization of Eastern and Central Europe and, on the other hand, that these investigations demonstrate negative consequences (such as growing public distrust) of partial, politicized and not very efficient implementations of policies dealing with past injustice for new democracies.

Among polices which have been implemented in Eastern European countries to deal with their communist past, the most common are: polices of lustration (screening the past of candidates for important positions with the aim of eliminating them from important public office), decommunization (excluding former Communist Party officials from high public positions), restitution of property, recompensation and rehabilitation of victims. The issue of lustration/decommunization emerged on the public agenda of almost all postcommunist countries (Schwartz 1995) and in the majority of them it has been a source of great controversy (Kritz 1995). Only in the Czech Republic has the policy of lustration been fully adopted, ensuring the disqualification of employees from high-ranking government posts for a period of five years if they were found to have been agents or informants of the secret police (Trucker 1999). In Russia and in the former republics of the USSR 'the abstention from pursuing retroactive justice happened more or less by default' (Elster 1998: 18). Poland's long and protracted history of legislative attempts to introduce lustration law started with the first Polish postcommunist government trying to 'let bygones be bygones' in the name of reconciliation and transformation. This forward-looking approach, aiming to smooth and stabilize the transformation process (Los 1995; Misztal 1999), very quickly attracted criticism for preserving intact the identity of the former communists. Ten years later, in 1999, due to continuous calls to address the past, Poland passed a lustration law which imposed a forced compromise, the importance of which was reduced by conflicts over previous misfired lustration bills. A decade-long controversy over how to address the communist past, which convinced Poles that the way justice is defined and the decision of whose vision of the past is adopted depends wholly on who holds political power, illustrates that 'justice is more political in transitional situations than under normal circumstances' (Elster 1989: 16).

Studies of the many fragile democracies in Latin America examine how post-authoritarian societies cope with the legal, moral and practical difficulties connected with the choice between truth and justice, forgiving and forgetting (Weschler 1990; Huntington 1991; Huyse 1995; Kritz 1995; Linz and Stepan 1997; Osiel 1997). Although they show that securing justice for past wrongdoings has always been an extremely flawed exercise, these investigations argue that by allowing victims to tell their stories and by undermining the previous official version of history such approaches are necessary and justified. As all post-liberated or post-authoritarian societies, despite the pain and the cost induced, continue to search for truth, it becomes clear that a new institutional order cannot avoid confronting people's long memories and desire for justice. Countries as diverse as Chile, Argentina and Honduras have found ways to hold former officials accountable for offences.

Of all the new democracies that struggled with the issue of retrospective justice in the 1990s, the operations of the South Africa Truth and Reconciliation Commission (TRC), which between 1994–8 investigated gross violations of human rights, seem to be the most comprehensive attempt at confronting the past and coming to terms with it (Nuttall and Coetzee 1998). The people responsible for the TRC's success understood the importance of justice and truth, and knew that the policy of trading justice for truth entails a moral sacrifice (Gutmann 1999; Jeffery 1999; Johnson 1999). The TRC may not have managed to ensure total justice, but as Richard Goldstone, a South African constitutional court judge, remarked 'making public the truth is itself a form of justice' (quoted in Ash 1997: 20). All the truth commissions that were set up around the world to investigate certain aspects of human rights violations under authoritarian rule (see e.g. Ensalaco 1994; Hayner 1994; Huyse 1995; Wilson 2000), tried to revitalize citizens' respect for the rule of law and promote a new culture of human rights, as well as a national consensus and solidarity. They aimed to help reconciliation by simultaneously discovering historical truth and facilitating a national unity. While all truth commissions faced many problems and criticisms, their establishment and functioning, as well as the recent creation of a world criminal court at The Hague, are indicative of new attitudes toward the past. With the willingness of nation states to apologize for past wrongs committed in their name becoming a worldwide phenomenon, we are witnessing the emergence of a new international morality, one which is rooted in both the power of human rights and the power of identity politics (Barkan 2000).

All the above examples suggest that attempts to silence oppositional memory may actually have the opposite effect. Many studies show that attempts to simply 'draw a line' under the past satisfy nobody. Consequently, various nations are, particularly now in the context of the globalization of the language of human rights and the importance of memory as a source of collective identity, forced to pay more attention to the ways in which they deal with the past (Osiel 1997). Yet investigations of various attempts at retrospective justice warn that we cannot rely solely on memory to render perfect justice, and that judicial outcomes cannot capture the complexity of history. Since memory, viewed as the representation of the past in the present rather than really the past, is always subject to change and can be irrational, subjective, inconsistent and self-serving, we should aim to achieve a balance between memory, which requires a narrator whose credibility can always be questioned, and a critical, scientific and objective distance by checking documents and archives which inform us of the 'facts' of what happened (Ricoeur 2001). However, because such confrontation does not necessarily solve all tensions between memory and history, and because of the problematic nature of memory, we need to depend upon a plurality of contending narratives and the civility of rules in the management of these strains. In other words, what happened can be discovered only under conditions of diversity and discourse, by relying 'not on a single narrator, but rather on a plurality of contending voices speaking to one another' (Sennett 1998: 14).

To sum up, this survey of the four fields of studying memory shows their richness and their contribution to our understanding of the relationship between nation states and their respective pasts, and the construction of preserved collective memories. In studies of memory trauma – now a major field of intellectual inquiry – debates about the past in the public sphere focus on the meaning of traumatic events, and tend to argue that revealing and acknowledging the truth about the past is an essential step in the preservation of moral order.

The chapter also shed light on the process of political change and the role of social memory in any successful transformation from an authoritarian to a democratic regime. An increasing recognition of the role of legal systems in shaping collective memory has focused research efforts on new questions concerning the relationship between memory and justice.

Further reading

Adorno, T.W. (1986) What does coming to terms with the past mean?, trans. T. Bahti and G. Hartman, in G. Hartman (ed.) *Bitburg in Moral and Political Perspective*, pp. 114–29. Bloomington, IN: Indiana University Press.

Ashplant, T.G., Dawson, G. and Roper, M. (2000) The politics of war memory and commemoration: contexts, structures and dynamics, in T.G. Ashplant, G. Dawson and M. Roper (eds) *The Politics of War Memory and Commemoration*, pp. 1–87. London: Routledge.

Booth, W.J. (1999) Communities of memory: on identity, memory, and debt, *American Political Science Review*, 93(2): 249–68.

Gillis, J.R. (1994) Introduction: memory and identity, in J.R. Gillis (ed.) *Commemorations. The Politics of National Identity*, pp. 3–26. Princeton, NJ: Princeton University Press.

Elster, J. (1998) Coming to terms with the past, *European Journal of Sociology*, XXXIX(1): 7–48.

Winter, J. and Sivan, E. (eds) (1999) *War and Remembrance in the Twentieth Century*. Cambridge: Cambridge University Press.

EPILOGUE

*'Man is a history-making creature who can neither repeat his
past nor leave it behind'*
(Auden 1962)

Our examination of social theories of remembering and current research
into various aspects of collective memory illustrates that the status and
the content of collective memory can provide essential insights into our
understanding of modern societies. Researching collective memory is an
important part of sociological investigation into the ways we give meaning
to the world, as our ability to make sense of the present is connected
with the fact that what we have learned from prior experiences has
been retained in memory. Studying memory is likewise significant
because the sense of continuity that is essential for understanding the
world is a result of our remembrance of past experiences. Investigating
memory is crucial because memory is also a site where contradictions of
identities are often contested. Since remembering offers a shared sense
of ideals about the past that can link people together and secure a sense
of continuity 'with what they think they know in order to be able to
deal with what they don't know' (Hamer 1994: 184), memory is also an
essential field for the study of the articulation between public and private
representations.

Memory discourse has also become the language through which we
address some of the most pressing concerns of modern societies, because the
situation of memory under modern conditions is indicative of the dilemma
of a democratic political identity. This is because in modernity, as memory
becomes the key to personal and collective identity, we are faced with the
tensions between the particularism of realms of memory and the universalism of democratic rights, or the friction between the vision of a 'rational

identity' and an identity laden with the responsibility of remembrance (Touraine 2000).

The recent shifts towards the openness of modern identity and the critical revision of national membership have affected societies differently. In the case of the liberal, stable and integrated democracies of the West, where the process of recalling and selecting from past experiences takes place under the conditions of open debate, there is the necessity of balancing the growing pluralization and individualization of societies with the state's interest in stability. In the case of new and fragile democracies, in which the search for a usable past requires the reopening of taboos and the overcoming of many disappointments with the past, there is the necessity of balancing the human need for justice and retribution with the state's interest in stability and reconciliation.

Consequently, two questions are urgently in need of an answer. First, how do we foster social cooperation without a shared recollection of the past? And second, how do we preserve the ability to settle conflicts in the context of the multiplication of particularistic memories? Answers to these questions are connected, on the one hand, with the limits to the level of abstraction from particularity that can be achieved and, on the other, with particularism's threat to the openness of universal democratic structures. An examination of how these tensions are accommodated in different types of society can be helped by studies of social memory.

By investigating memory we can grasp how public representations of the past, combined with private memories, contribute to the working of democracy. In today's global, ethnically and culturally pluralistic societies, there is a need to prevent collective memory from becoming an obstacle to democratic cooperation between groups. Hence, solving tensions between multiple memories is an essential concern. Efforts to enhance mutual trust by fostering reflective memory in all communities are therefore the crucial element of a democratic pedagogy. In its attempts at public enlightenment, such a strategy should explore the past and prevent forgetfulness that 'too easily goes with and justifies what is forgotten', because amnesia is a symptom of the social weakening of autonomy (Adorno 1986: 125) and leads to the erosion of civil society (Heller 1999). Memory, moreover, seems to be not only at the heart of democracy but also the cornerstone of the process of democratization, since the basic task of newly democratized societies is to deal with past injustices in such a way that facilitates critical revision of groups' memories but at the same time does not undermine national cohesion.

More generally, memory is also closely link with the process of change, which is the central aspect of contemporary personal and collective experience. Paradoxically, accelerated change gives rise to two different attitudes towards the past. On the one hand we insist on the relative merits of the future while on the other we exhibit a sentimental nostalgia for our past. This deep ambivalence in modern societies with respect to their past manifests itself in both 'the memory boom' and the expansion of the heritage industry (Nora 1996a; Hervieu-Leger 2000; Touraine 2000). Despite social amnesia, seen as a result of the demise of the traditional notion of the self and a decline in the power of many communities to allocate collective identities, memory tends to underpin the search for identity. Accordingly, the process of the atrophy of collective memory is accompanied by the privatization of the past and consequently manifests itself in the pluralization of memories (Hervieu-Leger 2000: 124–7). This form of forgetting either reduces us to being 'mosaics of behavioural patterns that are so diverse that they cannot generate any unitary personal principle' or encourages us to 'seek that unity in a cultural heritage, a language, a memory' (Touraine 2000: 39). Thus, in the context of a general orientation towards the future, the expanding heritage industry fills up popular memory with images of the 'good old days' and endows a select group with prestige and common purpose.

Equally important is the normative dimension of memory, because our choices about how to use the past and to what ends affect social reality. The moral claims of remembrance of past injustices not only help to establish facts about specific traumatic events, but also make it possible for a traumatized community to restore its unity (Booth 2001). Recent research within rational choice theory confirms that remembering past behaviour sharpens our moral standards. It has been discovered, while testing the notion that individuals tend to behave as rational and egoistic creatures, that people not only value fairness but also that memory is the essential remedy against egoistical behaviour. When participants in this experiment could get information about the past action of other players, they tended to reward them with the reputation for fair play. Knowing their partners' past allowed the players to make choices, evaluate what was good behaviour and which not, and then decide what kind of attitudes were important and what were not (Ahuja 2001: 6). In other words, social remembering enhances moral sensitivity and is an antidote to the narrowing and distorting of our self-understanding.

However, this does not mean that we should value memory for its own sake, as 'sacralizing memory is another way to render it sterile' (Todorov 1996: 15). Since remembering about the past can be one of the greatest antidotes against the parochialism of place and the provincialism of time, the study of social remembering should be used first of all to develop our systematic thinking about the present and its main characteristic – change. Second, it ought to enhance our understanding of other people, as remembering the past can provide us with rich, imaginative and critical insights into different cultures. Because both these characteristics are essential for living in a global world which demands from us reflexive judgement, we can conclude that studying memory practices, as the central feature of contemporary cultural formations, should become an important part of any examination of modern society.

GLOSSARY

adolescence: a stage in life that separates childhood from adulthood.

amnesia: refers to the loss of memory of events or experiences due to some physical or psychological trauma.

art of memory: *ars memoria*, attributed to the poet Simonides (c.556–468 BC), was a technique employed by orators to remember long passages that involved locating each element to be remembered in an imaginary palace of memory so that it could be easily recovered in its proper place by tracing a mental path through the palace.

autobiographical memory: memory about the self that provides a sense of identity and continuity. It is a source of information about our lives, as we reconstruct the past when telling others and ourselves the story of our life.

Cold War: the ideological battle between capitalist democratic states, led by the USA, and the now fallen communist systems, led by the Soviet Union, over the period 1947–89.

collective or social, memory: a group's representation of its past, both the past that is commonly shared and the past that is collectively commemorated, that enacts and gives substance to that group's identity, its present conditions and its vision of the future.

commemoration: ceremonial services to remember and honour the memory of past heroes or crucial national events; the word 'commemoration' derives from the Latin *com* (together) and *momorare* (to remember).

corporeal memory: a kind of somatic memory in which recollection is helped by the body into which memory is inscribed by – for example, pain or disfigurement.

counter-memory: an alternative view of the past which challenges the dominant representation of the past.

cultural memory: memory constructed from cultural forms and which thus refers to the recollection of events of which we do not necessarily have first-hand knowledge.

discourse: a coherent set of statements presenting a particular view of the world.

dominant ideology thesis: the theory, with roots in the Marxist tradition, argues that the ruling class controls the production of ideas as well as material production; it therefore creates and sustains sets of beliefs and ideas that claim objectivity and thus inveigle subordinate classes and minority groups into accepting their disadvantaged condition.

embodied: refers to the significance of bodies in conferring identities based on age, physical characteristics, sex and skin colour.

flashbulb memories: memories that are distinctly vivid, precise, concrete, long-lasting recollections of the personal circumstances surrounding people's experience of unusual events.

frame: an element out of which definitions of situations are built up. Framing was Goffman's (1974) notion to describe our ways of organizing experiences into meaningful activities, and ensures the clarity and simplicity of the definition of a situation.

generation: a cohort of people who are more or less the same age and who, by virtue of undergoing similar experiences, perceive historical events from more or less a similar perspective.

generational memory: the memory shared by people born at about the same time who have grown up in the same historical period, which shapes their views.

habit-memory: memory that allows us to recall the signs and skills we use in everyday life as well as to reproduce routine activities and ritual performances.

habitus: the system of durable thoughts, behaviours and tastes produced by objective structures and conditions but which are also capable of producing and repro-ducing those structures (Bourdieu 1977: 72). *Habitus* organizes the way in which individuals see the world and act in it.

hegemony: the all-embracing cultural and social dominance of a ruling group that legitimates its leadership by creating and sustaining an ideology presenting its dominance as fair and in the best interests of society as a whole.

hermeneutic: a theory of interpretation and understanding of texts and works of art that studies the problem of how to give meaning to cultural products.

heritage industry: the marketing of the past, closely connected with people's need for a sense of the past, belonging and identity as well for entertainment; associ-ated with the development of forms of tourism that promote 'historic' places, such as old towns, villages and museums, and with preserving or re-enacting the past.

historiography: the art of writing history and the study of historical writings. To study historiography is to study the methodological questions formulated in historical accounts of the past.

identity: a relatively stable set of perceptions by which we define ourselves and which allow us to project ourselves into the future.

ideology: a coherent set of ideas and beliefs that shapes a group's view of the world, and which provides the basis for the justification of that group's social status and political action.

invented traditions: traditions, which, in according to the presentist approach, were manipulated by the dominant sectors of society through public commemorations, education systems, mass media, official records and chronologies. Traditions are 'invented' in the sense of being deliberately designed and produced with a view to creating new political realities, defining nations and sustaining national communities (Hobsbawm and Ranger 1983).

keying: refers to Goffman's (1974) concept of the key – the set of conventions by which a given activity, one already meaningful in terms of some primary framework, is transformed into something patterned on, but independent of, it.

legitimacy: the belief of citizenry that power is lawful and that a political leadership and political order are well-founded, fair and binding.

lustration: the policy of checking or screening the past for candidates to some important positions, the main being the elimination from important public office people who worked in, or collaborated with, the communist security forces.

memory: a faculty by which we remember. Although there is a lack of consensus on how memory works, both the recent neuroscientific argument that memory is a set of encoded neural connections and the suggestion in interdisciplinary studies of the role of subjectivity in remembering seem to be accepted as the way forward in the conceptualization of memory. In the sociological perspective, memory is best understood as representations of the past which involve emotions and reconstructions of past experiences in such a way as to make them meaningful in the present (Schacter 1996; Prager 1998).

mnemonic communities: groups that socialize us to what should be remembered and what should be forgotten. These communities, such as the family, the ethnic group or the nation, provide the social contexts in which memories are embedded and mark the emotional tone, depth and style of our remembering.

mnemonic socialization: the process by which people, especially children, learn what should be remembered and what should be forgotten; they are familiarized with their collective past so that the continuity and identity of the group are sustained.

narrative: an account, or narration, of events, stories or tales.

official memory: memory that is the dominant national narrative, strategically employed by political élites who revise national history in such a way as to secure the status quo. Official memory is expressed most explicitly in the form of monuments, textbooks and the public remembrance and commemoration of key events.

popular memory: discursive practice, subordinated in its relation to the dominant discourse, which, as an aspect of political cultures, reproduces the established consensual view of the past.

public memory: beliefs and ideas about the past that help a society interpret its past and present as well as project its future. Public memory, according to Bodnar (1992) is a cognitive device to mediate competing interpretations, although it privileges some explanations over others.

realms of memory: Nora's (1996a) notion for various cultural forms, such as archives, organized celebrations, museums, cemeteries, festivals, statues and monuments, that are (when living memory disappears) constructed by modern societies to remind us about the past and history.

retrospective justice: attempts by post-authoritarian, newly democratized regimes to settle the wrongs that were committed during the previous era.

rhetoric: the art of using language effectively; the systematic study of how public speaking can be persuasive.

ritual: a form of patterned social practice that serves, among other things, to create and recreate the sense of individual and collective identity.

screen memories: memories which, according to Freud, block access to more disturbing memories of a traumatic past.

social constructionism: theories that emphasize the socially created nature of collective life and therefore underline the importance of inquiry into the manner in which whatever passes as natural reality is in fact socially constructed.

sociology of memory: a study of the content and social formation of collective memory by way of exploring its conditions and factors, (e.g. language, rituals, physical objects) that make remembering in common possible. Based on the argument that memory is intersubjectively constituted, the sociology of memory is interested in the ways in which social and cultural dimensions are woven together to create collectively significant representations of the past (Funkestein 1993; Schudson 1997; Zerubavel 1997; Prager 1998; Sherman 1999).

totalitarianism: an undemocratic political system in which power is concentrated in the hands of a dictator and in which the dominance of one ideology, the role of a secret police and lack of freedom of the mass media ensure the subordination of the masses.

tradition: a set of long-established social practices or beliefs that are handed down from one generation to the next.

trauma: initially referring to the physical effects of accidents, trauma came to be associated with an unforgettable shock causing a deep psychological wound.

traumatic memory: memory that has its origin in some terrible experience and which is particularly vivid, intrusive, uncontrollable, persistent and somatic.

BIBLIOGRAPHY

Ackerman, B. (1992) *The Future of Liberal Revolution.* Cambridge, MA: Harvard University Press.

Adam, B. (1990) *Time and Social Theory.* Oxford: Polity Press.

Adam, B. (1998) *Timescapes of Modernity.* London: Routledge.

Adorno, T.W. (1967) *Prisms*, trans. S. and S. Weber. London: Neville Spearman.

Adorno, T.W. (1973) *Negative Dialectics*, trans. E.B. Ashton, London: Routledge.

Adorno, T.W. (1986) What does coming to terms with the past mean?, trans. T. Bahti and G. Hartman, in G. Hartman (ed.) *Bitburg in Moral and Political Perspective*, pp. 114–29. Bloomington, IN: Indiana University Press.

Ahuja, A. (2001) The give and take game, *The Australian*, 6 January: 20.

Alcorn, G. (2002) It's democracy versus evil, *The Sydney Morning Herald*, 22 September: 6.

Anderson, B. (1983) *Imagined Communities.* London: Verso.

Antze, P. and Lambek, M. (eds) (1996a) *Tense Past: Cultural Essays in Trauma and Memory.* London: Routledge.

Antze, P. and Lambek, M. (1996b) Introduction: forecasting memory, in P. Antze and M. Lambek (eds) *Tense Past: Cultural Essays in Trauma and Memory*, pp. vii–xi. London: Routledge: vii–xi.

Appleby, J., Hunt, L. and Jacob, M. (1994) *Telling the Truth about History.* New York: Norton.

Aries, P. (1981) *At the Hour of Our Death*, trans. H. Weaver. New York: Knopf.

Arnold, J.H. (2000) *History.* Oxford: Oxford University Press.

Ash, G.T. (1996) Neo-pagan Poland, *The New York Review of Books*, 11 January: 10–14.

Ash, G.T. (1997) *The File: A Personal History.* London: HarperCollins.

Ashplant, T.G., Dawson, G. and Roper, M. (eds) (2000a), *The Politics of War Memory and Commemoration*, pp. 1–87. London: Routledge.

Assmann, J. (1995) Collective memory and cultural identity, *New German Critique*, 65, (Spring–Summer): 125–35.

Assmann, J. (1997) *Moses the Egyptian.* Cambridge, MA: Harvard University Press.

Auden, W.H. (1962) *The Dyer's Hand.* London: Faber & Faber.

Baddeley, A. (1989) The psychology of remembering and forgetting, in T. Butler (ed.) *Memory: History, Culture and the Mind*, pp. 33–60. Oxford: Basil Blackwell.

Baert, P. (1992) *Time, Self and Social Being*. Aldershot: Avebury.

Baert, P. (1998) *Social Theory in the Twentieth Century*. Oxford: Polity Press.

Bakhtin, M.M. (1981) *The Dialogic of Imagination: Four Essays by M.M. Bakhtin*, ed. M. Hoquiast, Austin TX: University of Texas Press.

Barbalet, J. (1998) *Emotion, Social Theory and Social Structure*. Cambridge: Cambridge University Press.

Barclay, C.R. (1988) Schematization of autobiographical memory, in D.C. Rubin (ed.) *Autobiographical Memory*, pp. 82–99. Cambridge: Cambridge University Press.

Barclay, C.R. and DeCooke, P.A. (1988) Ordinary everyday memories: some of the things of which selves are made, in U. Neisser and E. Winograd (eds) *Remembering Reconsidered: Ecological and Traditional Approaches to the Study of Memory*, pp. 91–126. Cambridge: Cambridge University Press.

Barkan, E. (2000) *The Guilt of Nations: Restitution and Negotiating Historical Injustices*. New York: Norton.

Barry, B. (2001) *Culture and Equality. An Egalitarian Critique of Multiculturalism*. Cambridge, MA: Harvard University Press.

Bartlett, F. (1932) Remembering: *A Study in Experimental and Social Psychology*. Cambridge: Cambridge University Press.

Bartoszewski, W. (1991) *The Convent at Auschwitz*. New York: George Braziller.

Bartov, O. (2000) An infinity of suffering, *Times Literary Supplement*, 15 September: 5–6.

Bauman, Z. (1982) *Memories of Class*. London: Routledge.

Baumeister, R.F. and Hastings, S. (1997) Distortions of collective memory, in J.W. Pennebaker, D. Paez and B. Rime (eds) *Collective Memory of Political Events*, pp. 277–94. Mahwah, NJ: Lawrence Erlbaum.

Bayley, J. (2001) What happened to the hippopotamus's wife? *The New York Review of Books*, 17 May: 16–19.

Bellah, R.N., Madsen, R., Sullivan, W.M., Swidler, A. and Tipton, S.M. (1985) *Habits of the Heart*. New York: Harper & Row.

Ben-Amos, D. and Weissberg, L. (eds) (1999) *Cultural Memory and the Construction of Identity*. Detroit, MI: Wayne State University Press.

Benjamin, W. (1968) *Illuminations: Essays and Reflections*, trans. H. Zohn, ed. H. Arendt. New York: Schocken Books.

Benjamin, W. (1986) *Berlin Chronicle in Reflections*. New York: Schocken Books.

Berdahl, D. (1999) *Where the World Ended: Reunification and Identity in the German Borderland*. Berkeley, CA: University of California Press.

Bergson, H. ([1896] 1996) *Matter and Memory*. trans. N.M. Paul and W.S. Palmer. New York: Zone Books.

Berlin, I. (1991) *The Crooked Timber of Humanity*. New York: Alfred A. Knopf.

Berlin, I. (1993) *Conversation with Isaiah Berlin*, ed. R. Jahanbegloo. New York: Phoenix Press.

Berlin, I. (1999) *The Roots of Romanticism*, ed. H. Hardy. Princeton, NJ: Princeton University Press.

Bernstein, R. (1992) French collaborators: the new debate, *The New York Review of Books*, 25 June: 12–15.

Billig, M. (1990) Collective memory, ideology and the British royal family, in D. Middleton and D. Edwards (eds) *Collective Remembering*, pp. 60–80. London: Sage.

Billig, M. (1995) *Banal Nationalism*. London: Sage.

Block, A. (1998) The narcissism of minor differences, *European Journal of Social Theory*, 1(1): 33–56.

Bodnar, J. (1992) *Remaking America: Public Memory, Commemoration, and Patriotism in the Twentieth Century*. Princeton, NJ: Princeton University Press.

Bodnar, J. (1994) Public memory in an American city: commemoration in Cleveland, in J.R. Gillis (ed.) *Commemorations: The Politics of National Identity*, pp. 74–104. Princeton, NJ: Princeton University Press.

Bommes, M. and Wright, P. (1982) Charms of residence: the public and the past in making histories, in R. Johnson, G. McLennan, B. Schwartz and D. Sutton (eds) *Studies in History Making and Politics*, pp. 253–302. London: Hutchinson.

Booth, W.J. (1999) Communities of memory: on identity, memory, and debt, *American Political Science Review*, 93(2): 249–68.

Booth, W.J. (2001) The unforgotten: memories of justice, *American Political Science Review*, 95(4): 777–89.

Bouchard, D.F. (1977) Introduction, in M. Foucault, *Language, Counter-memory, Practice: Selected Essays and Interviews*, ed. D.F. Bouchard, pp. 15–28. Ithaca, Cornell University Press.

Bourdieu, P. (1977) *Outline of a Theory of Practice*, trans. R. Nice. Cambridge: Cambridge University Press.

Bourdieu, P. (1984) *Homo Academicus*. Stanford, CA: Stanford University Press.

Bourdieu, P. and Wacquant, L.J.D. (1992) *An Invitation to Reflexive Sociology*. Oxford: Polity Press.

Boym, S. (2001) *The Future of Nostalgia*. New York: Basic Books.

Brison, S. (1999) Trauma narratives and the remaking of the self, in M. Bal, J. Crewe and L. Spitzer (eds) *Acts of Memory, Cultural Recall and the Present*, pp. 39–54. Hanover, VT: University Press of New England.

Brown, L.N.R., Shevell, S.K. and Rips, L.J. (1988) Public memories and their personal context, in D.C. Rubin (ed.) *Autobiographical Memory*, pp. 137–58. Cambridge: Cambridge University Press.

Burke, P. (1989) History as social memory, in T. Butler (ed.) *Memory: Culture and the Mind*, pp. 1–32. Cambridge: Blackwell.

Burke, P. (1998) Interview, in E. Domanska (ed.) *Encounters*, pp. 211–33. Charlottesville, VA: University Press of Virginia.

Byatt, A.S (1998) Memory and the making of fiction, in P. Fara and K. Patterson (eds) *Memory*, pp. 47–73. Cambridge: Cambridge University Press.

Byatt, A.S. (2001) *On Histories and Stories*. Cambridge, MA: Harvard University Press.

Caldwell, J.T. (2000) *Electronic Media and Technoculture*. New Brunswick: Rutgers University Press.

Calhoun, C.J. (1983) The radicalism of tradition, *American Journal of Sociology*, 88(5): 886–914.

Carrier, C. (2000) Places, politics and the archiving of contemporary memory, in S. Radstone (ed.) *Memory and Methodology*, pp. 37–58. Oxford: Berg.

Carruthers, M. (1990) *The Book of Memory: A Study of Medieval Culture.* Cambridge: Cambridge University Press.

Caser, H.A. (1996) Post-war Italian narratives: an alternative account, in D. Forgacs, and R. Lumley (eds) *Italian Cultural Studies*, pp. 248–60. Oxford: Oxford University Press.

Castells, M. (1997) *The Power of Identity.* Oxford: Polity Press.

Cerulo, K.A. (1997) Identity construction, *Annual Review of Sociology*, 23: 385–409.

Clendinnen, I. (2000) *Tiger's Eye.* Melbourne: Text.

Clifford, M. (2001) *Political Genealogy After Foucault.* New York: Routledge.

Cohen, D. (2001) The rhetoric of justice: strategies of reconciliation and revenge in the restoration of Athenian democracy in 403 BC, *European Journal of Sociology*, XLII (2): 335–56.

Cohen, S.B. (1983) Representing authority in Victorian India, in E. Hobsbawm and T. Ranger (eds) *The Invention of Tradition*, pp. 165–210. Cambridge: Cambridge University Press.

Cohen, S.J. (1999) *Politics Without Past.* Durham, NC: Duke University Press.

Collini, S. (1999) *English Past.* Oxford: Oxford University Press.

Collins, R. (1988) The theoretical continuities in Goffman's work, in A. Drew and A. Wooton (eds) *Erving Goffman: Exploring the Interaction Order*, pp. 41–63. Oxford: Polity Press.

Comaroff, J. and Stern, M. (1994) New perspectives on nationalism and war, *Theory and Society*, 23(1): 147–50.

Confino, A. (1997) Collective memory and cultural history: problems and method, *American Historical Review*, December: 1386–405.

Connerton, P. (1989) *How Societies Remember.* Cambridge: Cambridge University Press.

Conway, M.A. (1997) The inventory of experience, in J.W. Pennebaker, D. Paez and B. Rime (eds) *Collective Memory of Political Events*, pp. 21–46. Mahwah, NJ: Lawrence Erlbaum.

Cook, J. (1999) The techno-university and knowledge, in B. Mieke and H. de Vries (eds) *Cultural Memory in the Present*, pp. 303–26. Stanford, CA: Stanford University Press.

Coser, L.A. (1992) Introduction, in L.A. Coser (ed.) *Maurice Halbwachs: On Collective Memory*, pp. 1–36. Chicago: University of Chicago Press.

Crane, S.A. (ed.) (2000a) *Museum and Memory.* Stanford, CA: Stanford University Press.

Crane, S.A. (2000b) Introduction: on museum and memory, in S.A. Crane (ed.) *Museum and Memory*, pp. 1–17. Stanford, CA: Stanford University Press.

Creeber, G. (2001) Taking our personal lives seriously: intimacy, continuity and memory in the television drama serial, *Media, Culture and Society*, 23(4): 439–55.

Cressy, D. (1994) National memory in early England, in J.R. Gillis (ed.) *Commemorations: The Politics of National Identity*, pp. 61–73. Princeton, NJ: Princeton University Press.

Culbertson, R. (1995) Embodied memory, transcendence, and telling: recounting trauma, re-establishing the self, *New Literary History*, 26: 169–95.

Evans, M. and Lunn, K. (eds) (1997) *War and Memory in the Twentieth Century.* Oxford: Berg.

Damousi, J. (2002) *Living with the Aftermath*. Cambridge: Cambridge University Press.

Davis, C. (1999) Reviewing memory: Wiesel, testimony and self-reading, in H. Peitsch, C. Burdett and C. Gorra (eds) *European Memories of the Second World War*, pp. 122–9. Oxford: Berghahn Books.

Davis, J. (1989) The social relations of the production of history, in E. Tonkin, M. McDonald and M. Chapman (eds) *History and Ethnicity*, pp. 104–20. London: Routledge.

Davis, N.Z. and Starn, E. (1989) Introduction to special issue on memory, *Representations*, 25(Spring): 2–6.

de Man, P. (1970) Literary history and literary modernity, *Daedalus*, 90: 384–404.

de Tocqueville, A. (1968) *Democracy in America*, vol. 2. London: Fontana.

Debouzy, M. (1986) In search of working-class memory, *History and Anthropology*, 2: 261–82.

DiMaggio, P. (1997) Culture and cognition, *Annual Review of Sociology*, 23: 263–83.

Douglas, M. (1986) *How Institutions Think*. Syracuse, NY: Syracuse University Press.

Draaisma, D. (2000) *Metaphors of Memory: A History of Ideas About Mind*. Cambridge: Cambridge University Press.

Duby, G. (1988) Solitude: eleventh to thirteenth century, in G. Duby (ed.) *A History of Private Life*, vol. 2, pp. 619–20. Cambridge, MA: Harvard University Press.

Durkheim, E. ([1893] 1964) *The Division of Labour in Society*. New York: Free Press.

Durkheim, E. ([1912] 1965) *Elementary Forms of the Religious Life*. New York: Free Press.

Durkheim, E. ([1925] 1973) *Moral Education*. New York: Free Press.

Eisenstein, E. (1966) Clio and chronosm, *History and Theory*, 6: 36–64.

Eley, G. (1997) Foreword, in M. Evans and K. Lunn (eds) *War and Memory in the Twentieth Century*, pp. vii–xiv. Oxford: Berg.

Ellias, N. (1992) *Time: An Essay*. Oxford: Blackwell.

Elster, J. (1989) *The Cement of Society*. Cambridge: Cambridge University Press.

Elster, J. (1998) Coming to terms with the past, *European Journal of Sociology*, XXXIX(1): 7–48.

Ensalaco, M. (1994) Truth commission for Chile and El Salvador: a report and assessment, *Human Rights Quarterly*, 16: 656–75.

Evans, J. (1999) Introduction: nation and representation, in D. Bowell and J. Evans (eds) *Representing the Nation: A Reader*, pp. 1–9. London: Routledge.

Evans, M. and Lunn, K. (eds) (1997) *War and Memory in the Twentieth Century*. Oxford: Berg.

Evans-Pritchard, E.E. (1968) *The Nuer*. Oxford: Clarendon Press.

Eyerman, R. and Turner, B. (1998) Outline of a theory of generations, *European Journal of Social Theory*, 1(1): 91–106.

Farmer, S. (2000) Postwar justice in France: Bordeaux, in I. Deak, J.T. Gross and T. Judt (eds) *The Politics of Retribution in Europe*, pp. 194–211. Princeton NJ: Princeton University Press.

Fentress, J. and Wickham, C. (1992) *Social Memory*. Oxford: Blackwell.

Fine, G. (1996) Reputational entrepreneurs and the memory of incompetence, *American Journal of Sociology*, 101: 1159–93.

Finkelstein, N.G. (2000) *The Holocaust Industry: Reflection on the Exploitations of Jewish Suffering*. London: Verso.

Finkenauer, C., Gisle, L. and Luminet, O. (1997) When individual memories are specially shaped, in J.W. Pennebaker, D. Paez and B. Rime (eds) *Collective Memory of Political Events*, pp. 191–208. Mahwah, NJ: Lawrence Erlbaum.

Finkielkraut, A. (1989) *Remembering in Vain: The Klaus Barbie Trial and Crimes against Humanity*. New York: Columbia University Press.

Flood, S. (1994) *Mabo: A Symbol of Sharing. The High Court Judgment Examined*. Glebe, NSW: Fink.

Fortier, A-M. (2000) *Migrant Belongings. Memory, Space Identity*. Oxford: Berg.

Foucault, M. (1976) *The History of Sexuality*, vol. 1, trans. R. Hurley. New York: Random House.

Foucault, M. (1977) *Language, Counter-memory, Practice: Selected Essays and Interviews*, ed. Donald F. Bouchard and Sherry Simon. Ithaca, NY: Cornell University Press.

Foucault, M. (1978) Politics and the study of discourse, *Ideology and Consciousness*, 3: 3–26.

Freud, S. (1966) *Psychopathology of Everyday Life*. London: Ernest Benn.

Freud, S. (1984) *On Metapsychology: The Theory of Psychoanalysis*. Harmondsworth: Pelican.

Friedland, R. and Boden, D. (1994) NowHere: an Introduction, in R. Friedland and D. Boden (eds) *NowHere: Space, Time and Modernity*, pp. 1–60. Berkeley, CA: University of California Press.

Friedlander, S. (1993) *Memory, History and the Extermination of the Jews of Europe*. Bloomington, IN: Indiana University Press.

Friedlander, S. and Seligman, A.B (1994) The Israeli memory of the Shoah: on symbols, rituals and ideological polarization, in R. Friedland and D. Boden (eds) *NowHere: Space, Time and Modernity*, pp. 356–7. Berkeley, CA: University of California Press.

Frijda, N.H. (1997): Commemorating, in J.W. Pennebaker, D. Paez and B. Rime (eds) *Collective Memory of Political Events*, pp. 103–31. Mahwah, NJ: Lawrence Erlbaum.

Funkenstein, A. (1993) *Perception of Jewish History*. Berkeley, CA: University of California Press.

Fussell, P. (1975) *The Great War and Modern Memory*: New York: Oxford University Press.

Gadamer, H.G. (1975) *Truth and Method*. London: Sheed & Ward.

Gaskel, G.D. and Wright, D.B. (1997) Group differences in memory for a political event, in J.W. Pennebaker, D. Paez and B. Rime (eds) *Collective Memory of Political Events*, pp. 175–90. Mahwah, NJ: Lawrence Erlbaum.

Gedi, N. and Elam, Y. (1996) Collective memory – what is it? *History and Memory*, 8(1): 30–50.

Geertz, C. (1973) *The Interpretation of Cultures*. New York: Basic Books.

Gellner E. (1965) *Thought and Change*. Chicago: University of Chicago Press.

Gellner, E. (1993) *Nations and Nationalism*. Oxford: Blackwell.

Giddens, A. (1981) *A Contemporary Critique of Historical Materialism*. Berkeley, CA: University of California Press.
Giddens, A. (1984) *The Constitution of Society*. Oxford: Polity Press.
Giddens, A. (1991) *Modernity and Self-Identity*. Oxford: Polity Press.
Giddens, A. (1992) *The Transformation of Intimacy: Sexuality, Love, and Eroticism in Modern Societies*. Cambridge: Polity Press.
Giddens, A. (1999) *Tradition*. BBC Reith Lectures 3, BBC onLine network: http://news.bbc.co.uk/hi/english/static/events/reith_99/week 3/week3.htm
Gillis, J.R. (ed.) (1994a) *Commemorations: The Politics of National Identity*. Princeton, NJ: Princeton University Press.
Gillis, J.R. (1994b) Introduction: memory and identity, in J.R. Gillis (ed.) *Commemorations: The Politics of National Identity*, pp. 3–26. Princeton, NJ: Princeton University Press.
Gilloch, G. (1996) *Myth and Metropolis: Walter Benjamin and the City*. Oxford: Polity Press.
Ginzburg, V. (1994) Fiction as historical evidence, in M.S. Roth (ed.) *Rediscovering History: Culture, Politics, and the Psyche*, pp. 378–88. Stanford, CA: Stanford University Press.
Goffman, E. (1959) *The Presentation of Self in Everyday Life*. Hamondsworth: Penguin.
Goffman, E. (1974) *Frame Analysis: An Essay on Face-to Face Behaviour*. New York: Harper & Row.
Goffman, E. (1983) The interaction order, *American Sociological Review*, 48 (February): 1–17.
Goody, J. (1977) *The Domestication of the Savage Mind*. Cambridge: Cambridge University Press.
Goody, J. (1998) Memory in oral tradition, in P. Fara and K. Patterson (eds) *Memory*, pp. 73–94. Cambridge: Cambridge University Press.
Goody, J.R. and Watt, I. (1968) The consequences of literacy, in J. Goody (ed.) *Literacy in Traditional Societies*, pp. 27–84. Cambridge: Cambridge University Press.
Gordon, R. (1999) Primo Levi, the duty of memory, in H. Peitsch, C. Burdett and C. Gorra (eds) *European Memories of the Second World War*, pp. 130–40. Oxford: Berghahn Books.
Gray, P. and Oliver, K. (2001) The memory of catastrophe, *History Today*, 5: 9–19.
Gross, D. (1993) Rethinking tradition, *Telos*, Winter: 5–10.
Gross, J.T. (2000) Themes for a social history of war experience, in I. Deak, J.T. Gross and T. Judt (eds) *The Politics of Retribution in Europe*, pp. 15–37. Princeton, NJ: Princeton University Press.
Gunn Allen, P. (1999) Who is your mother? Red roots of white feminism, in C. Lemert (ed.) *Social Theory: The Multicultural and Classic Readings*, pp. 585–594. Boulder CO: Westview.
Gutmann, A. (1999) Liberty and pluralism in pursuit of the non-ideal, *Social Research*, 66(4): 1039–53.
Habermas, J. (1996) *Between Facts and Norms: Contributions to a Discourse Theory of Law and Democracy*, trans. W. Rehg. Oxford: Polity Press.
Habermas, J. (1997) *A Berlin Republic: Writing on Germany*, trans. S. Rendall. Lincoln, NE: University of Nebraska Press.

Hacking, I. (1995) *Rewriting the Soul*. Princeton, NJ: Princeton University Press.

Hacking, I. (1996) Memory sciences, memory politics, in P. Antze and M. Lambek (eds) *Tense Past: Cultural Essays in Trauma and Memory*, pp. 67–88. London: Routledge.

Halbwachs, M. ([1926] 1950) *The Collective Memory*, trans. F.J. and V.Y. Ditter. London: Harper Colophon Books.

Halbwachs, M. (1941) *La Topographie Legendarie de Evangiles en Teore Sainte*. Paris: Presses de Universitaires de France.

Halbwachs, M. ([1926] 1992) *On Collective Memory*. Chicago: Chicago University Press.

Hamer, H. (1994) Identity, process and reinterpretation, *Anthropos*, 89: 190–1.

Harper, S. (1997). Popular film, popular memory: the case of the second war, in M. Evans and K. Lunn (eds) *War and Memory in the Twentieth Century*, pp. 163–76. Oxford: Berg.

Hartman, G.H. (1986) Introduction, in G.H. Hartman (ed.) *Bitburg in Moral and Political Perspective*. Bloomington, IN: Indiana University Press.

Hassard, J. (ed.) (1990) *The Sociology of Time*. London: Macmillan.

Hayner, P.B. (1994) Fifteen truth commissions – 1974 to 1994: a comparative study. *Human Rights Quarterly*, 16: 597–655.

Heelas, P. (1996) *The New Age Movement: The Celebration of the Self and the Sacrilization of Modernity*. Oxford: Blackwell.

Heller, A. (1999) *A Theory of Modernity*. Oxford: Blackwell.

Heller, A. (2001) A tentative answer of the question: has civil society cultural memory?, *Social Research*, 68(4): 103–42.

Herf, J. (1997) *Divided Memory: The Nazi Past in the Two Germanys*. Cambridge, MA: Harvard University Press.

Hervieu-Leger, D. (2000) *Religion as a Chain of Memory*. Oxford: Polity Press.

Hewison, R. (1987) *Heritage Industry*. London: Methuen.

Hewison, R. (1999) The climate of decline, in D. Bowell and J. Evans (eds) *Representing the Nation: A Reader*, pp. 151–62. London: Routledge.

Hirsch, M. (1997) *Family Frames: Photography, Narrative, and Postmemory*. Cambridge, MA: MIT Press.

Hobsbawm, E. (1983) Introduction: inventing traditions, in E. Hobsbawm and T. Ranger (eds) *The Invention of Tradition*, pp. 1–14. Cambridge: Cambridge University Press.

Hobsbawm, E. and Ranger, T. (eds) (1983) *The Invention of Tradition*. New York: Cambridge University Press.

Hoepken, W. (1999) War, memory and education in a fragmented society: the case of Yugoslavia, *East European Politics and Societies*, 13(1): 190–227.

Holmes, S. (1995) The end of decommunization, in N.J. Kritz (ed.) *Transitional Justice*, vol. 1, pp. 116–20. Washington, DC.: United States Institute for Peace.

Holub, R.C. (1994) Habermas among the Americans, *German Politics and Society*, 12(3): 1–23.

Hosking, G.A. (1989) Memory in a totalitarian society, in T. Butler (ed.) *Memory, History, Culture and the Mind*, pp. 97–114. Oxford: Blackwell.

Huntington, S. (1991) *The Third Wave: Democratisation in the late Twentieth Century*. Norman, OK: University of Oklahoma Press.

Hutton, P. (1988) Collective memory and collective mentalities, *Historical Reflections*, 15(2): 311–22.

Hutton, P. (1993) *History as an Art of Memory*. Hanover, VT: University Press of New England.

Huyse, L. (1995) Justice after Transition, *Law and Social Enquiry*, 1: 51–78.

Huyssen, A. (1995) *Twilight Memories*. London: Routledge.

Igartua, J. and Paez, D. (1997) Art and remembering traumatic collective events, in J.W. Pennebaker, D. Paez and B. Rime (eds) *Collective Memory of Political Events*, pp. 79–130. Mahwah, NJ: Lawrence Erlbaum.

Ignatieff, M. (1996) *Blood and Belongings*. London: Primedia BBC Works.

Inglehart, R. (1999) Trust, well-being and democracy, in M.E. Warren (ed.) *Democracy and Trust*, pp. 88–120. Cambridge: Cambridge University Press.

Inglis, K. (2002) *Sacred Places: War Memorials in the Australian Landscape*. Melbourne: Melbourne University Press.

Innes, M. (1988) Memory, orality and literacy in an early medieval society, *Past and Present*, 158: 3–37.

Irwin-Zarecka, I. (1993) In search of usable past, *Society*, 30(2): 21–5.

Irwin-Zarecka, I. (1994) *Frames of Remembrance*, New Brunswick: Transactions Book.

Isbister, J.N. (1985) *Freud: An Introduction to His Life and Work*. New York: Basic Books.

Jedlecki, J. (1999) Historical memory as a source of conflicts in eastern Europe, *Communist and Post-Communist Studies*, 32: 225–32.

Jeffery, A. (1999) *The Truth About the Truth Commission*, Johannesburg: South African Race Relations.

Joas, H. (1997) *G.H. Mead: A Contemporary Re-examination of His Thought*. Cambridge, MA: MIT Press.

Johns, A. (1998) *The Nature of the Book: The Print Knowledge in the Making*. Chicago: Chicago University Press.

Johnson, R., McLennan, G., Schwarz, B. and Sutton, D. (eds) (1982) *Making Histories: Studies in History Writing and Politics*. London: Hutchinson.

Johnson, R.W. (1999) Why there is no easy way to dispose of painful history, *London Review of Books*, 14 October: 9–14.

Kammen, M. (1995a) Review of *Frames of Remembrance, History and Theory*, 34(3): 245–66.

Kammen, M. (1995b) Some patterns and meanings of memory, in D.L. Schacter (ed.) *Memory Distortion*, pp. 329–44. Cambridge, MA: Harvard University Press.

Kartiel, T. (1999) The past in Israeli pioneering museums, in D. Ben-Amos and D. Weissberg (eds) *Cultural Memory and the Construction of Identity*, pp. 99–135. Detroit, MI: Wayne State University Press.

Keneally, T. (1994) *Schindler's List*. London: Sceptre.

Kertzer, D.I. (1983) Generation as a sociological problem, *Annual Review of Sociology*, 9: 125–49.

Kirmayer, L.J. (1996) Landscapes of memory, in P. Antze and M. Lambek (eds) *Tense Past: Cultural Essays in Trauma and Memory*, pp. 173–98. London: Routledge.

Klein, K. (2000) On the emergence of memory in historical discourse, *Representations*, Winter: 127–53.

Koonz, C. (1994) Between memory and oblivion: concentration camps in German memory, in J.R. Gillis (ed.) *Commemorations: The Politics of National Identity*, pp. 258–80. Princeton, NJ: Princeton University Press.

Koselleck, R. (2001) The reasons for the upsurge of memory. www.iwm.at/a_cor103.htm

Koshar, R. (1994) *From Monuments to Traces: Artifacts of German Memory, 1870–1990*. Berkeley, CA: California University Press.

Kritz, N.J. (1995) The dilemma of transitional justice, in N.J. Kritz (ed.) *Transitional Justice*, vol. 1, pp. xix–xxx. Washington, DC: United States Institute for Peace.

Kugelmass, J. (1996) Missions to the past: Poland in contemporary Jewish thought and deed, in P. Antze and M. Lambek (eds) *Tense Past: Cultural Essays in Trauma and Memory*, pp. 199–214. London: Routledge.

Kundera, M. (1980) *The Book of Laughter and Forgetting*. New York: King Penguin.

LaCapra, D. (1997) Revisiting the historians' debate, *History and Memory*, 9(1/2): 80–112.

Landsberg, A. (1997) America, the Holocaust, and the mass culture of memory, *New German Critique*, 71 (Spring–Summer): 63–86.

Lane, C. (1981) *The Rites of Rulers: Rituals in an Industrial Society*. Cambridge: Cambridge University Press.

Langer, L. (1995) *Admitting the Holocaust: Collected Essays*. Oxford: Oxford University Press.

Laqueur, T.W. (1994) Memory and naming in the Great War, in J.R. Gillis (ed.) *Commemorations: The Politics of National Identity*, pp. 150–66. Princeton, NJ: Princeton University Press.

Laqueur, T.W. (2000) Introduction, *Representations*, Winter: 1–7.

Lash, S. (1999) *Another Modernity: A Different Rationality*. Oxford: Blackwell.

Layder, D. (1994) *Understanding Social Theory*. London: Sage.

Le Goff, J. (1992) *History and Memory*, trans. S. Rendall and E. Claman. New York: Columbia University Press.

Leak, A. and Paizis, G. (eds) (1999) *The Holocaust and the Text: Speaking the Unspeakable*. London: Macmillan.

Levi, P. (1988) *The Drowned and the Saved*, trans. R. Rosenthal. New York: Summit Books.

Levi-Strauss, C. (1966) *The Savage Mind*. London: Weidenfeld & Nicolson.

Levy, D.S. and Sznaider, N. (2002) The Holocaust and the formation of cosmopolitan memory, *European Journal of Social Theory*, 5(1): 87–106.

Lewis, B. (1975) *History: Remembered, Recovered, Invented*. New York: Simon & Schuster.

Linz, J. and Stepan, A. (1997) *Problems of Democratic Transition and Consolidation: Southern Europe, South America and Post-Communist Europe*. Baltimore, MD: Johns Hopkins University Press.

Lipset, S.M. (1996) *American Exceptionalism: A Double-Edged Sword*. New York: W.W. Norton.

Lipsitz, G. (1990) *Time Passages: Collective Memory and American Popular Culture*. Minneapolis, MN: University of Minnesota Press.

Lipstadt, D. (1993) *Denying the Holocaust: The Growing Assault on Truth and Memory*. New York: Free Press.

Locke, J. ([1690] 1975) *An Essay Concerning Human Understanding*. Oxford: Clarendon Press.
Loewen, J. (1995) *Lies My Teacher Told Me: Everything Your American Textbooks Got Wrong*. New York: New Press.
Los, M. (1995) Lustration and truth claims: unfinished revolution in Central Europe, *Law and Social Inquiry*, 20(1): 117–62.
Lowenthal, D. (1985) *The Past is a Foreign Country*. Cambridge: Cambridge University Press.
Lowenthal, D. (1994) Identity, heritage and history, in J.R. Gillis (ed.) *Commemorations: The Politics of National Identity*, pp. 40–57. Princeton, NJ: Princeton University Press.
Lowenthal, D. (1998) *The Heritage Crusade and the Spoils of History*. Cambridge: Cambridge University Press.
Luban, D. (1987) The legacies of Nuremberg, *Social Research*, 54(4): 62–87.
Luke, T.W. (1996) Identity, meaning and globalization, in P. Heelas, S. Lash and P. Morris (eds) *Detraditionalization: Critical Reflections on Authority and Identity*, pp. 109–33. Oxford: Blackwell.
Lyotard. J.F. (1988) *The Postmodern Condition: A Report on Knowledge*, trans. G. Bennington. Manchester: Manchester University Press.
Macdonald, S. (1996) Theorizing museums: an introduction, in S. Macdonald and G. Fyfe (eds) *Theorizing Memory*, 1–20. Oxford: Blackwell.
Maier, C.S. (1988) *The Unmasterable Past: History, Holocaust and German National Identity*. Cambridge, MA: Harvard University Press.
Maier, C.S. (1993) A surfeit of memory: Reflection on history, melancholy and denial, *History and Memory*, 5: 136–51.
Maier, C.S. (2001) 'Hot' memory and 'cold' memory: on the political half-life of nazism and communism. IWM Lectures in Human Sciences, http://univie.ac.at/iwm/a-human.htm
Mannheim, K. (1952) *Ideology and Utopia*. New York: Harvest HBJ.
Mannheim, K. (1972) *Essays on the Sociology of Knowledge*. London: Routledge.
Marias, J. (1970) *Generations. A Historical Method*. Tuscaloosa, AL: Alabama University Press.
Marx, K. ([1852] 1973) The Eighteenth Brumaire of Louis Bonaparte, trans. B. Fowkes, in K. Marx (ed.) *Surveys from Exile*, pp. 143–249. London: Lawrence & Wishart.
Mason, J.W. (2000) Hungary's battle for memory, *History Today*, 50(3): 28–34.
Matsuda, M.K. (1996) *The Memory of the Modern*. New York: Oxford University Press.
McAdams, A.J. (2001) *Judging the Past in Unified Germany*. Cambridge: Cambridge University Press.
McConkey, J. (ed.) (1996) *The Anatomy of Memory: An Anthology*. New York: Oxford University Press.
McLuhan, M. (1962) *Gutenberg Galaxy: The Making of Typographic Man*. Toronto: Toronto University Press.
Mead, G.H. (1929) The nature of the past, in J. Coss (ed.) *Essays in Honor of John Dewey*, pp. 235–42. New York: Henry Holt.
Mead, G.H. (1932) *The Philosophy of the Present*. LaSalle, IL: Open Court Publishing.

Mead, G.H. (1938) *The Philosophy of Act.* Chicago: University of Chicago Press.

Megill, A. (1999) History, memory and identity, *History of the Human Sciences,* 11(3): 37–62.

Melling, P. (1997) War and memory in the New World Order, in M. Evans and K. Lunn (eds) *War and Memory in the Twentieth Century,* pp. 255–68. Oxford: Berg.

Merridale, C. (1999) War, death and remembrance in Soviet Russia, in J. Winter and E. Sivan (eds) *War and Remembrance in the Twentieth Century,* pp. 61–83. Cambridge: Cambridge University Press.

Michaels, W.B. (1996) You who never was there: Slavery and the new historicism, deconstruction and Holocaust, *Narrative,* 4: 5–29.

Middleton, D. and Edwards, D. (1988) Conversation, remembering and family relationships: how children learn to remember, *Journal of Social and Personal Relationships,* 5: 3–25.

Milosz, C. (2001) *New and Collected Poems.* New York: Penguin.

Misztal, B.A. (1996) *Trust in Modern Societies.* Oxford: Polity Press.

Misztal, B.A. (1999) How not to deal with the past, *European Journal of Sociology,* XL(1): 31–55.

Misztal, B.A. (2001) Legal attempts to construct collective memory, *Polish Sociological Review,* 133(1): 61–76.

Mitchell, J. (1998) Memory and psychoanalysis, in P. Fara and K. Patterson (eds) *Memory,* pp. 95–112. Cambridge: Cambridge University Press.

Modejska, D. (2000) Refreshing the memory, *The Australian Review of Books,* August: 5–6 and 26.

Morgan, R. (1999) Collective memory and foreign policy, *Government and Opposition,* 27(4): 429–32.

Morrison, T. (1990) *Out There.* Cambridge: MA: MIT Press.

Mosse, G.L. (1990) *Fallen Soldiers: Reshaping the Memory of the World Wars.* Oxford: Oxford University Press.

Neal, A.G. (1998) *National Traumas and Collective Memory: Major Events in the American Century.* New York: Sharpe.

Neisser, U. (1982) Memory: what are the important questions? in U. Neisser (ed.) *Memory Observed: Remembering in Natural Context,* pp. 3–19. San Francisco: W.H. Freeman.

Nietzsche, F.W (1969) *On the Genealogy of Morals,* trans. W. Kaufmann. New York: Vintage.

Nietszche, F.W. (1980) *On the Advantage and Disadvantage of History for Life.* New York: Hackett.

Nietzsche F.W. (1983) *Untimely Meditations,* trans. R.J. Hollingdale. Cambridge, MA: Cambridge University Press.

Nisbet, R.A. (1966) *The Sociological Tradition.* London: Heinemann.

Noakes, L. (1997) Making histories: experiencing the Blitz in London's museums in the 1990s, in M. Evans and K. Lunn (eds) *War and Memory in the Twentieth Century,* pp. 89–103. Oxford: Berg.

Nora, P. (1989) Between memory and history, *Representations,* 26 (Spring): 7–25.

Nora, P. (ed.) (1996a) *Realms of Memory,* vols 1–3, trans. A. Goldhammer. New York: Columbia University Press.

Nora, P. (1996b) General introduction: between memory and history, in P. Nora (ed.) *Realms of Memory*, vol. 1, trans. A. Goldhammer, pp. 1–20. New York: Columbia University Press.

Nora, P. (1996c) Generation, in P. Nora (ed.) *Realms of Memory*, vol. 1, trans. A. Goldhammer, pp. 499–531. New York: Columbia University Press.

Nora, P. (2001) The reasons for the upsurge of memory. IWM Lectures in human sciences, http://univie.ac.at/iwm/a-human.htm.

Novick, P. (1999) *The Holocaust in American Life*. Boston, MA: Houghton Mifflin.

Novotny, H. (1994) *Time: The Modern and Postmodern Experiences*, trans. N. Plaice. Oxford: Polity Press.

Noyes, D. and Abrahams, R.D. (1999) From calendar to national memory: European commonplace, in D. Ben-Amos and D. Weissberg (eds) *Cultural Memory and the Construction of Identity*, pp. 77–98. Detroit, MI: Wayne State University Press.

Nussbaum, M.C. (2001) *Upheavals of Thought*. Cambridge: Cambridge University Press.

Nuttall, S. and Coetzee, C. (eds) (1998) *Negotiating the Past: The Making of Memory of South Africa*. Cape Town: Oxford University Press.

Oakeshott, M. (1983) *On History*. Cambridge: Blackwell.

Olick, J.K. (1999) Genre memories and memory genres, *American Sociological Review*, 64: 381–402.

Olick, J.K. and Levy, D. (1997) Collective memory and cultural constraint: Holocaust myth and rationality in German politics, *American Sociological Review*, 62: 927–36.

Olick, J.K. and Robbins, J. (1998) Social memory studies, *Annual Review of Sociology*, 24(1): 105–41.

Ong, W. (1983) *Ramus: Methods and the Decay of Dialogue: from the Art of Discourse to the Art of Reason*. Cambridge, MA: Harvard University Press.

Oretga y Gasset, J. ([1926] 1960) *The Revolt of Masses*. New York: Norton.

Osiel, M. (1997) *Mass Atrocity, Collective Memory and the Law*. New Brunswick: Transaction Publishers.

Ourdan, R. (2000) Elections deepen Bosnia's divisions, *Guardian Weekly*, 23 November: 31.

Ozouf, M. (1988) *Festivals and the French Revolution*. Cambridge, MA: Harvard University Press.

Paez, D., Basabe, N. and Gonzales, J.L. (1997) A cross-cultural approach to remembering, in J.W. Pennebaker, D. Paez and B. Rime (eds) *Collective Memory of Political Events*, pp. 147–74. Mahwah, NJ: Lawrence Erlbaum.

Parks, T. (2001) The luck of Letty Fox, *New York Review of Books*, 20 December: 90–3.

Passerini, L. (1979) Work ideology and consensus under Italian Fascism, *History Workshop*, Autumn: 88–9.

Passerini, L. (1987) *Fascism in Popular Memory: The Cultural Experience of the Turin Working Class*. Cambridge: Cambridge University Press.

Payne, D.G. and Blackwell, J.M. (1998) Truth in memory: caveat emptor, in S.J. Lynn and K.M. McConkey (eds) *Truth in Memory*, pp. 32–47. New York: Guilford Press.

Pearce, S.M. (1992) *Museums, Objects and Collections: A Cultural Study*. Leicester: Leicester University.

Pearson, R. (1999) Custer loses again: the contestation over commodified public memory, in D. Ben-Amos and D. Weissberg (eds) *Cultural Memory and the Construction of Identity*, pp. 176–201. Detroit, MI: Wayne State University Press.

Peitsch, H., Burdett, C. and Gorra, C. (eds) (1999) *European Memories of the Second World War*. Oxford: Berghahn Books.

Pennebaker, J.W. and Banasik, B.L. (1997) On the creation and maintenance of collective memory, in J.W. Pennebaker, D. Paez and B. Rime (eds) *Collective Memory of Political Events*, pp. 3–20. Mahwah, NJ: Lawrence Erlbaum.

Piccone, P. (1993) Introduction: symposium on 'The Past in Ruins', *Telos*, Winter: 3–4.

Pickering, W.S.F. (1998) Introduction, in N.J. Allen, W.S.F. Pickering and W. Watts Miller (eds) *On Durkheim's Elementary Forms of Religious Life*, pp. 1–12. London: Routledge.

Plicher, J. (1994) Mannheim's sociology of generation: an undervalued legacy, *British Sociology*, 45(3): 481–95.

Plumb, J.H. (1969) *The Death of the Past*. London: Macmillan.

Polanyi, M. (1958) *The Study of Man*. Chicago: University of Chicago Press.

Polanyi, M. (1967) *The Tacit Dimension*. New York: Doubleday.

Polanyi, M. (1969) *Knowing and Being*. London: Routledge.

Popular Memory Group (1982) Popular memory: theory, politics and method, in R. Johnson, G. Mclennan, B. Schwartz and D. Sutton (eds) *Making Histories: Studies in History Making and Politics*, pp. 205–52. London: Hutchinson.

Prager, J. (1998): *Presenting the Past: Psychoanalysis and the Sociology of Misremembering*. Cambridge, MA: Harvard University Press.

Price D.W. (1999) *History Made, History Imagined*. Urbana, IL: University of Illinois Press.

Proust, M. ([1922] 1989) *Remembrance of Things Past*, trans. C.K. Scott Moncrieff and T. Kilmartin. Harmondsworth: Penguin.

Radstone, S. (2000) Working with memory: an introduction, in S. Radstone (ed.) *Memory and Methodology*, pp. 1–24. Oxford: Berg.

Ranger, T. (1983) The invention of tradition in Africa, in E. Hobsbawm and T. Ranger (eds) *The Invention of Tradition*, pp. 211–62. Cambridge: Cambridge University Press.

Ray, L.J. (1999) Memory, trauma and genocidal nationalism, *Sociological Research Online*, 4(2), www.socresonline.org.uk.

Renan, E. ([1882] 1990) What is a nation? in H.K. Bhabha (ed.) *Nation and Narration*. London: Routledge.

Reynolds, H. (2000) The public role of history, *Dissent*, Spring: 2–5.

Ricoeur, P. (1986) *Time and Narrative*. Chicago: Chicago University Press.

Ricoeur, P. (1999) Memory and forgetting, in R. Kearney and M. Dooley (eds) *Questioning Ethics*, pp. 5–12. London: Routledge.

Ricoeur, P. (2001) History and memory. IWM Lectures in Human Sciences, http://univie.ac.at/iwm/a-human.htm.

Rieff, P. (1979) *Freud: The Mind of the Moralist*. Chicago: Chicago University Press.

Rime, B. and Christophe, V. (1997) How individual emotional episodes feed collective memory, in J.W. Pennebaker, D. Paez and B. Rime (eds) *Collective Memory of Political Events*, pp. 131–46. Mahwah, NJ: Lawrence Erlbaum.

Rittnar, C. and Roth, J.K. (1993) *Memory Offended: The Auschwitz Convent Controversy.* New York: Praeger.

Rojek, C. (1999) Fatal attractions, in D. Bowell and J. Evans (eds) *Representing the Nation: A Reader,* pp. 208–32. London: Routledge.

Rosen, N. (1974) The Holocaust and the American-Jewish novelist, *Midstream,* 20(3): 54–62.

Rosenberg, T. (1995) *The Haunted Land.* New York: Random House.

Roth, M.S. (1995) *The Ironist's Cage: Memory, Trauma and the Construction of History.* New York: Columbia University Press.

Rousso, H. (1991) *The Vichy Syndrome.* Cambridge, MA: Harvard University Press.

Rubin, D.C. (1988) Introduction, in D.C. Rubin (ed.) *Autobiographical Memory,* pp. 1–18. Cambridge: Cambridge University Press.

Rubin, D.D., Rahhal, T. and Poon, L.W. (1998) Things learned in early adulthood are remembered best, *Memory and Cognition,* 26: 3–19.

Rushdie, S. (1980) *Midnight's Children.* New York: Penguin.

Sa'dah, A. (1998) *Germany's Chance: Trust, Justice and Democratisation.* Cambridge, MA: Harvard University Press.

Sabel, C.F. (1993) Studied trust: building new forms, in R. Swedberg (ed.) *Explorations in Economic Sociology,* pp. 103–43. New York: Russell Sage.

Samuel, R. (ed.) (1981) *People's History and Socialist Theory.* London: Routledge & Kegan Paul.

Samuel, R. (1994) *Theatres of Memory,* vol. 1: *Past and Present in Contemporary Culture.* London: Verso.

Samuel, R. (1999) Resurrectionism, in D. Bowell and J. Evans (eds) *Representing the Nation: A Reader,* pp. 163–84. London: Routledge.

Sandage, S. (1993) A marble house divided: the Lincoln memorial, the civil rights movement, and the politics of memory: 1939–1963, *Journal of American History,* 800(1): 135–67.

Sartre, P. (1972) *The Psychology of Imagination,* trans. H. Barnes. London: Methuen.

Savage, K. (1994) The politics of memory: black emancipation and the civil war monument, in J.R. Gillis (ed.) *Commemorations: The Politics of National Identity,* pp. 127–47. Princeton, NJ: Princeton University Press.

Schachtel, E.G. (1982) On memory and childhood amnesia, in U. Neisser (ed.) *Memory Observed,* pp. 1–26. San Francisco: W.H. Freeman.

Schacter, D.L. (1996) *Searching for Memory: The Brain, The Mind, and The Past.* New York: Basic Books.

Schama, S. (1995) *Landscape and Memory.* New York: Alfred A. Knopf.

Schudson, M. (1989) The present in the past versus the past in the present, *Communication,* 11: 105–13.

Schudson, M. (1992) *Watergate in American Memory.* New York: Basic Books.

Schudson, M. (1995) Distortion in collective memory, in D.L. Schacter (ed.) *Memory Distortion,* pp. 346–63. Cambridge MA: Harvard University Press.

Schudson, M. (1997) Lives, laws and language: commemorative versus non-commemorative forms of effective public memory, *The Communication Review,* 2(1): 3–17.

Schuman, H. and Corning, A.D. (2000) Collective knowledge of public events: the Soviet era from the Great Purge to Glasnost, *American Journal of Sociology,* 105(4): 913–43.

Schuman, H. and Scott, J. (1989) Generations and collective memories, *American Sociological Review*, 54 (June): 359–81.

Schuman, H., Belli, R.F. and Bischoping, K. (1997) The generational basis of historical knowledge, in J.W. Pennebaker, D. Paez and B. Rime (eds) *Collective Memory of Political Events*, pp. 47–78. Mahwah, NJ: Lawrence Erlbaum.

Schwartz, B. (1982) The social context of commemoration: a study in collective memory, *Social Forces*, 61(2): 374–402.

Schwartz, B. (1990) The reconstruction of Abraham Lincoln, in D. Middleton and D. Edwards (eds) *Collective Remembering*, pp. 108–20. London: Sage.

Schwartz, B. (1996) Introduction: the expanding past, *Qualitative Sociology*, 9(3): 275–82.

Schwartz, B. (2000) *Abraham Lincoln and the Forge of National Memory*. Chicago: Chicago University Press.

Schwartz, B., Zerubavel, Y. and Barnett, B. (1986) The recovery of Masada: a study in collective memory, *Sociological Quarterly*, 127(2): 164–74.

Schwartz, H. (1995) Lustration in eastern Europe, in N.J. Kritz (ed.) *Transitional Justice*, vol. 1, pp. 461–83. Washington, DC: United States Institute of Peace Press.

Sennett, R. (1998) Disturbing memories, in P. Fara and K. Patterson (eds) *Memory*, pp. 10–46. Cambridge: Cambridge University Press.

Sherman, D.J. (1994) Art, commerce and the production of memory in France after World War I, in J.R. Gillis (ed.) *Commemorations: The Politics of National Identity*, pp. 186–213. Princeton, NJ: Princeton University Press.

Sherman, D.J. (1999) *The Construction of Memory in Interwar France*. Chicago: Chicago University Press.

Shils, E. (1981) *Tradition*. Chicago: University of Chicago Press.

Shotter, J. (1990) The social construction of remembering and forgetting, in D. Middleton and D. Edwards (eds) *Collective Remembering*, pp. 120–38. London: Sage.

Sicher, E. (2000) Countermemory and postmemory in contemporary American post-Holocaust narratives, *History and Memory*, 12(2): 56–87.

Sider, G. and Smith, G. (1997) Introduction, in G. Sider and G. Smith (eds) *Between History and Histories: The Making of Silences and Commemorations*, pp. 1–31. Toronto: University of Toronto Press.

Silverman, M. (1999) *Facing Postmodernity*. London: Routledge.

Skutlans, V. (1998) *The Testimony of Lives*. London: Routledge.

Smith, A.D. (1986) *The Ethnic Origins of Nations*. Oxford: Blackwell.

Smith, A.D. (1997) The 'Golden Age' and national renewal, in G.A. Hosking and G. Schopflin (eds) *Myths and Nationhood*, pp. 36–59. London: Hurst & Company.

Sontag, S. (2001) In Plato's cave, in J. Thomas (ed.) *Reading Images*, pp. 40–53. New York: Palgrave.

Spillman, L. (1997) *Nation and Commemoration*. Cambridge: Cambridge University Press.

Sturken, M. (1997) *Tangled Memories: The Vietnam War, the AIDS Epidemic, and the Politics of Remembering*. Berkeley, CA: University of California.

Sutton, J. (1998) *Philosophy and Memory Traces*, Cambridge: Cambridge University Press.

Swidler, A. (1986) Culture in action, *American Sociological Review*, 51: 273–86.

Swidler, A. and Arditi, J. (1994) The new sociology of knowledge, *Annual Review of Sociology*, 20: 305–29.

Szacka, B. (1997) Systematic transformation and memory of the past, *Polish Sociological Review*, 118(2): 119–32.

Szacki, J. (1971) *Tradition*. Warsaw: PWN.

Szacki, J. (1992) *Dilemmas of the History of Ideas and Other Essays*. Warsaw: PWN.

Taylor, C. (1989) *Sources of the Self: The Making of the Modern Identity*. Ithaca, NY: Cornell University Press.

Taylor, T. (1971) *Nuremberg and Vietnam: An American Tragedy*, New York: Bantam.

Terdiman, R. (1993) *Present Past: Modernity and the Memory Crisis*. Ithaca, NY: Cornell University Press.

Tester, K. (1999) The moral consequentiality of television, *European Journal of Social Theory*, 2(4): 469–84.

Thompson, J.B. (1996) Tradition and self in a mediated world, in P. Heelas, S. Lash and P. Morris (eds) *Detraditionalization: Critical Reflections on Authority and Identity*, pp. 89–108. Oxford: Blackwell.

Thompson, K. (1998) Durkheim and sacred identity, in N.J.B. Allen, W.S.F. Pickering and W. Watts Miller (eds) *On Durkheim's Elementary Forms of Religious Life*, pp. 92–104. London: Routledge.

Thomson, A. (1994) *Anzac Memories: Living with the Legend*. Melbourne: Oxford University Press.

Todorov, T. (1996) The abuse of memory, *Common Knowledge*, 6(22): 6–26.

Tonkin, E. (1992) *Narrating Our Past*. Cambridge: Cambridge University Press.

Tosh, J. (1991) *The Pursuit of History*. London: Longman.

Touraine, A. (2000) *Can We Live Together? Equality and Difference*, trans. D. Macey. Stanford, CA: Stanford University Press.

Trigg, R. (2001) *Understanding Social Science*. Cambridge: Blackwell.

Trouillot, M.R. (1995) *Silencing the Past Power and the Production of History*. Boston, MA: Beacon Books.

Trucker, A. (1999) Paranoids may be persecuted, *European Journal of Sociology*, XL(1): 56–102.

Tulving, E. and Craik, F.I.M. (2000) Preface, in E. Tulving and F.I.M. Craik (eds) *The Oxford Handbook of Memory*, pp. i–vii. Oxford: Oxford University Press.

Urry, J. (1996) How societies remember the past, in S. Macdonald and G. Fyfe (eds) *Theorizing Memory*, pp. 45–68. Oxford: Blackwell.

Vansina, J. (1972) *Oral Tradition*. London: Routledge.

Vidial-Naquet, P. (1992) *Assassins of Memory: Essays in the Denial of the Holocaust*. New York: Columbia University Press.

Walder, D. (2000) Records of a people's shame, *Times Literary Supplement*, 17 November: 31.

Walzer, M. (1997) *On Toleration*. New Haven, CT: Yale University Press.

Wanner, C. (1998) *Burden of Dreams*. Philadelphia, PA: Pennsylvania State University Press.

Warnock, M. (1976) *Imagination*. Berkeley, CA: University of California Press.

Warnock, M. (1987) *Memory*. London: Faber & Faber.

Watchel, N. (1986) Introduction: between memory and history, *History and Anthropology*, 2: 2–7.

Weber, M. (1978) *Selections in Translation*. Cambridge: Cambridge University Press.
Wegner, G. (2000) The power of selective tradition: Buchnewald concentration camp and the Holocaust education, in L. Hein and M. Selden (eds) *Censoring History: Citizenship Memory in Japan, Germany, and the US*, pp. 226–55. Armonk, NY: M.E. Sharpe.
Weigl, S. (1996) *Body- and Image-space: Re-reading Walter Benjamin*, trans. G. Paul. London: Routledge.
Weissberg, L. (1999) Introduction, in D. Ben-Amos and L. Weissberg (eds) *Cultural Memory and the Construction of Identity*, pp. 1–22. Detroit, MI: Wayne State University Press.
Weschler, L. (1990) *A Miracle, A Universe*. New York: Pantheon Books.
Whyte, H. (1978) *Topics of Discourse: Essays in Cultural Criticism*. Baltimore, MD: Johns Hopkins University Press.
Wilson, R.A. (2000) Reconciliation and revenge in post-apartheid South Africa, *Current Anthropology*, 41(1): 75–103.
Wingfield, N.M. (2000) The politics of memory: constructing national identity in the Czech land, *East European Politics and Societies*, 14(2): 246–60.
Winter, J. (1995) *Sites of Memory, Sites of Mourning: The Great War in European Cultural History*. New York: Cambridge University Press.
Winter, J. and Sivan E. (eds) (1999a) *War and Remembrance in the Twentieth Century*. Cambridge: Cambridge University Press.
Winter, J. and Sivan, E. (1999b) Setting the framework, in J. Winter and E. Sivan (eds) *War and Remembrance in the Twentieth Century*, pp. 3–29. Cambridge: Cambridge University Press.
Wohl, R. (1979) *The Generation of 1914*. Cambridge, MA: Harvard University Press.
Wolin, S.S. (1989) *The Presence of the Past*. Baltimore, MD: Johns Hopkins University Press.
Wood, D. (1991) Introduction, in D. Wood (ed.) *On Paul Ricoeur: Narrative and Interpretation*, pp. 1–20. London: Routledge.
Wright, P. (1985) *On Living in an Old Country*. London: Verso.
Wrightson, K. (2001) Passion and politeness, *Times Literary Supplement*, 13 April 34.
Wrong, D. (1994) *The Problem of Order*. Cambridge, MA: Harvard University Press.
Wuthnow, R. (1998) *After Heaven: Spirituality in America Since the 1950s*. Berkeley, CA: University of California Press.
Yarrington, A. (1988) *The Commemoration of the Hero, 1800–1864*. New York: Garland Publishing.
Yates, F.A. (1966) *The Art of Memory*. London: Routledge
Yeo, R. (2001) *Encyclopedic Visions*. Cambridge: Cambridge University Press.
Yerushalmi, Y. (1982) *Zakhor: Jewish History and Jewish Memory*. Seattle, WA: University of Washington Press.
Young, A. (1996) Bodily memory and traumatic memory, in P. Antze and M. Lambek (eds) *Tense Past: Cultural Essays in Trauma and Memory*, pp. 89–102. London: Routledge.
Young, J.E. (1993) *The Texture of Memory: Holocaust Memorials and Meaning*. New Haven, CT: Yale University Press.

Young, J.E. (2000) *At Memory's Edge: After-Images of the Holocaust in Contemporary Art and Architecture*. New Haven, CT: Yale University Press.

Young, M. (1988) *The Metronomic Society: Natural Rhythms and Human Timetables*. London: Thames & Hudson.

Zelizer, B. (1993) *Covering Body: The Kennedy Assassination and the Media*. Chicago: Chicago University Press.

Zelizer, B. (1995) Reading the past against the grain, *Critical Studies in Mass Communication*, 12: 214–39.

Zelizer, B. (1998) *Remembering to Forget: Holocaust Memory Through the Camera's Eye*. Chicago: Chicago University Press.

Zemon Davis, N. (1987) *Fiction in the Archives: Pardon Tales and their Tellers in Sixteenth Century France*. Stanford, CA: Stanford University Press.

Zerubavel, E. (1981) *Hidden Rhythms: Schedules and Calendars in Social Life*. Chicago: Chicago University Press.

Zerubavel, E. (1997) *Social Mindscape: An Invitation to Cognitive Sociology*. Cambridge, MA: Harvard University Press.

INDEX

adolescent memories, 85, 86–8
Adorno, T., 21, 143, 145
Africa
    invention of traditions in colonial
        Africa, 58
    oral culture in, 29
    South Africa, 147, 152
African-Americans
    and generational memory, 90
    and the Lincoln Memorial, 131
Albertus Magnus, 3, 32
alternative memories, 68, 130
amnesia
    and amnesty, 147–8
    and collective memory, 156, 157
    and Nazi Germany, 149
    structural, 30
    and trauma memories, 140, 141
    see also forgetting
analogies of memory, 3
ancient Greece
    and the art of memory, 30–2
    and generation, 83
    and history and memory, 110
    and imagination and memory, 115
    reconstruction of democracy in,
        147–8
    and sites of remembrance, 16
Anderson, Benedict, 17, 60, 136
Annales school, 102
appropriated memories, 76

Aquinas, St Thomas, 32, 34
archives, 43, 105
    and new technology, 48
Aristotle, 31, 109
art of memory (ars memoria), 30–2,
    34–5
artistic world and memory, 44–5
Assmann, J., 23–4
Auden, W.H., 155
Augustine, St, 32
Auschwitz concentration camp, and
    Holocaust memory, 121–2, 143,
    144
Australia
    creating national identities in, 136
    war memorials in, 130
autobiographical (personal) memory,
    9–10, 78–9, 87
autonomy, and collective memory,
    14–15

Bacon, Francis, 38
    The Advancement of Learning,
        35
Balzac, Honoré de, 116
Barclay, C.R., 78–9
Bartlett, Frederic, 82, 118–19
Bauman, Z., 119
Benjamin, Walter, 16–17, 45, 141
Bergson, Henri, 44, 118
    on time and memory, 109–11, 112

and retrospective justice, 153
and trauma, 143
History of the Peloponnesian War,
116
Hobbes, Thomas, 108, 117, 146
Hobsbawm, E., 58
and Ranger, T., *Invention of
Tradition*, 56, 57, 59, 93, 127
Holocaust memory, 2, 8, 48, 90, 121–4,
139
in American life, 123–4
and the convent controversy at
Auschwitz, 121–2
and Holocaust denial, 122–3
and retrospective justice, 149–50
sacralization of, 123
and trauma, 142–4
Holy Land, and communities of
memory, 16
human rights
and justice, 145, 146, 147, 153
and the legal system, 20
and national memories, 18
Hume, David, 117
hysteria, 139, 140

identity aspect of tradition, 93–4
identity and memory, 1–2, 8, 14, 36–7,
132–9, 155–6
and collective identity, 132–3, 135,
138–9
and contested memories, 120–5
generational memory, 88
Halbwachs on the social context of,
52, 55
and heritage, 135
history and French cultural identity,
104
and the media, 25
and personal identity, 133
and postmodernism, 134
see also national identities
identity politics, 47, 134, 135, 138
and ethnic group memories, 18,
136–7
and justice, 145, 153
ideology
and the invention of traditions, 61

popular memory and the dominant
ideology, 61–7
images and words, and the status of
memory, 22–3
imagination and memory, 115–20,
124–5
philosophers on, 117–18
rationalization and individual
memories, 118–19
imagined communities, 17, 60, 136
India, invention of traditions in British
India, 58
individual memories
autobiographical, 9–10, 78–9, 87
cultural context of, 81–2
and the embodied self, 75–83
flashbulb memory, 76, 81, 87
Halbwachs on the social context of,
51, 52–5
and imagination, 118–19
and oral cultures, 29
and social memory, 5–6, 7, 11
tradition in, 98
industrial capitalism, and the
disintegration of collective memory,
45–6
Inglis, K., 130
institutions of memory, 19–22
interdisciplinary integration of memory
studies, 7–8
internet, 3, 48
and family memories, 19
intersubjectivist approach to memory, 6,
10–11
and the embodied self, 77, 78
intuition, Bergson's theory of, 110–11
invention of traditions (presentist
approach), 7, 55, 56–61
and the dynamics of memory
approach, 67–8, 73
and generational memory, 89
and popular memory, 61–2
Irving, David, 122
Italy, invention of traditions in, 58

Jerusalem, and communities of memory,
16
John Paul II, Pope, 121

GENDER AND SOCIAL THEORY

Mary Evans

- What is the most significant aspect of current literature on gender?
- How does this literature engage with social theory?
- How does the recognition of gender shift the central arguments of social theory?

We know that gender defines and shapes our lives. The question addressed by *Gender and Social Theory* is that of exactly how this process occurs, and what the social consequences, and the consequences for social theory, might be. The emergence of feminist theory has enriched our understanding of the impact of gender on our individual lives and the contemporary social sciences all recognise gender differentiation in the social world. The issue, however, which this book discusses is the more complex question of the extent to which social theory is significantly disrupted, disturbed or devalued by the fuller recognition of gender difference. We know that gender matters, but Mary Evans examines whether social theory is as blind to gender as is sometimes argued and considers the extent to which a greater awareness of gender truly shifts the concerns and conclusions of social theory. Written by an author with an international reputation, this is an invaluable text for students and an essential reference in the field.

Contents
Series foreword – Acknowledgement – Introduction – Enter women – The meaning of work – The world of intimacy – The gendered self – The real world – Now you see it, now you don't – Notes – Bibliography – Index.

160pp   0 335 20864 9 (Paperback)   0 335 20865 7 (Hardback)

ECONOMY, CULTURE AND SOCIETY
A SOCIOLOGICAL CRITIQUE OF NEO-LIBERALISM

Barry Smart

... excellent ... a probing survey of classical and contemporary social theory ... extremely well written and organized ... one of the best overviews of contemporary economy, culture and society I have read.

Professor Douglas Kellner, UCLA

... an authoritative analysis and a definitive defence of sociology as a critical theory of the market, politics and social institutions. A balanced and thorough critique of the neo-liberal revolution.

Professor Bryan Turner, University of Cambridge

- How have economic processes and transformations been addressed within classical and contemporary social thought?
- What impact have the market system and market forces had on social life?
- How has the imbalance between the public and private sectors been felt in contemporary society?

Economic factors and processes are at the heart of contemporary social and cultural life and this book is designed to refocus social theorizing to reflect that fact. The author re-interprets the work of classical theorists and, in the context of the move towards social regulation and protection in the 19th and early 20th centuries, he discusses more recent transformations in capitalist economic life that have led to greater flexibility, forms of disorganization, and a neo-liberal regeneration of the market economy. As our lives have become subject to a process of commodification, market forces have assumed an increasing prominence, and the imbalance in resources between private and public sectors has been aggravated. This illuminating text addresses these central concerns, drawing on the work of key social and economic thinkers.

Contents
Series editor's foreword – Sociological reason and economic life – No alternative? capit-alist economic life and the closing of the political universe – Cultures of production and consumption – Without regard for persons: the market economy – Affluence and squalor: the private and public sectors – Conclusion: new economic conditions and their social and political consequences – Further reading – References – Index.

208pp   0 335 20910 6 (Paperback)   0 335 20911 4 (Hardback)